Michael Heatley

FOOTBALL FACT BOOK

Michael Heatley

Lost League Football Grounds
Michael Heatley

First published 2010

ISBN 978 0 7110 3508 9

Published by Ian Allan Publishing

an imprint of Ian Allan Publishing Ltd, Hersham, Surrey KT12 4RG.
Printed in England by Ian Allan Printing Ltd, Hersham, Surrey KT12 4RG.

Visit the Ian Allan Publishing website at www.ianallanpublishing.com
Distributed in the United States of America and Canada by BookMasters Distribution Services.

Contents

INTRODUCTION

Non-League Football. The name sounds a bit negative, like semi-skimmed milk…a product lacking cream. Yet compared with the cash cows of the Premier League and some of the wannabes in the divisions below there's an honesty and camaraderie available at the lower levels of the Pyramid that may well prove attractive. You can stand and let off steam in congenial company – sometimes even smoke. Just try to forget the name: grassroots football would be a more appropriate label.

There are many hundreds of decent clubs being run within their means. Yet scratch the surface and you'll also find a boom and bust culture at boardroom level where money is injected into clubs on the brink of League status only to be withdrawn with often catastrophic results. This is where supporters' trusts prove their worth because owners and players come and go but the fans will be there for the long term.

On the positive side, non-League offers a communal experience in terms of making friends and influencing people. There's always something around the corner, from quiz nights through fundraising entertainment to sponsored walks, that you can get yourself involved with. It's good for fans to feel they can make a difference in some way or another, and very hard to walk away on Saturday at ten to five and forget about things for a week. If fans hang around in the clubhouse bar, you can even tell the players where you think they're going wrong (or right).

Many fans also support a 'proper' team – but when it comes to meeting friends, relishing a bit of banter with opposing fans or simply enjoying 90

minutes of good honest football you know where you'll find them.

With playing standards on the up as foreign imports push home-grown talent down the Pyramid, non-League Football may even surprise the purists. Take a look at the grass roots after reading this book and it will have achieved its aim.

Michael Heatley
August 2010

Acknowledgements

Special thanks to Alan Kinsman, who contributed much to this book; Nick Grant for commissioning it; Mark Beynon for editing it; and Mark Hardy for checking it. Dedicated to all the author's fellow fans of the non-League game – especially Iain McNay, who took him to his first; Dave Workman; and the 18 Yarders @ Farnborough.

ORGANISATION

THE PYRAMID
How non-League football is structured and administered

In the present climate of spiralling costs within the game, it is becoming increasingly difficult for clubs from the lower reaches of the game to aspire to playing in the Football League. The structure referred to as The Pyramid is intended to allow them to make that enormous transition. What it means in effect is that a team currently playing in Division Six of the Weston-super-Mare League could find itself performing in Division Two of the Football League after a number of successful seasons provided they havethe necessary financial backing and meet the criteria for ground standards.

The converse is also true, and these days a Premiership side which hits tough times could easily slip out of the main four divisions and into the non-League game. One only has to look at the recent examples of Luton and Oxford, both top-flight teams in relatively recent times, to see how far and fast the mighty can tumble. Leeds, Southampton and Charlton could conceivably suffer the same fate in years to come.

But for many years, things were very different. The system whereby the least successful clubs in the Football League were required to seek re-election was introduced soon after the competition itself, and in the early days there were many casualties. In the years leading up to the First World War, there was a steady turnover of clubs, and some found themselves leaving and rejoining the League two or three times.

After a number of revisions, the system by which clubs were voted in and out of the Football League was settled with the introduction of Division Three (North) and Division Three (South) in 1921. The League's 'full members' (those clubs in the top two divisions) were given one vote for each available

League place, while 'associate members' (those in the lower divisions) had to be content with a small number of votes between them. In the inter-war years, the number of clubs that lost their Football League status dropped significantly, and between 1946 and 1987, when automatic promotion and relegation between the Conference National and the Football League was introduced, only seven clubs lost their League status – New Brighton (1951), Gateshead (1960), Bradford Park Avenue (1970), Barrow (1972), Workington (1977), Southport (1978) and Lincoln (1987).

The introduction of automatic promotion and relegation between the Conference and the Football League thus put a stop to decades of what amounted to complacency among under-achieving League clubs. Voting worked in favour of existing League sides, who could usually count on enough support from colleagues to avoid the drop. Some non-League sides put themselves up for election and suffered the disappointment of rejection on numerous

occasions. Bedford Town and Chelmsford City share the unwanted distinction of being refused admission no fewer than 18 times, while Kettering Town (16), Worcester City (15) and Telford United (14) were among the other perennial hopefuls. Some came agonisingly close, Altrincham falling just two votes short of ousting Rochdale in 1980 and Bath City polling only three votes less than Wigan Athletic and Southport in 1978, when Wigan were elected to the League in Southport's place.

Things currently are very different from the way they were just a quarter of a century ago. Now, at the summit of the English game stands the Premiership, closely followed by the Championship, League One and League Two, between them encompassing the traditional 92 clubs of what was once the (pre-Premiership) Football League. But the 'glass ceiling' maintained for so many years by an outmoded, and essentially arbitrary, voting system has been swept aside in favour of a much fairer and more transparent arrangement.

The initial goal for non-League clubs is to make it into the Football Conference National (currently sponsored by Blue Square), the champions of which automatically gain promotion to League Two. Another promotion place is available via the play-off system, introduced in 2003, which involves those clubs finishing in positions second to fifth.

The Conference National is fed in turn by Conference North and Conference South, two teams from each replacing four relegated clubs. Again, the champions of each are promoted automatically, with play-offs to determine who will join them in non-League's top flight. Clubs relegated from the Conference National are placed in the lower divisions according to their geographical location.

Below Conference North and Conference South lie three competitions, the Northern Premier League, Southern League and Isthmian League Premier Divisions, and promotion and relegation arrangements are similar to those at the higher levels. Once a team finds itself at this level of the game, attaining Football League status becomes a tangible possibility. One rung further down the non-League ladder are the Northern Premier League, Southern League and Isthmian League feeder divisions, each currently known as Division One and each arranged in two regional sections.

Outside of the above, leagues are run on a regional basis either for a specific area, county or urban district, the United Counties League, Dorset Premier League and Brighton, Hove & District League being good examples. Because of the Pyramid system, the incentive to perform well on a local basis is a strong factor for the hundreds of clubs playing in the lesser leagues. Promotion is not always obtainable by playing record alone because facilities are still an issue when it comes to acceptance in a higher division.

There are thousands of clubs jockeying for advancement across more than 20 designated levels within the football Pyramid structure. The Conference National is Level 5, and the levels from there down to Level 11 fall under the jurisdiction of the Football Association. These seven levels are referred to as the National League System. At Level 11 you will find such leagues as the Kent County League Premier, the Suffolk & Ipswich Football League Senior Division and Northampton Town Premier League. While Sunday League has always been a strong element in the football world, these clubs fall outside the Pyramid, although there is no barrier to any of them entering the higher levels.

There are a number of Welsh clubs involved within the Pyramid structure but there is an anomaly in that Wales has a similar Pyramid system of its own, with the Welsh Premier League (formerly the League Of Wales) at its apex. The WPL winners have entry into the Champions League and those finishing in the next two positions earn a place in the Europa League. As things stand, there is little chance of any of the teams from the WPL making it into the English set-up.

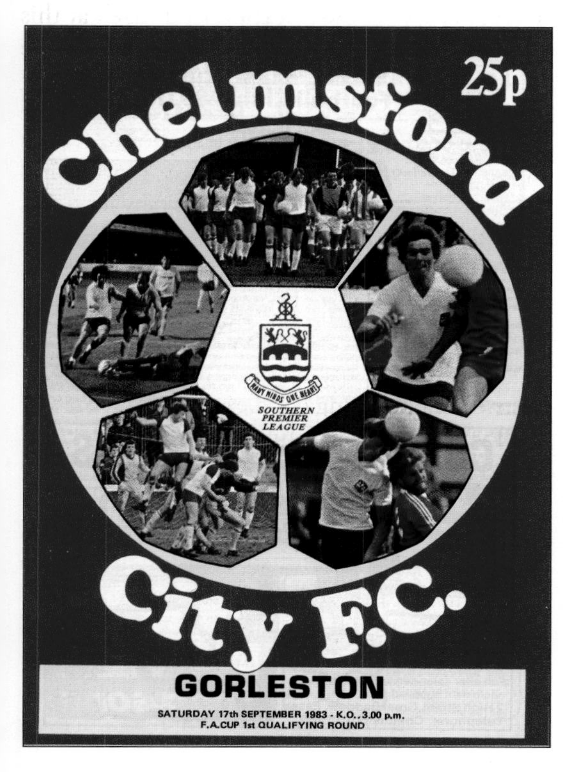

THE MAJOR LEAGUES

The Conference's three divisions atop the non-league Pyramid and the three leagues that feed it

The Football Conference

The Football Conference may be still outside the Football League but few would argue with the idea that it is now League Three in all but name. Its origins lie in the changes that occurred in the non-League game in the mid-seventies, with the abolition of amateur status in 1974 and a growing appreciation of the need to provide a clear route into the Football League for the leading non-League clubs.

Although it would be another seven years before the name was adopted, the Football Conference was formed in 1979 as the Alliance Premier League, its 20 founder members being drawn from the then top teams in the Southern League and the Northern Premier League. The Isthmian League initially refused permission for any of its clubs to join – it would be 1985 before the Isthmian League champions were granted promotion to the Alliance – but two Isthmian League sides, Enfield and Dagenham, decided to jump ship in 1981. Enfield went on to enjoy considerable success in the early years of the new competition, with two championships and a runners-up place to their credit, but the front-runners at the very beginning were Cheshire side Altrincham, champions in each of the first two seasons.

The Alliance was the first real attempt to create a national division below the lowest tier of the Football League, then known as Division Four. But while the idea of a clearly defined path to the Football League was gaining ground, there was initially no automatic promotion and relegation between the Alliance and Division Four. For the time being, at least, the system whereby clubs applied for election or re-election to the League remained in place. In the seasons immediately before the formation of the Alliance, two League clubs, Workington in 1977 and Southport in 1978, had failed to secure re-election, but between 1979 and 1986 there were no further casualties, and none of the early Alliance champions achieved the goal of Football League status.

Between 1984 and 1986, the arrival of sponsorship meant that the league was known as the Gola League, but by the time Scarborough won the championship at the end of the 1986-87 season a new sponsorship deal had seen it become the GM Vauxhall Conference. That year, Lincoln City were voted out of the League and Scarborough became the first Conference side to step up to Division Four. In fact, Lincoln were the very last club to lose their League status at the ballot box – after much discussion, the Football League had finally bowed to pressure and, from the 1987-88 season onwards, agreed to automatic promotion and

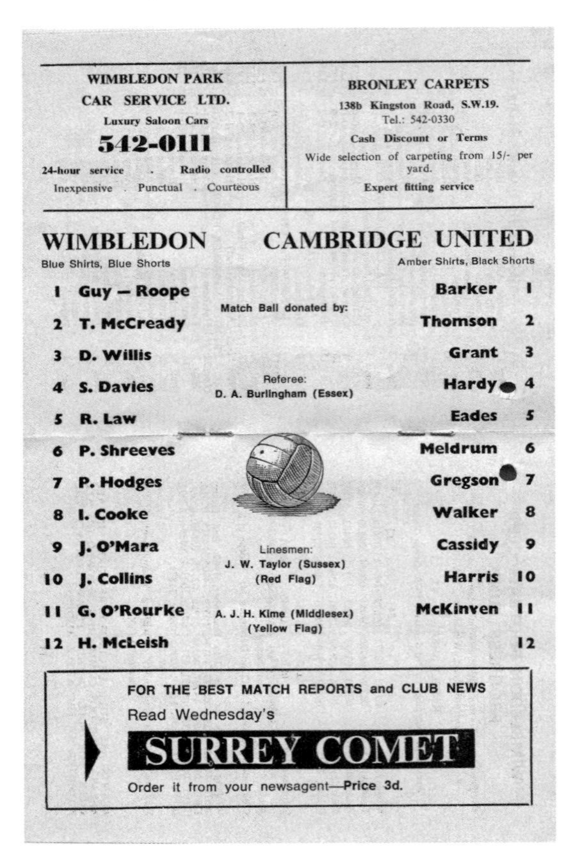

WIMBLEDON PARK
CAR SERVICE LTD.
Luxury Saloon Cars
542-0111
24-hour service . Radio controlled
Inexpensive . Punctual . Courteous

BRONLEY CARPETS
138b Kingston Road, S.W.19.
Tel.: 542-0330
Cash Discount or Terms
Wide selection of carpeting from 15/- per yard.
Expert fitting service

WIMBLEDON Blue Shirts, Blue Shorts		CAMBRIDGE UNITED Amber Shirts, Black Shorts
1 Guy – Roope	Match Ball donated by:	Barker 1
2 T. McCready		Thomson 2
3 D. Willis		Grant 3
4 S. Davies	Referee: D. A. Burlingham (Essex)	Hardy 4
5 R. Law		Eades 5
6 P. Shreeves		Meldrum 6
7 P. Hodges		Gregson 7
8 I. Cooke		Walker 8
9 J. O'Mara	Linesmen: J. W. Taylor (Sussex) (Red Flag)	Cassidy 9
10 J. Collins		Harris 10
11 G. O'Rourke	A. J. H. Kime (Middlesex) (Yellow Flag)	McKinven 11
12 H. McLeish		12

FOR THE BEST MATCH REPORTS and CLUB NEWS
Read Wednesday's
SURREY COMET
Order it from your newsagent—Price 3d.

relegation provided clubs could meet the League's ground standards. Since 1997, each winner has made it into the League, but three successive years earlier in the decade had seen disappointment for Kidderminster Harriers, Macclesfield Town and Stevenage Borough, each of whose facilities had not come up to scratch.

Between 1998 and 2007, the Conference was sponsored by the Nationwide Building Society and was known as the Nationwide Conference. During this time, there were further significant changes to the competition's structure and its relationship with the Football League.

In 2003, a second promotion place was made available to the winners of a play-off tournament contested by those finishing in second to fifth positions. The second-placed team takes on the fifth and the third plays the fourth, both ties taking place over two legs. A single game featuring the winners of these semi-finals, held at a neutral venue, determines who will join the Conference champions in what is now Division Two of the Football League.

The following year saw a major development when the Conference was restructured and one became three, with the Conference National being designated as the top league and fed by two new divisions, Conference North and Conference South. As before, this new level was created from the top clubs of the feeder leagues, a process that was, understandably, not welcomed by those leagues that considered themselves both weakened and reduced in importance.

With the introduction of the new divisions came a system where four teams are relegated from the Conference National and allocated to the most geographically appropriate feeder league. Both Conference North and South must have 22 clubs each and so occasionally a little juggling has to be done to maintain the status quo. The situation is equally difficult to manage when it comes to clubs promoted from the feeder leagues. This can lead and has led to anomalies, such as in 2009 when Gloucester

City were admitted to the Conference North, despite being south of Conference South neighbours Worcester City.

In 2007, a new three-year sponsorship deal for all three Conference divisions was brokered with online betting firm Blue Square. The deal, which was renewed for a similar period in 2010, covers the naming rights to the leagues, sponsorship of perimeter boards, corner flags, patches and match officials, and the introduction of Blue Square Player and Manager of the Month awards.

The Conference has also had its own League Cup competition, although this has always been regarded as of lesser importance than the FA Vase and the FA Trophy. Introduced at the same time as the league itself, the Conference League Cup was contested each year until 2001, when it was discontinued after unsuccessful attempts to secure sponsorship. In 2004, it was reintroduced as the Football Conference Challenge Cup, but discontinued again after only one season because the additional fixtures were considered undesirable in the light of the proposed enlargement of the Conference National to 24 clubs. However, the competition was revived in 2007-08 under a new sponsorship deal, becoming the Setanta Shield, although the failure of Setanta GB in June 2009 meant the competition was put on indefinite hiatus.

Football Conference North and South

Clearly, the two feeder leagues for Conference National have little history to speak of, having come into existence in the overhaul of the National League System that took place in 2004. Promotion to the Conference National is automatic for the champions of each feeder league, and further promotion places are available to the winners of the respective league play-offs, subject, of course, to the usual ground grading criteria.

While the play-offs take place between teams placed second to fifth in the North and South, in 2004-05, the first year of Conference North and Conference South, the play-off winners in each division played each other to determine who would secure a third promotion place. Altrincham beat Eastbourne Borough 2-1 in the play-off final held at Stoke City's Britannia Stadium. Altrincham were promoted to the Conference National, while Eastbourne Borough remained in the Conference South. This only happened once.

It is worth noting that the majority of promoted clubs have so far held their own in Conference National, the concept of yo-yo clubs having yet to occur. Those taking a tumble from the Conference set-up at the other end of the table find themselves in either the Southern League Premier, Isthmian League Premier or Northern Premier League Premier, depending on their geographical location.

The Northern Premier League

Formed in 1968, the Northern Premier League, or NPL, was intended as a northern equivalent of the Southern League and the Isthmian League, and therefore (in the pre-Conference era) sat at the highest level of football outside the Football League itself. At first it had equal standing with the long-established amateur Northern League, but the abolition of amateur status in 1974 left the Northern League having to find a new niche within non-League football, and the NPL gradually became the major competition in the area.

In 1979, the introduction of the Alliance Premier League meant that the NPL took a step down in the overall structure of the game, and a further drop down the Pyramid came with the introduction of the Conference regional divisions in 2004. In between times, the NPL underwent expansion, the introduction of a second division resulting in the creation of the NPL Premier Division and NPL Division One in 1987. From 2007-08, Division One was itself split in two, creating the NPL Division One North and South.

At the end of the season, the NPL Premier League champions, plus the winners of a play-off tournament that includes the teams in second to fifth positions, are promoted to Conference North, while the four basement clubs are relegated to NPL Division One North or South, which supply their replacements.

Famous former NPL clubs include Wigan Athletic, who were league champions twice before moving on to bigger and better things, and Scottish club Gretna, who also moved up in the world, reaching the dizzy heights of the Scottish Premier League before financial difficulties consigned them to a life in non-League football north of the border.

The NPL's first sponsorship deal came in 1985 when it became the Multipart League for a single season. There was no sponsor for the following two campaigns, but a new five-year deal was struck before the 1988-89 season, and until 1993 the NPL was known as the HFS Loans League. Another two seasons without sponsorship followed before the NPL linked up with UniBond in 1995 and this association, the longest to survive at this level of non-League football, continued until 2010 when a new three-year deal was concluded with Evo-Stik.

The Southern League

The highly historic Southern League dates back to 1894, and owes its existence to the determination of a number of clubs in the south of England to create a professional football league in the face of fierce opposition from the Old Boys' network of clubs from public schools that was still dominant in the region. The initial idea was put forward in 1891 by Woolwich Arsenal, one of the first clubs in the south to embrace professionalism, but there was little enthusiasm at the time, and Woolwich Arsenal opted instead to join the Football League. But the seeds had been sown, and in 1894 the idea came to fruition.

The initial set-up saw 16 clubs in two divisions, and the new competition soon became the most prestigious outside the Football League. There were some famous names among those founder members, including Luton Town, Millwall (as Millwall Athletic), Reading, Swindon Town, Gillingham (as New Brompton) and Southampton (as Southampton St Mary's). The quality of the Southern League became obvious in 1901 when Tottenham Hotspur, who joined the Southern League in 1896, won the FA Cup, the only occasion since the Football League was founded on which a non-League side has done so.

This quality was recognised by the Football League in 1920, when almost all the clubs in the Southern League's top division were absorbed into the new Division Three. Over the years that followed other Southern League clubs found their way into the Football League via the voting process. Fulham, Ipswich, and Wimbledon, who won the championship three seasons running in the seventies, are among the famous clubs who rose to prominence from the Southern League.

In 1979, the Southern League became a feeder to the newly constituted Alliance Premier, and thus took a step down the pecking order, a process repeated when the Conference expanded to three divisions in 2004, and many of the top SL clubs joined the new set-up.

Since its inception the Southern League has been reorganised on several occasions, and at various times there have been two or three divisions, often organised regionally. These have included English, Welsh, Eastern, Western, North Western, South Eastern, Central and Midland Divisions, the current arrangement being yet another permutation, the Southern League Premier Division, Division One Midlands and Division One South & West.

Clubs promoted from the Premier Division join the Conference North or South, as appropriate, with the champions automatically promoted, and play-offs for those finishing second to fifth. Those relegated from Division One Midlands and Division One South & West are absorbed by various regional leagues.

Sponsorship came relatively late to the Southern League, whose first deal, with Beazer Homes, came in 1987. Between then and 1996, the Southern League was known as the Beazer Homes League, then between 1996 and 2004 it became the Dr Marten's League before reverting to the Southern League for two seasons. In 2006, British Gas stepped up to the plate, and for three seasons it became the British Gas Business League, but a new two-year deal with InterContinental Brands was struck in 2009, and the league currently bears the name of one of ICB's products, Zamaretto.

The Isthmian League

The Isthmian League, whose member clubs take their place by invitation only, was formed in 1905 with an initial membership of only six teams. It was the first league created exclusively for amateur clubs who had previously been able to test their mettle only in cup competitions. Strongly committed to the ideals of amateurism, the Isthmian League attracted clubs who were unwilling or unable to compete financially with the professionals, and quickly established itself as the top amateur league in the south. Over the years, many of its clubs won the FA Amateur Cup, but even though the quality of Isthmian League football was clearly high, the league was always regarded as the poor relation to the Southern League and its northern counterpart.

In the years that followed there was slow but steady expansion, and by the early twenties there were 14 clubs in the league. Over the next five decades, however, there were few changes, with new clubs admitted mainly to replace those who dropped out. In general, those who joined came from the Athenian League, another notable southern amateur competition.

Major changes took place in the seventies – a second division was added in 1973, at which point the top division was renamed as the Isthmian League Premier Division with the new Division One below it. Four years later a third division was added.

TOOTING AND MITCHAM UNITED F.C.

Member of the Football Association
Affiliated to London F.A. and
Surrey F.A.

T.&M.U.F.C.

Hon. Secretary: L. W. HELLARD
71, Manor Road
Mitcham, Surrey

OFFICIAL PROGRAMME

No. 31 THREEPENCE

Saturday, 23rd January, 1965

Tooting & Mitcham v. Wycombe Wdrs.

Isthmian League—SENIOR SECTION

Kick-Off 3 p.m.

RANDOM NOTES

After our jaunt into the country last week at Whyteleafe we return today to our own enclosure to give a warm welcome to the players, officials and supporters of Wycombe Wanderers. Their team will be very anxious to retrieve some of the goals inflicted against them by our boys when the teams last met at Loakes Park (6—1) earlier in the season.

Last Saturday Enfield just managed to score the extra goal at Wycombe in a 3—2 victory. Our team returned from Whyteleafe victorious 4—1 and were worthy winners under the very wet and muddy conditions. Each of the forwards scored one each with the exception of Alf Barrett who was an important link in this revised line. Jim Pittuck returned with far more verve than he has shown for some time and Bob Winter and Eddie Green gave us some good wing play, with Tony Hacker always a danger to the "Leafs". Our coach has selected the same team for today.

The Reserve XI was successful at Barking by 4 goals to 2 scored by Keith Ashton (3) and Tony Algar. This was a fine performance as the side was reduced to nine men in the late stages of the game because of injury to Alan Webb and Bob Jenkins. Today the side travel to Kent to play Maidstone Reserves. We are pleased to welcome Ken Fulks to the team who has joined us from Maidstone F.C. and plays his qualifying game against his "old" club. Another newcomer to the club and reserve side is Dave Sinclair who last week made his debut with the 'A' side and who was previously with Hendon. We are glad to report that the injuries to Webb and Jenkins are not serious although neither are fit for today. The chosen team is: A. Baldwin; R. Marsh, M. Pepper; K. Jones, L. Burns, C. Willmott; A. Algar, D. Leonard, K. Ashton, K. Fulks, D. Sinclair. D. Grindrod and L. Paskell travel as reserves.

[*Continued on back page.*

There was also the issue of professionalism. As a purely amateur league, the Isthmian had always thought of itself as the top division in that area of the game and, until the mid-sixties, had one of the best teams outside the Football League in the shape of Wimbledon. At the start of the 1964-65 season, Wimbledon elected to go semi-professional and join the Southern League. Ten years later, the Isthmian had to accept the inevitable fact that players under its jurisdiction wanted and indeed warranted money for their services.

When the Alliance Premier League was formed in 1979, the Isthmian League declined to participate, and for the next few years stood outside the Pyramid. As a result, two Isthmian League sides defected to the Alliance in 1981 and, although the league stood apart for a while longer, by 1985 promotion and relegation between the Alliance and the Isthmian leagues had been introduced.

The last 25 years have seen several divisional

reorganisations. In 1984, Division Two was split into North and South regional sections, additional clubs joining from the Athenian League, which was then discontinued. Seven years later, these regional divisions were reorganised again into Division Two and Division Three. Further changes were made in 2002, with Divisions One and Two being merged and reorganised to form Division One North and South, resulting in Division Three being renamed Division Two. But this was a short-lived arrangement, and Division Two was disbanded in 2004. Just to confuse matters, the regional structure of Division One was again abandoned at this point, and the clubs placed in new versions of Division One and Division Two!

The current set-up, with the Premier Division sitting above Division One North and Division One South, was introduced for the 2006-07 season. Promotion from the Premier Division takes a club into the Conference South, while the drop from Division One North or South will result in a place in one of the many leagues around the London and South-East area.

Scotland and Wales

Unlike England and Wales, Scotland has no pyramid structure to enable lesser teams to work their way up to the level of those playing in the Scottish League or the Scottish Premier League, which constitutes the professional game north of the border.

Some sort of reform has been proposed on a number of occasions over the years, but as yet there is no sign of the Scottish FA changing the current set-up, in which the only way a senior non-League side can make it into Division Three is if a side from that division is automatically relegated after finishing bottom for three consecutive seasons. The members of the SFA can then vote for a replacement. (Annan Athletic were latest to join in 2008, but this was as a result of the demise of Gretna. Spartans, Cove Rangers, Edinburgh City and Preston Athletic were unsuccessful applicants.)

Outside the Scottish Football League, there are more than 50 senior and 160 junior clubs. The senior clubs play in the Highland Football League (which covers an area beyond the Highlands), the South of Scotland Football League or the East of Scotland Football League. Many of these senior clubs also make an effort to participate in the Scottish FA Cup, which they achieve via a qualifying competition.

The junior clubs, meanwhile, fall under the jurisdiction of the Scottish Junior Football Association, and play in three regionalised leagues: East, West and North. In addition to the league competitions, there is a Scottish Junior Cup, the winners of which automatically qualify for a place in the Scottish FA Cup first round, where they are joined by the champions of the three regional leagues. These automatic places are a recent concession, having been introduced in the 2007-08 season.

Welsh non-League football, meanwhile, has a pyramid structure similar to its English counterpart, although there are differences as you go further down through the levels.

At the top of the tree sits the Welsh Premier League, formerly known as the League of Wales, which was proposed in 1991 by Alun Evans, Secretary General of the Football Association of Wales, in response to a perceived threat to the Welsh international football team. Evans was convinced that the International Football Association Board was looking to force the home nations into having a single, combined UK national side, and that having a Welsh national league competition would strengthen the case for retaining a separate Welsh national side.

Prior to this, Wales was unusual in having no national league competition. Traditionally, the premier Welsh clubs had played their football in the English Football League, as Cardiff City and Swansea City still do and Aberdare Athletic, Merthyr Town, Newport County and Wrexham have in the past. The introduction of the new competition, which started in the 1992-93 season, provoked a bitter row between the

Football Association of Wales and several non-League sides who wanted to remain as part of the English set-up, but the dust eventually settled in the mid-nineties with Colwyn Bay, Merthyr Tydfil and Newport County remaining in the English leagues, and Barry Town, Rhyl, Newtown, Caernarfon Town and Bangor City moving across to the League of Wales.

The Welsh Premier League winners secure a place in the UEFA Champions League, with those clubs in second and third positions entering into the first qualifying round of the UEFA Europa League (formerly UEFA Cup). If the Premier League winners win the Welsh Cup, then the team in fourth place will also claim a place in the Europa League. At the start of the 2009-10 season the WPL consisted of 18 clubs, but there are plans to reduce this to 12, necessitating restructuring in the lower divisions.

The WPL is currently fed by both the Welsh Football League Division 1 and the Cymru Alliance, the former covering South Wales, the latter encompassing the north and central parts of the country. The champions of both leagues are entitled to promotion to the WPL but, as with the English system, grounds still have to meet certain criteria if elevation is to be achieved. It is possible for the runners-up in either league to be considered for promotion if the winners fail to come up to scratch. The two sides relegated from the WPL are placed in either of these two lower leagues.

The Welsh Football League is actually comprised of three divisions with a regular promotion and relegation system in place, but the Cymru Alliance has no such structure, relying on three regional feeder leagues for such purposes. The three leagues concerned are the Welsh League, which covers the area around Wrexham; the Mid-Wales League; and the Welsh Alliance. The three league winners gain automatic promotion if their respective grounds meet the required standards, but once again the runners-up can enter the frame if the top sides fall short.

Thereafter, the Welsh League has two further divisions: the Welsh Alliance sits atop a mini-pyramid, which includes leagues based in Clwyd, Gwynedd and Anglesey, and the Mid-Wales League has leagues from Aberystwyth, Cardiganshire and Montgomeryshire to draw on. Below its three divisions the Welsh League's tentacles spread as far down as the Barry & District League, Aberdare Valley League and the Port Talbot & District League. While normal promotion and relegation does exist in the lower reaches of Welsh non-League football, the manner in which teams gain promotion can often be mystifying to the uninitiated. In the western part of the country, teams confronted by a step up the ladder will often opt to stay in their own localised league rather than face the financial implications of playing at a higher level.

Women's Football

The women's game had its first golden age in the UK in the early twenties when crowds of up to 5,000 came to watch, but this was stopped on 5 December 1921 when England's Football Association voted to ban the game from grounds used by its member clubs. The ban lasted until 1971, but recent decades have seen many male clubs form women's teams.

Women's and girls' football continues to grow with more players competing in affiliated competition than any other team sport. The number of players, clubs, leagues and competitions has increased from 10,400 in 1993 to over 150,000 today.

Sport England's Active People survey in 2008 highlighted that 260,000 women and 1.1 million girls play some form of football in England. There are 26 million females playing across the world, of whom 4.1 million are playing affiliated football – this is a 54% growth since the year 2000.

Women's football has a well-regarded player pathway and a strong Centre of Excellence infrastructure. The number of national players emerging from these Centres is evidence of their success. There are 52 licensed FA Centres of Excellence in operation across England providing weekly quality coaching and a localised fixture programme for talented girls from the age of 8 to 16.

In 2000 it was announced that the women's game would be going professional with the sanctioning of a professional women's league at the start of the 2003-04 season. But that target was not met, clubs being reluctant to follow the lead set by Fulham, who turned professional in 2000 to become, at the time, the country's only full-time pro women's club. The game has now reverted to its former basis.

Arsenal Ladies FC have traditionally been the strongest English club, but their four-year grip on the FA Cup was loosened by Everton in 2010. The Gunners had been hit by defections by key players to the US professional game.

Sixth European Championship for National Representative Women's Teams 1993/95
Group 7 Qualifying Match

England v Slovenia
Sunday 17th April 1994

Kick-off 11.00 am
Brentford Football Club
Programme 60p

THE MAJOR CUPS

The Amateur Cup and the competitions that have replaced it remain prestigious today

The FA Amateur Cup

Staged for the first time in the 1893-94 season, the FA Amateur Cup was introduced in response to the rise of the professional clubs, who were becoming increasingly dominant in the game in general, and the FA Cup in particular, at the time. The initial idea came from Sheffield FC, who approached the FA in 1892 with proposals for a separate cup competition open only to amateur teams, but the concept was rejected despite Sheffield's offer to provide the trophy themselves.

A year later, however, the Football Association reversed their decision and announced the introduction of the FA Amateur Cup. At the time, the amateur game in the south of England was dominated by teams representing the old boys of leading public schools, and the inaugural tournament included a dozen such sides among the 81 who entered. One of them, Old Carthusians, the team for former pupils of Charterhouse School, became the first to lift the new silverware, and in the process achieved a distinction that would remain theirs alone for almost a century – Old Carthusians had won the FA Cup in 1881, and no other club would be able to boast victories in both competitions until Wimbledon, FA Amateur Cup winners in 1963, lifted the FA Cup in 1988.

Although the early years of the competition were dominated by teams from the north-east, the old boys' sides continued to play in the Amateur Cup until 1902, when a dispute with the FA led to the introduction of the Arthur Dunn Cup, a competition specifically for such teams. They left on a winning note, however, the 1901-02 competition being won by the Old Malvernians. Middlesbrough, Bishop Auckland and Stockton each claimed two victories in the years leading up to the First World War, but southern clubs were beginning to make their presence felt and were to enjoy considerable success in the years that followed, winning 15 of the 20 competitions held between the wars.

Interest in the FA Amateur Cup peaked in the years immediately after the Second World War. From 1949 until the competition ended in 1974, the final was held at Wembley Stadium, having previously been held at a variety of venues, the normal practice being to select a suitable ground lying somewhere between the home towns of the participating teams. Crowds of 100,000 were recorded on several occasions in the fifties, but in later years the final was played out in front of less than half this number.

In 1957, Bishop Auckland completed a unique hat-trick of victories in the competition that brought their total number of wins to 10, a figure never surpassed or even approached, their nearest rivals, Clapton and Crook Town, only being able to boast the same number of wins between them.

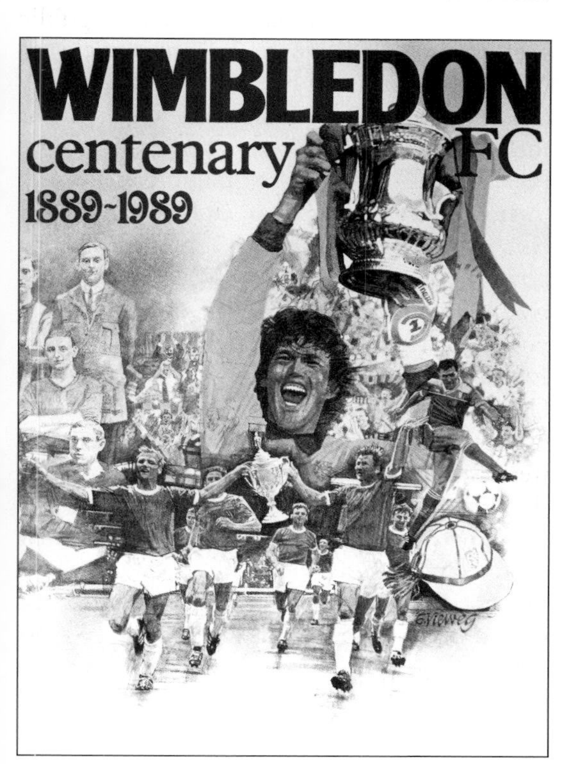

The later years of the tournament were again dominated by clubs from the south, with many of the winners coming from the Isthmian League, based in London and the Home Counties. The last club to lift the trophy was Bishop's Stortford, who beat Ilford in the 1974 final. In the same year, the Football Association took the decision to abolish the official distinction between 'amateur' and 'professional' footballers and this meant the end not only of the Amateur Cup but also Amateur Internationals involving England.

Thereafter, depending on the level at which they played, clubs would enter either the existing FA Trophy competition or the newly created FA Vase. The FA Trophy had been set up a few years earlier for professional clubs who played their football outside the Football League, but with the demise of the FA Amateur Cup, the strongest of the amateur sides, including Enfield, Hendon, Dagenham and Skelmersdale United, were allocated to the FA Trophy. The FA Vase, meanwhile, was introduced to cater for the remaining amateur clubs, and is generally regarded as a direct replacement for the earlier competition.

There were some famous names among the winners of the FA Amateur Cup, and those who later turned professional and gained entry to the Football League include Wimbledon, Wycombe Wanderers and Barnet.

The FA Vase

As we have seen, the FA Vase effectively replaced the FA Amateur Cup in 1974, although many of the clubs that had achieved pre-eminence in the earlier competition would henceforth contest the FA Trophy. The result was that, for the first time, the smaller clubs – even village sides – would have the chance of playing in a national final at Wembley.

The story of the FA Vase wouldn't be complete without mention of the man whose idea the new competition was. The trophy itself bears the inscription: 'Presented by Frank Adams, Life Member of the Football Association and Patron of Wycombe Wanderers FC'. Frank

Adams was a man who dedicated his life to football and, in particular, to the amateur game. Born in High Wycombe in 1891, Adams spent all but one season of his playing career at Wycombe Wanderers, helping them step up from the Spartan League to the Isthmian League in 1921. He was also selected for several England Amateur International squads, but sadly never represented his country. After retiring as a player in 1929, he remained part of the Wanderers' administrative team until 1947, when he was elected to the FA. During the 1966 World Cup, Adams was part of the International Selection committee, but no matter how far he rose in the football hierarchy, he remained a true Corinthian. It was at his suggestion that a new competition for the lesser sides was introduced after the abandonment of the FA Amateur Cup.

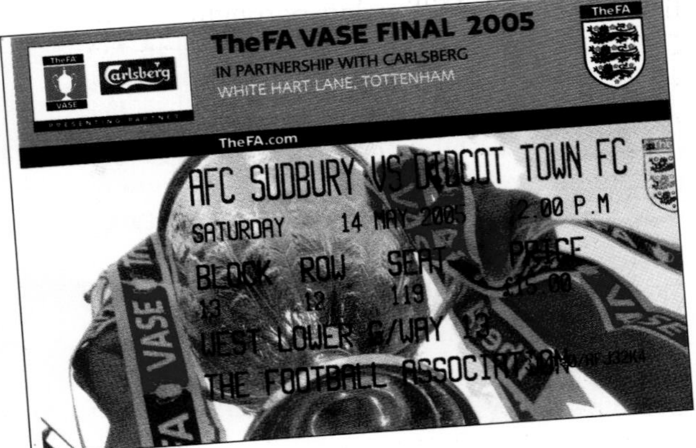

The first FA Vase competition attracted over 200 entries and the winners were Spartan League side Hoddesdon Town whose 2-1 Wembley victory over Surrey Senior League side Epsom & Ewell was witnessed by 9,000 fans. But the early front-runners were Essex Senior League side Billericay Town, who won the trophy three times in four years at the end of the seventies. They certainly worked hard for the silverware, needing extra time to beat Stamford in 1976, and a replay to overcome Sheffield FC the following year, but they had an easier time in 1979, when a hat-trick by Dick Young, the first in a Wembley final since the 1966 World Cup, smoothed the path to a 4-1 win over Gloucestershire County League side Almondsbury Greenway.

In the eighties, it was West Midlands League side Halesowen Town who featured heavily, with two wins in three final appearances. After losing out by a single goal to VS Rugby in 1983, Halesowen bounced back to record consecutive victories against Fleetwood Town in 1985 and Southall in 1986.

Of all the names inscribed on the FA Vase, the 1988 winners, Colne Dynamoes, almost certainly have the most unusual history. Formed in 1963 by local businessman Graham White, Colne spent almost twenty years in the lower reaches of non-League football before White's spectacular financial success led to him investing heavily in the club. The squad was strengthened, and the club rose rapidly through the North West Counties League and the Northern Premier League, gathering the FA Vase along the way. In 1989, they went full-time, won the Northern Premier League Premier Division by a staggering 26 points, and then found themselves refused promotion to the Conference because their Holt House ground wasn't up to scratch. After failing to entice Football League club Burnley into a ground-sharing arrangement, White dramatically folded the club in the summer of 1990.

Meanwhile, a new attendance record for an FA Vase match was set in 1989, when 26,489 fans watched Sudbury Town and Tamworth draw 1-1 at Wembley. Despite the closeness of the first match Tamworth ran out comfortable 3-0 winners in the replay at Peterborough, one of their goals coming from Ian Moores, a former Tottenham Hotspur player.

The 1992 final is regarded by many as the best so far, an eight-goal thriller that saw Wessex League club Wimborne recover from going a goal down after 14 minutes to run out 5-3 winners against high-flying Guiseley. The Dorset side had never progressed beyond the third round of the competition before, while Guiseley were not only the current FA Vase holders, they had also been losing semi-finalists in 1990, and were enjoying their first season in the Northern Premier League Division One after securing promotion from the Northern Counties East League. It was a memorable game that recently made it into a *Daily Mail* Top 50 Wembley finals feature.

While Wembley Stadium was being rebuilt, four different Premiership grounds hosted the FA Vase finals, two being held at Villa Park, two at St Andrews and one each at Upton Park and White Hart Lane. On its return to Wembley in 2007, the final saw a new record attendance figure for the competition, 36,232 fans raising the rafters at the new stadium as Truro City came from behind to beat AFC Totton 3-1. Not that anyone knew it at the time, though – it wasn't until June 2008 that the real attendance figure was confirmed when the FA admitted that the official total released initially had been skewed by a faulty turnstile and a failure to include 'walk-up' ticket sales.

As if to confirm that the original spirit of the FA Vase lives on, Kirkham & Wesham of the North West Counties League lifted the trophy in 2008 in their very first season in the competition, beating Lowestoft Town 2-1, while in 2009 Whitley Bay were guided to victory by manager Ian Chandler, who had scored the only goal of the game when Whitley Bay beat Tiptree United in the 2002 final. Whitley Bay thus became the fifth club to lift the trophy for a second time, sharing the distinction with Billericay (the only club to have won on three occasions), Halesowen Town, Tiverton Town and Brigg Town.

The FA Trophy

The FA Trophy was introduced in 1969 to give semi-professional sides a more realistic chance of playing in a Wembley final. Amateur clubs had this opportunity via the FA Amateur Cup, but many of the more successful non-League clubs were, by this stage, making some form of payment to their players and were therefore ineligible for the Amateur Cup. The FA Cup offered their only route to Wembley, but virtually no chance of success.

Nine of the first ten winners of the competition came from the Northern Premier League, Southern League Telford United being the only outsiders to lift the trophy, but southern clubs featured almost as heavily in the final itself, with Hillingdon Borough, Barnet, Dartford, Dagenham and Leatherhead all suffering the agony of defeat at Wembley during this period.

Despite the fact that fans were slow to embrace the new competition, the big non-League clubs have always taken it seriously, and past winners have included a number of future Football League sides. As well as the first winners, Macclesfield Town, seven others have spent time in the Football League – Scarborough, Morecambe, Kidderminster Harriers, Colchester United, Wycombe Wanderers, Cheltenham Town and Yeovil Town.

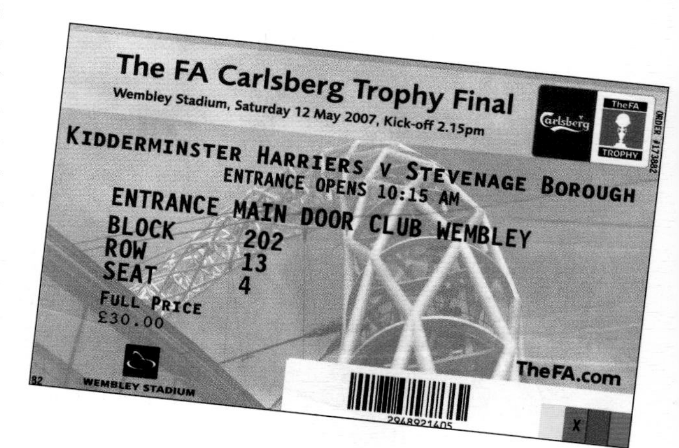

The discontinuation of the FA Amateur Cup in the wake of the Football Association's decision to abolish the official distinction between amateur and professional sides in 1974 had the effect of dramatically increasing the number of clubs that entered the FA Trophy, this rising to more than 300. The number dropped over the next 15 years, with some amateur sides electing to compete for the newly introduced FA Vase, and by the early nineties the number of entries had dipped to just under 200. In the years that followed, steps were taken to restrict eligibility to the two competitions on the basis of each club's position within the Pyramid, and these days the FA Trophy attracts about 250 entries every season.

In 1979, the formation of the Alliance Premier League from the leading Northern Premier League and Southern League clubs inevitably meant that Alliance clubs all but dominated proceedings in the forthcoming decade, although Bishop's Stortford, who plied their trade in the Isthmian League, made their way from the Preliminary Round to Wembley to record a surprise win in 1981. It was a decade in which only one club, Telford United, lifted the trophy more than once, their 1989 win making them the second side to win the FA Trophy for a third time, equalling Scarborough's achievement in the previous decade.

The nineties, however, were rather different, with three clubs and two famous managers virtually monopolising the competition. In 1991, Wycombe Wanderers were led to victory by former Northern Ireland international Martin O'Neill, then in the first year of his managerial career. In 1993, O'Neill went one better, taking Wanderers to their second FA Trophy win and adding the Conference National title and promotion to the Football League for good measure. Wanderers thus became the second club to complete this non-League 'double' – Wealdstone had achieved the same feat in 1985 but, with automatic promotion still two years away, had failed to secure a Football League place.

In the second half of the nineties the FA Trophy virtually belonged to the legendary Geoff Chapple, who took Woking to the first of their wins in the competition in 1994. He had managed the side since the mid-eighties, guiding them from the obscurity of the Isthmian League Division Two South to the Conference, and masterminding their famous 1991 FA Cup run along the way. Woking lifted the FA Trophy again in 1995 and 1997 before Chapple moved on to Kingstonian, where the success story continued. The Ks secured the Isthmian League Premier Division title in 1998, won the FA Trophy in 1999 and 2000, and were seconds away from achieving an historic appearance in the fifth round of the FA Cup in 2001.

The next four years saw the FA Trophy go to first-time winners Canvey Island, Yeovil Town, Burscough and Hednesford Town, but another of the competition's legendary figures was waiting in the wings. Mark Stimson, a former Football League player, had been part of the 2001 FA Trophy-winning Canvey Island side, and had moved into management at Grays Athletic the following year. In 2005, Grays won the FA Trophy in the competition's first penalty shoot-out and ended the season as Conference South champions an impressive 23 points ahead of runners-up Cambridge City. In 2006, Grays retained the FA Trophy but not Stimson, who moved on to take the reins at Stevenage Borough, taking them to victory in the 2007 FA Trophy final and thus becoming the first manager to win the competition in three successive seasons.

Interestingly, although teams have competed for it only since 1969, the FA Trophy itself is more than 100 years old, having been presented to the FA as long ago as 1905 for use in a proposed international tournament between England, Canada and the US that was intended to promote the game in North America. The earlier tournament never materialised, and it was more than 60 years before the trophy would finally be held aloft by a winning captain.

REGIONAL REORGANISATION

Balancing economic factors with the quality of football at non-League's top levels

These days, the Conference is generally regarded as the Premier/Football League's fifth division, but while the idea of a national non-League competition has raised the profile of the game, the distances involved in travelling between such far-flung outposts as Lewes and Barrow have often resulted in poor attendance figures, not to mention added expense for the clubs.

There are some persuasive arguments for regionalising the Conference, but those with memories of the time before automatic promotion and relegation were introduced suggest this shouldn't be done in isolation but in combination with the Football League, taking all the clubs in League Two and the Conference and then splitting them into two geographical divisions.

Fans of a certain age will remember the days of regionalisation in the Football League, with Division Three split into North and South. That came to an end in 1958, but regionalisation remained the norm in non-League football until the formation of the Alliance (now the Conference) in 1979.

Grays chairman Mick Woodward supports the idea of upward amalgamation. 'League Two should be 44 clubs split into two divisions, with current Conference National clubs making it up. The Conference National should be the same with Conference North and South teams going into it knowing that it is strictly part-time.' Less money spent, fewer risks taken and less heartbreak – a return to the successful old days. (After their relegation from the Conference in 2010, Grays took a voluntary two-division demotion in an attempt to find financial stability.)

Former Woking chairman David Taylor came out in favour of regionalisation of the Conference National as the club prepared for the withdrawal of owner Chris Ingram's £300,000 a year investment in May 2009. Taylor was then of the opinion that, in the prevailing financial climate, the expense of long away trips was too much for teams in the top tier of non-League football. But he felt regionalisation would bring other benefits too, with fans having to pay less to follow their team around, and therefore being able to go to more matches, boosting gates and generating more income for the clubs. 'Clubs like ours really can't afford the overnights anymore,' he said. 'I think regionalisation has to come – Wrexham away is a huge journey for fans who want to see a game of football.'

The suggestion has divided fans, with some seeing the advantages of less travelling and more local derbies and others arguing that such a move would reduce the quality of lower-league football. It has also divided those within the game, and not quite along the lines that might be expected.

Before losing their place in the Conference National at the end of 2008-09, Woking were covering more than 5,500 miles a year, including long trips to York, Wrexham and Barrow. Although this dropped by around 40 per cent in 2009-10 in Conference South, Taylor's general point holds true for the clubs they left behind.

In 2008-09, 15 per cent of Barrow's annual expenditure went on travelling an estimated 15,000 miles, their nearest derby game, at Altrincham, involving a round trip of 206 miles. But surprisingly, Barrow chairman Brian Keen is one of those who disagrees with David Taylor's point of view, and feels that regionalising the Conference would 'end with the Football League slamming the door in our face'. He sees that scenario as involving an amalgamation with Conference North and South, thereby diluting the quality of football.

Histon's former chairman, Gareth Baldwin, who presided over one of the smallest teams in the Conference for 17 years before stepping down in late 2009, has gone as far as to call the suggestion 'nonsense'. Baldwin and Keen are both convinced that any sort of regionalisation would be to the detriment of the leagues they are currently in. They argue that if the Conference National were to be regionalised, then teams from the Conference North and Conference South, and possibly from the level below that, would be needed to make up the numbers.

Barrow's Keen summed up the argument in the *Non-League Paper*, saying: 'If we weren't facing the same level of opposition, our own standards would no doubt drop and if we were to make it to the League we would be a far weaker outfit than we are now and we'd come straight back. If that were to happen, then sooner or later the gulf would get so wide that the League would say thanks but no thanks, and we'd be scrapping just to get one club promoted again.'

He has a point, given that the difference in standard between the Conference National and League Two is really not that great as things stand at present. Any dilution of quality in the Conference could only work against those striving to make the step up.

Football League regionalisation came to an end in 1958, after almost 40 years. Curiously, its origins could be traced back to the arrival of professionalism in the game during its earliest years. Northern clubs embraced the idea of paying their players far more readily than their southern counterparts, attracted many of the better players and, in turn, came to dominate the game in the last years of the Victorian era. When it was formed in 1888, the Football League was entirely composed of northern clubs, and this situation barely changed in its first 30 years.

Meanwhile, the Southern League had grown in strength, and in the period immediately after the First World War there were rumblings about starting another professional league in the south in direct competition with the Football League. The League reacted by admitting the Southern League clubs in 1921, using the simple expedient of effectively taking over the Southern League's top division and renaming it Division Three. The establishment of a northern equivalent the following year meant that the northern bias was restored to some extent, but at least the League could now boast almost 30 southern clubs among its 86 members, a better average than the seven from 44 that had been the case prior to 1920.

One drawback of two regionalised divisions of equal standing was that promotion to Division Two was restricted to the champions of each, which meant that the chances for advancement were relatively slim.

Outside the League, there have been frequent reorganisations, almost all of them along regional lines. Indeed, it took until 1979, and the formation of the Alliance Premier League, for a national competition to be introduced, and non-League football has undoubtedly benefited. Below the top flight, regionalisation is the norm for exactly the reasons that its advocates put forward – it allows the smaller clubs to keep their expenses down. The further down the Pyramid you go, the more regionalised things become, with the Conference National sitting above Conference North and South, Conference North and South sitting above the top divisions of the Northern Premier League, the Southern League and the Isthmian League, and each of these having regionalised lower divisions. So it goes right the way down to the county leagues and beyond.

So, how would the reorganisation of the current national league competitions be achieved, and how would it affect the game?

Reintroducing the idea to the Football League alone probably wouldn't have much effect on the non-League game. A regionalised League One, amalgamating the current League One and League Two and dividing the clubs into two divisions along geographical lines, would probably change the way in which relegation from the League was handled, with only the bottom club from each division being relegated in favour of two sides from Conference National.

If the Conference were to be regionalised, however, the effect would be much more noticeable. In all probability, Conference National would disappear, along with Conference North and South, the best teams from which would be divided between two new top-flight non-League divisions. Unless new regionalised divisions were introduced within the Conference immediately below the top flight, those who didn't make the cut would find themselves in the NPL, the Southern League or the Isthmian League, with a possible knock-on effect for those in the lower reaches of each.

But far more important is the effect this would have on non-League sides trying to get into the Football League. The idea of introducing a three-up, three-down system between the current League Two and the Conference has been mooted, but the League clubs have so far resisted. Little chance, then, of them being receptive to the idea of having four clubs relegated from the League, which would leave a regionalised Conference with just two available League places to fill, restricting promotion to the champions of each of the non-League top-flight divisions. There would be no play-offs, and for clubs outside the top, say, three or four in each division, there would be little to play for other than pride.

Following this argument, it's perhaps hard to see what advantages Conference regionalisation might offer, but set David Taylor's comments in the context of Woking's recent history and they make more sense. Woking may have lost their fight to stay in the top flight of the Conference at the end of the 2008-09 season, but for several years earlier in the decade they were in with a shout of promotion to the Football League and, like any club in that position, ended up spending money in the pursuit of the dream. Money is tight, and anything that offers a way to reduce unnecessary outgoings has to be given serious consideration. Any club is going to favour investing in players or facilities over hotel and fuel bills. Not only that, but a change would also offer security, since a club threatened with relegation from a national division would find themselves sitting comfortably mid-table in a regional set-up.

Brian Keen, meanwhile, thinks that clubs need to spend more carefully. 'If somebody goes out and signs four new strikers, they can't complain that they can't afford to travel to Barrow,' he said recently in the *Non-League Paper*, and his is not an isolated point of view in the non-League game. There are several other clubs, the likes of Histon and Kidderminster Harriers, who have done well in recent years by spending sensibly and building slowly.

The non-League game has never been stronger, and that, in part, has been due to the introduction of a national league competition. Money will always be an issue at this level, and clubs need to achieve a balance between ambition and resources in order to survive and progress. For many, the idea that the overall quality of the league should be compromised in order to protect clubs who are unable – or unwilling – to manage their spending is simply unthinkable. They argue that the additional costs involved are one of the prices clubs have to pay for success, and it's down to each club to work out how to cover them. Those who can't – or won't – should be allowed to fall by the wayside, leaving the field open to those who get the balance right.

The arguments for and against regionalisation will doubtless rumble on in an argument almost as old as the game itself.

CONTROVERSIES

Non-League football and its constituent clubs have seen more that their fair share of controversial decisions and incidents. Here are just a few from recent times

Kettering Town's sponsorship deal 1976

The introduction of shirt sponsorship to the British game came not through Manchester United, Chelsea or Liverpool but homespun Kettering Town FC. Their Southern League game against Bath City on 24 January 1976 was first to see a British club play with a sponsor's name printed on their shirts. Manager-cum-chief executive Derek Dougan was a forward-thinking character, having been PFA chairman while in the professional game, and decided that 'sponsors guarantee funds when the turnstiles cannot click sufficiently to wipe out overdrafts and debts'.

Signing a deal with local firm Kettering Tyres, he circumvented the Football Association's objections by abbreviating the on-shirt slogan to Kettering T – which could just as easily have stood for Kettering Town. The club backed down and removed the offending slogan in the face of a £1,000 fine, but it took only a year for the practice to be accepted in the professional game.

Kettering's next claim to fame would be exactly thirty years later – Paul Gascoigne's brief and ill-fated management stint in late 2005.

Burton Albion v Leicester City 1985

Neil Warnock was in charge at Burton Albion during an infamous FA Cup third-round tie with Leicester City in 1985, which had to be replayed after Burton keeper Paul Evans was knocked unconscious by a missile hurled from the Filbert Street terraces. At that time, the then Northern Premier side were holding their illustrious top-flight opponents 1-1. The felled keeper claimed he could remember nothing about the second and third goals as the home team routed Burton 6-1. He continued this claim under FA cross-examination (ironically Evans was a solicitor in his day job) and the match was ordered to be replayed. The second game was staged behind closed doors as a message that crowd trouble would not be tolerated. Leicester won, but by only a single goal. It was the first time such a decision had been made, and 11 years since the FA had ordered a replay of any kind.

Stevenage denied a Football League place 1996

Stevenage Borough won the Conference title in 1996, but were denied entry to the Football League because they had not fulfilled ground grading requirements in time. They mounted a £250,000 legal challenge over their failure to gain promotion on the basis of restraint of trade, but were unsuccessful. The judge rejected their plea because a precedent had been set in earlier cases involving Kidderminster Harriers and Macclesfield Town. However, he accepted many of their arguments, and the League subsequently shifted its ground-grading deadline to three months later in the year.

Torquay United were the club that retained their League status in 1996 thanks to Stevenage's debarring, and their chairman Mike Bateson added a twist to the tale when he alleged that Stevenage had asked them for a £20,000 'incentive' to encourage their players to win the title. It was to the Devon club's advantage for Stevenage to prevail, since the other main Conference title contender, Woking, would have taken Torquay's League place as their ground was already up to standard. A Football Association inquiry confirmed the allegations and imposed a suspended £25,000 fine on Stevenage for their audacity.

Stevenage had known constant success since Paul Fairclough took over the management seven years earlier, but, in the aftermath of their failure to achieve League status, had to sell skipper Paul Barrowcliff, Nigerian youth international Efe Sodje and leading scorer Barry Hayles. Chairman Victor Green denied, however, that their sale had been required to cover court fees. After several near misses Stevenage Borough finally made the jump to League Two in 2010.

Stevenage Borough v Newcastle 1998

Stevenage were the centre of controversy again two years later when they were rewarded for their FA Cup giant-killing heroics at Swindon with a fourth-round draw at home to Newcastle United. It was assumed that Borough, struggling in the lower half of the Conference and with a small ground, would opt to switch the tie to St James' Park to increase their financial windfall – FA Cup receipts being split between the clubs – but they were given the go-ahead to stage the biggest game of their history at their home ground, Broadhall Way.

Newcastle were not convinced of the ground's safety, however, and the FA's Challenge Cup committee brought in safety experts to approve the ground and the temporary seating planned to increase its capacity to 8,000. A fresh dispute then arose over the cost of tickets for the match, Stevenage having announced that they were to raise prices for the game. 'There's no doubt that there will be an increase,' manager Paul Fairclough said. 'There has to be, unfortunately. We are going to be seeing £50 million worth of class players on this pitch and I think the prices will reflect that.'

The match resulted in a 1-1 draw, which meant Stevenage had to travel to St James' Park anyway. Stevenage striker Giuliano Grazioli scored the non-leaguers' equaliser, a header cancelling out an early strike from his more illustrious counterpart, Alan Shearer. Ironically Giuliano was then injured in a game at Gateshead, mere miles from St James' Park, and, without him in their ranks for the replay, Stevenage slipped to a 2-1 defeat.

The most bizarre victim of the war of words between Stevenage Borough and Newcastle United was Graham Roberts. The former Tottenham and England defender lost his manager's job at Yeovil Town because of his alleged involvement in sending a fax to St James' Park prior to the replay. The fax, which found its way into the Hertfordshire team's dressing-room, was apparently on Yeovil Town headed paper and reportedly said: 'We are not all arseholes in the Vauxhall Conference.' Ironically, Stevenage visited Yeovil in their first match after the replay defeat.

Northern Premier League fiasco 2005

In 2005 the Northern Premier League championship was decided in controversial fashion at the end of the season. League officials had to adjudicate after one team, Spennymoor United, failed to complete its fixtures.

The League's Board of Directors decided to expunge Spennymoor's playing record, a decision that was disputed by Gateshead, Radcliffe Borough, Hyde United and Workington. One of the grounds of their appeal to the FA was that the meeting making that decision did not have a quorum. A second, quorate board meeting on 1 May 2005 confirmed the decision to expunge Spennymoor United's record.

This meeting came a day after the final day of the Northern Premier League Premier Division season where Workington had finished in first place, Hyde United in second (having played 41 games to Workington and Farsley's 42) and Farsley in third. The deletion of Spennymoor's record led to Farsley finishing in first place, Hyde United in second and Workington third.

Gateshead, Hyde United, Radcliffe Borough and Workington continued to appeal to the FA, which, four days later, overturned the Northern Premier League Board's decision. As a result Spennymoor United's playing record was reinstated and, in addition, the FA awarded three points to teams for each game outstanding against Spennymoor, although no goals for or against were allocated. Hyde United were one of the teams awarded three points, and were thus finally awarded the 2004-05 Northern Premier League Premier Division championship.

Farsley Celtic, who had celebrated winning the championship on the last day of the season, ended up third in the table. Burscough, who had slipped out of the promotion play-offs thanks to

Prescot Cables being awarded six points for unplayed games against Spennymoor, attempted to get the FA to go to arbitration, and, when this was rejected, went with Farsley to the High Court.

On 13 May 2005 the FA and Northern Premier League confirmed that Hyde United were the champions of the Northern Premier League Premier Division, and they were presented with the trophy. Workington, who had finished first on the last day of the season having played a game more than Hyde, were promoted along with them, having beaten Farsley Celtic in the play-off final after a penalty shoot-out.

Chesterfield v Droylsden, FA Cup 2008

A second-round FA Cup game between League club Chesterfield and Blue Square North outfit Droylsden in December 2008 took four matches to be decided, and even then the result was overturned!

The first game was abandoned because of fog, with Droylsden one up, and the subsequent 2-2 draw ended with a controversial goal. With the match delicately poised at 1-1, the Blue Square North side put the ball out of play after an injury to their striker. However, when the ball was thrown back into play, rather than return it as convention demanded, Chesterfield's Jack Lester lobbed it past unprepared Droylsden goalkeeper Craig Mawson from 30 yards. A row that held the match up for five minutes was defused when Lee Richardson, the Chesterfield manager, ordered his players to allow Steve Halford to walk the ball into an empty net from the restart.

The third attempt at a result was abandoned with the visitors leading Droylsden 2-0 when floodlight failure ended the game on 70 minutes. A fourth match was necessary to decide who got a trip to Championship side Ipswich Town in the third round. But, despite winning 2-1, Droylsden were then disqualified thanks to fielding Sean Newton, the player who scored both their goals. He had picked up a fifth yellow card in the first completed match between the clubs, leading to an automatic suspension, and had therefore been ineligible.

Chester join Conference 2009

Having been relegated from the Football League in May 2009, Chester City were given the go-ahead to begin their season in the Blue Square Premier in the following August. However, their opening two matches of the season against Grays and Gateshead were both postponed as the Football Association held off granting affiliation to Chester.

They were showing their disapproval of the Conference offering Chester membership in return for a further deduction of 15 points on top of the usual 10-point penalty. The club had a spell in voluntary administration after relegation from the Football League, which was followed by a buy-out by former owner Stephen Vaughan.

A commission of the FA's sanctions and registrations committee fined the Conference £5,000, suspended until the start of the

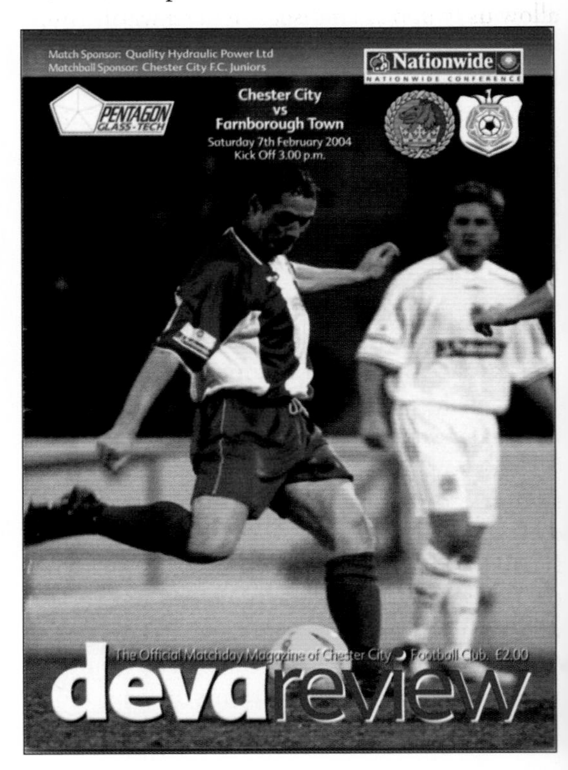

following season. In a statement, the FA declared that the proposition made to Chester was 'a clear breach of Conference rules', and insisted the Conference must bring their insolvency rules in line with FA standards by the end of 2009.

An FA spokesman said: 'In the interests of all parties, not least the supporters of Chester City, this has been dealt with as a matter of priority. It has been clear that the Conference would be breaking its own rules by proceeding with their proposal and this made it impossible for the FA to approve it. We would have liked to resolve this situation before the start of the season but important aspects of this arrangement have only come to light in recent days.'

Chester City signed what they described as a confidentiality agreement and were effectively banned from appealing their 25-point deduction. The agreement was entered into in return for their affiliation from the FA. City managing director Bob Gray said, 'They won't allow us to appeal or discuss it. The whole thing stinks, but we'll do anything just to play football.'

Conference chairman Brian Lee said, 'Embarrassing? Not at all, our main objective has been achieved, the Conference running with 24 teams, thus preserving the promotion and relegation arrangement we have with the Football League. To achieve this we've had to diversify and for that we have been fined £5,000. Thus I think it's fair to say we have contravened, but not broken our rules.'

Ultimately Chester City failed to see out the 2009-10 season and were expelled from the Conference in February 2010, their playing record being expunged. This caused yet another controversy, with clubs that had gained points from matches with the defunct club insisting that these should stand – especially as yellow and red cards awarded in the games were not rescinded.

FINANCIAL MATTERS

BOOM AND BUST

Many non-League clubs have risen up the Pyramid and fallen just as fast. Here's just a small selection

Team Bath

Team Bath, known as 'The Crescents' after the famous Royal Crescent, or 'The Scholars', were a football club affiliated with the University of Bath and were founded in 1999. Yet their history was to encompass just ten highly eventful years.

Their stated aim was to be a fully fledged football club within the environment of the University, allowing players to combine full-time training with a university course, something unique in British football. Team Bath recruited over 50 young former professionals, most of whom eventually graduated and many of whom subsequently returned to the professional game.

After winning promotion in a successful first season in the Southern League Division One West, and playing in the Southern League Premier Division, Team Bath won promotion to the Conference South in May 2008. They had been the first university side to reach the first round of the FA Cup in 122 years in 2002 and matched that achievement twice more in subsequent years, sharing rivals Bath City's Twerton Park ground.

After the Football Conference ruled in 2009 that Team Bath were not eligible to win promotion to the national division, a ruling which also meant that the club were no longer able to compete in Football Association cup competitions, they decided to fold at the end of the season.

'The Conference's decision means the club has gone as far as it can go without making significant changes to its structure,' said manager Ged Roddy. 'Team Bath has been an ambitious club and our long-term goal has always been to secure a place in the Football League. Unfortunately the Conference said that no further promotions would be possible, thereby denying us the opportunity to progress. Our dream has always been to promote a student football team into the Football League.'

Boston United

The rise of Boston United from the Southern League to the Football Conference in 2000 and to the Football League in 2002 was meteoric. They had lost their way somewhat after being founder members of the Conference (then Football Alliance) in 1979 and taking 12,000 supporters to Wembley in the FA Trophy final in 1985.

However, both promotions have since been overshadowed by revelations of off-the-field financial irregularities. A five-year tax scam resulted in £323,000 in taxes being withheld as the club operated a shadowy system of parallel contracts and secret payments which enabled them to recruit players of a quality they otherwise would not have been able to afford.

News of the irregularities emerged shortly after Boston won promotion and the FA punished the club by fining them £100,000 and docking them four League points. Manager Steve Evans and club chairman Pat Malkinson were also found guilty of impeding the inquiry. The club that should have gained League status in 2003 was Dagenham & Redbridge, who went up four years later.

Cammell Laird

Northern Premier League side Cammell Laird, who had over-achieved by gaining four promotions in five seasons – took cost-cutting to an extreme in late 2008 when they decided to revert to amateur status. Chief executive George Higham pointed out the fact that fresh sponsorship was hard to find in the credit crunch and that despite on-field success their attendances had actually fallen since promotion from the NPL Division One North in May 2008. 'We hope the footballing community of Wirral rally together with our existing die-hard supporters and ensure the football club has a future,' he said.

To make matters worse they finished fifth bottom of their division – high enough to avoid relegation – only to be compulsorily relegated for failing to meet ground regulations by the 31 March deadline. They failed to reach the C grading required to compete at Step 3, building work on a new enclosure at their Kirklands ground having not been completed. Their appeal to the FA in May failed and they began the following season in the NPL Division One South, Ironically, this rule is what got them promoted to the Northern Premier League Premier Division in the 2007-08 campaign when they finished second and leapfrogged the club above.

Canvey Island

Jeff King, a former player, took over ownership of Canvey Island FC in 1992 and both managed the team and funded the club's progress through the divisions between 1992 and 2006. The highlight was their 2001 FA Trophy win against Forest Green Rovers in front of over 10,000 people at Villa Park, while they arrived in the Football Conference in 2004.

Subsidy from King's building and entertainment businesses had sustained Canvey's climb up the non-League ladder but in 2006, with crowds that at times dipped below 500, he announced that he was terminating his association with Canvey and instead took over at Isthmian League Premier Division Chelmsford City.

He said: 'It's difficult when you are playing at home with gates of 4-500. We charge nothing like Football League clubs but if people choose not to go, we can choose not to waste our time and money. When you are talking to a counterpart from a Surrey club who says it's hard to make ends meet with an average gate of 1,900 that puts it into perspective. It looks like people in Canvey don't want to support a team in that league.'

Canvey faced a potentially crucial period of change – and while the players scattered, some following their erstwhile boss, the club took voluntary relegation to the Ryman League Division 1 North, the bulk of the squad the reserve side from the previous season. The Gulls narrowly missed out on a play-off place, but went one better the following season, gaining promotion to the Ryman Premier League through the play-offs.

Chelmsford City

Chelmsford City were formed as a professional club in 1938, the aim a place in the Football League. In pursuit of that end they spent a fortune developing their ground and assembling a squad of players capable of playing at that level. The public of Chelmsford turned up in large numbers and demonstrated their hunger for a higher class of football. Unfortunately the closed shop policy of the Football League proved their undoing. Indeed in 1962 the club employed a staff of full-time professionals, although it was all to end in tears when the Football League banned them from applying for membership for five years following a breach in regulations of which City were in fact innocent.

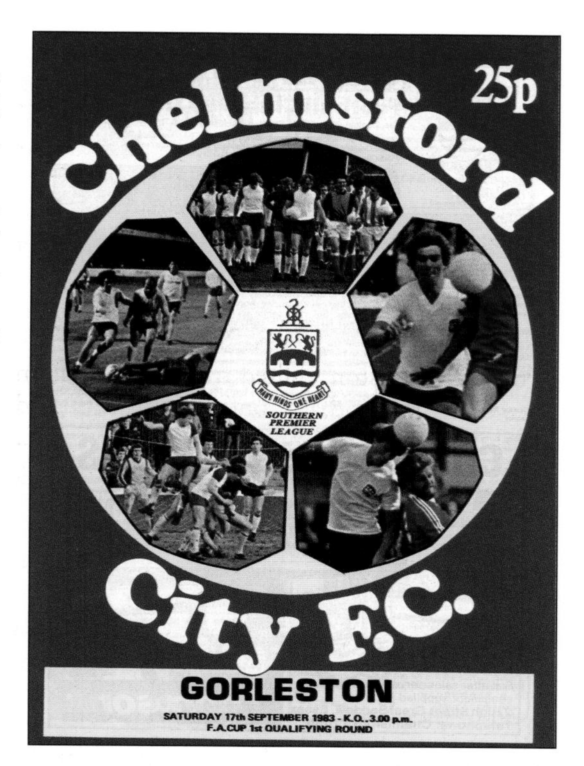

City's decline as a power in non-League football saw them miss out on the formation of the Alliance Premier League (now the Football Conference) in 1979, and encounter ever-increasing financial difficulties which saw the club surrender ownership of New Writtle Street, a development that led to City being kicked out of the ground in 1997.

When the official receivers sold the stadium, they had to spend a decade playing ten miles from Chelmsford, at nearby Maldon and Billericay, before returning to the town at the Melbourne Park athletics track. At least they survived, unlike neighbours Hornchurch FC, who were bankrolled by a company called Carthium Ltd but folded when on the point of promotion to the Conference in 2005. A new club, AFC Hornchurch, has since risen from the Essex Senior League to the Ryman League Premier Division.

Crawley Town

Formed in 1896, Crawley Town began life in the West Sussex League. They hit tough times in 1999, enduring a couple of months of administration, but had been dragged out of the mire by John Duly who took them through a very successful period in their history. In 2004 they reached the Conference for the first time ever. But this made them the target for a takeover which led to disaster.

In mid-2005, new owners – the SA Group – decided that they would now run Crawley as a full-time football club and money started to be spent, heralding the onset of problems both on and off the pitch. In the 2006 close season the club were fined £10,000 and deducted three points for financial irregularities, which led to another spell in administration. In August 2006 it was announced that Crawley would fold due to their £1.8 million debts and they came within an hour of the liquidation deadline. However, a last-minute rescue package saved the club and allowed them to carry on playing, albeit with a 10-point deduction for entering administration.

In May 2007 it was confirmed that all of Crawley Town's debts had been cleared. However, they were given a 6-point penalty and a transfer embargo was put in place due to 'financial irregularities'; it is believed that Crawley failed to confirm to the league that the debts had been paid. In April 2008 Prospect Estate Holdings Limited took control of Crawley after buying it from the SA Group in conjunction with former owner John Duly. Many fans who had boycotted the club during the SA Group reign returned, but the appointment of controversial manager Steve Evans brought yet more polarisation of opinion.

Farnborough Town

Farnborough Town's history began in 1968 in the Surrey Senior League and ended in May 2007 when the football club was liquidated and expelled from the Conference South.

Boro' had enjoyed success in the Spartan and Athenian Leagues with a formidable home record – they remained unbeaten on their own ground from August 1973 to April 1977, a total of 87 games and almost four seasons. Under long-serving boss Ted Pearce, who managed for 23 years, they were invited to join the GM Vauxhall Conference in 1989 when champions Leytonstone/Ilford were not promoted because of ground grading regulations. A decade of yo-yo relegation and promotion ended when wealthy Graham Westley arrived as club owner and team manager in 1999. Plans to shift the ground 30 miles to Kingston came to nothing amid fan opposition, but a first season in the Conference saw Farnborough finish seventh as

Westley, an unsuccessful would-be League player turned wealthy businessman, poured money into the team to fulfil his dream.

A lucrative FA Cup tie against Arsenal in early 2003 turned out to be Westley's last as he left in mid-season, taking his backroom staff and seven players to Conference rivals Stevenage Borough. Transfer embargoes, several shifts in ownership and a huge debt to the Inland Revenue, among others, combined to break the club he left behind in name if not in spirit, though they struggled on for four more eventful seasons as their Cherrywood Road ground fell apart around them.

The reformed Farnborough Football Club had both name and colours chosen by the fans, who elected to revert to the club's pre-Westley yellow and blue. They took a step back up the Pyramid at the first attempt, winning the Southern League South & West division in style, and achieved promotion to the Conference South in 2010. They were clearly on the up again. And this time around money was being invested in facilities as well as players by new chairman Simon Hollis.

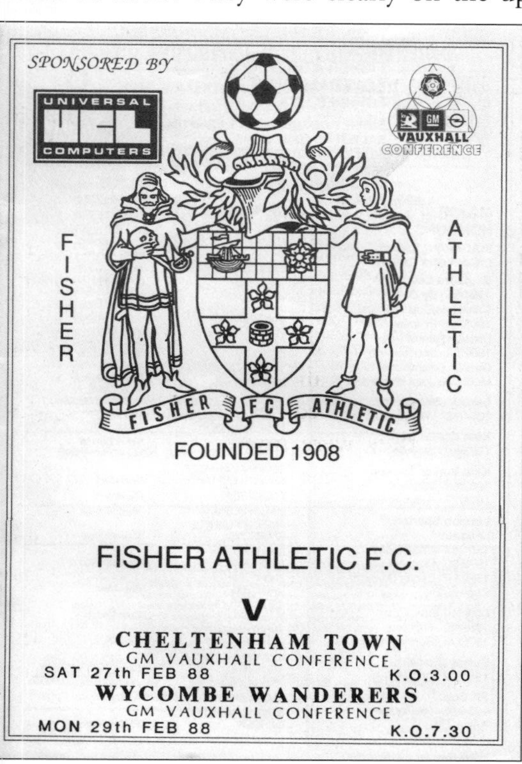

Fisher Athletic

Fisher Athletic FC was a semi-professional football club from South East London named after Catholic martyr St John Fisher and founded in 1908 by Michael Culiton, headmaster at Dockland School, to provide sporting facilities for underprivileged youths of Bermondsey. The club was elected to the Spartan League in 1974 and the Southern League in 1982, playing fortunes peaking with a rise to the Conference five years later.

The club left its docklands ground ostensibly to return after redevelopment, but found itself sharing Champion Hill Stadium with Dulwich Hamlet. The ground they left, Salter Road, still lies derelict, its outline planning permission for 129 dwellings not raising enough income to build a new ground, which the council insisted should be part of the plans.

Fisher Athletic were wound up by the High Court in May 2009 after failing to pay debts to the Inland Revenue, but the club name lives on in the shape of Fisher FC, formed to compete in the Kent League in the 2009-10 season.

Fan Joe Arif reflects on the demise and rebirth of Fisher Athletic:

'Generally when fellow non-League supporters hear of another club's demise, I find the term most commonly used is; 'I feel sorry for the true fans.'

'And, true, I felt very sorry for myself over the footballing death of Fisher Athletic (London) Ltd and angry it was left to us to effectively pick up the pieces. What I found surprising, however, was the sense of liberation brought on by the prospect of reforming my club. True, we are forced to ply our trade three leagues lower than we had become accustomed to but what we gain far outweighs any minor negatives. We've given ourselves the opportunity to right many of the wrongs that eventually brought the original club to its knees. To put an analogy on recent proceedings, we've watched the fall of a dictatorship and seen it replaced by democracy.

'Our chairman, along with the club's new committee, are all elected on an annual basis by our Supporters' Trust and they are accountable to its members. People who hold senior positions are there to provide a service to the club rather than fuel any egotistical power trips. The club, currently owned by 42 founding members who each hold an equal stake, have put measures in place to ensure no one person can hold a stake of any more than 10 per cent regardless of the cash injection put forward. We must learn from our past and aim to be fully self-sufficient. Success on the field, we hope, will be translated from excellent organisation off it.

'Sport is all about achievement, but this cannot be sustained long-term by the boom and bust environment that has plagued this club throughout its century-long existence. In non-League football, the 'sugar daddy' era is slowly coming to an end, and the number of fans-owned clubs is rising steadily. There may be less money rolling around but I still think it makes for a healthier non-League game going forward.'

Scarborough

Scarborough FC had played at the former Athletic Ground since it was first opened in 1898, moving from Scarborough Cricket Club. In 1988, under a sponsorship deal, they sold the naming rights and until its closure in 2007 the stadium was known as the McCain Stadium after the food company. The club enjoyed League status from 1987to 1999, but failed to bounce back from the Conference as hoped.

In March 2006 a plan was announced for a new stadium to be located in Eastfield, Scarborough, with a capacity of around 4,000. It would include offices that would be let to cover the club's operating losses. The McCain Stadium was to be sold to property developers Persimmon Homes for around £4.1 million, which would have been enough to pay off all the club's debts and fund the new stadium.

However, a covenant existed on the McCain Stadium that restricted its use only to sporting activities and Scarborough FC failed to convince the council that its proposals to sell to a housing developer would raise enough money to both pay off the debts and build a new ground.

In June 2007, Scarborough FC were given an eight-day stay of execution following a change of heart by the council. But on 20 June they were wound up in the High Court with debts of £2.5m. This ended 128 years of history. However, the supporters' trust formed a new club, Scarborough Athletic, which was entered in the Northern Counties East League, Division One with effect from 2007-08.

In December 2008 the council finally purchased the ground from the liquidators and Scarborough Athletic expressed an interest in moving back to the stadium, which had been torn apart by vandals in the interim.

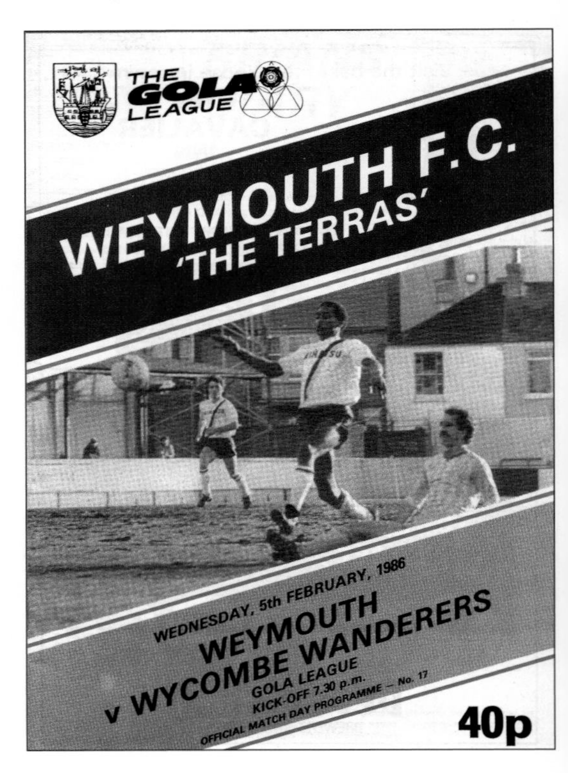

Scarborough Athletic currently play out of town in Bridlington with gates of less than 500.

Weymouth

Formed in 1890, Weymouth were founder members of the Dorset League and moved into the Southern League and thence the Conference. A move to a new ground, the Wessex Stadium, in 1987 brought further success, but the club was relegated from the Conference and see-sawed between the Premier and Southern Divisions of the Southern League. Finances suffered through lack of support both in real terms and commercially until the appearance of Ian Ridley and Steve Claridge as chairman and player-manager in 2003-04 saw a revolution.

However, differences in the boardroom saw Martyn Harrison take the reins on Ridley's departure, dismissing Claridge and in 2005 turning the club fully professional, the only full-time non-League side outside the Conference. Though promotion to the Conference was achieved in 2006, debts of £3 million were amassed in two years. A plan to sell the ground and build a new stadium on the proceeds fell through and Harrison sold the club to music promoter Mel Bush for £1. Bush stayed for four months, and then handed over to property developer Malcolm Curtis. His company bought the land around the ground, injecting £550,000 into the coffers, but this was soon swallowed up by losses.

Businessman Stephen Beer offered to buy the club, but this fell through when he had a suspected stroke. He then changed his mind about investing a day later; meanwhile, a youthful scratch team bolstered by journeymen players keen to be in the shop window was losing 11 consecutive games en route to relegation.

Ridley returned in 2009 and staved off administration by a mixture of fundraising and a cameo on-pitch return for Steve Claridge that made national headlines. In October, however, he announced that he was stepping down from his post for health reasons, and by the end of the season the club had seen four different managers take charge as well as three different chairmen. Little surprise they finished rock bottom of Conference South.

GROUND GRADING

In simple terms, the idea of ground grading is to ensure that any club competing in a given league have facilities appropriate to the level at which they're playing. It's a process that applies from the very top of the English game to the numerous leagues operating down as far as Level 11. The Premiership and the Football League set their own grading criteria, while those for non-League clubs are set by the Football Association. There are currently eight grades:

Grade A - for clubs at Level 5
(the Conference National division)
Grade B - for clubs at Level 6
(the Conference North and South divisions)
Grade C - for clubs at Level 7
(the Northern Premier League, Southern League and Isthmian League Premier divisions)
Grade D - for clubs at Level 8
(the Northern Premier League, Southern League and Isthmian League First divisions)
Grade E - for clubs being promoted to Level 8
(Grade D required within 12 months)
Grade F - for clubs at Level 9
Grade G - for clubs at Level 10
(if their league has a division at Level 9).
Grade H - is the minimum grade introduced in February 2010

In general, any promoted club has until 31 March of the year following their promotion to bring their ground up to the required grade. The exception, as can be seen from the list above, is at Level 8, where slightly longer has been allowed for the necessary steps to be completed.

Full details of the requirements for each grade can be found on the FA's website (www.thefa.com/Leagues/National-LeagueSystem/GroundGrading.aspx).

Although there are eight grades and each includes a substantial number of sections covering different aspects of the ground and its facilities, there is a lot of overlap and some sections apply to all grades. There are also several sections that apply to most grades, with only Grade A, or Grades A and B, different from the lower grades.

Some of the grading requirements are very specific, while others are surprisingly vague. For example, a Grade A ground must *'give an overall appearance and impression of being a football ground suitable for the highest Division of The National League System'*, although exactly what might be required in order to give the desired impression is not made clear. Grade A grounds must also *'have the potential of being upgraded to meet the criteria for membership of The Football League'*.

The rules covering the number of spectators a ground should be able to accommodate, and the proportion of those who should be seated and/or under cover, are almost certainly the most troublesome for the majority of clubs. These upgrades involve a significant outlay for clubs struggling to make ends meet, and the possibility that any investment made towards improving facilities will have an adverse effect on the size of the squad or the quality of players that can be attracted or retained is a constant worry.

Over the years, a number of clubs have either failed to make the necessary improvements, or failed to meet the deadline for doing so. In some cases, offenders have been denied promotion, among the most notable being Stevenage Borough, Conference champions in 1995-96, but prevented from taking their place in the Football League. Others have enjoyed the high life for a while before suffering an FA-imposed relegation, recent victims including Cambridge City, who finished fourth in Conference South in 2007-08 but started the following season back in the Southern League Premier Division, and King's Lynn, demoted from the Conference North after finishing seventh in 2008-09.

From Grade A down to Grade E, the requirements state that the ground should have a minimum operational capacity, referred to as 'X'

in the table below, as calculated by *'a competent person in accordance with the guidance given in the Guide To Safety At Sports Grounds (the Green Guide)'*. For Grade A to Grade D, there must also be the potential to increase the capacity, to a total referred to as 'Y' below, in the future. The relevant figures are:

Grade	X	Y
Grade A	X = 4,000	Y = 5,000
Grade B	X = 3,000	Y = 4,000
Grade C	X = 2,000	Y = 3,000
Grade D	X = 1,500	Y = 2,000
Grade E	X = 1,000	

In addition, to attain Grade A there must be final planning permission and a business plan in place, with realistic timescales, to allow the increase in capacity to 5,000 to be achieved. At lower levels, there are no rules covering the capacity of the ground, although clubs are encouraged to be *'mindful that the minimum requirement for Grade E is 1,000'*.

Other sections relating to the ground itself cover such things as the provision of a clubhouse, car parking arrangements, the size and standard of the playing surface, floodlights, barriers around the playing area, public address systems and emergency access. Section 2.6, relating to the provision of facilities for disabled spectators, highlights an important aspect of the ground grading system – while these regulations are designed, in part, to ensure a safe and suitable environment for both players and spectators, they are not intended to replace or override government legislation, and clubs still have obligations in these areas. In the case of disabled fans,

> *'No specific requirement is currently included in the grading criteria but the Football Association strongly recommends that access is provided to both a covered viewing area and toilet and refreshment facilities.'* Clubs are,

however, reminded that they *'must take account of the needs of disabled spectators'* and be mindful of their *'obligations under the provisions of the Disability Discrimination Act 1995'*.

As well as specifying the capacity required at each level, the sections dealing with spectator facilities also encompass the size and condition of terracing, the type of seating to be provided and how much of the spectator accommodation should be under cover. Again, the figures differ from level to level, but for each level there is a minimum requirement for covered accommodation, here referred to as 'X', of which at least a certain amount, here referred to as 'Y', has to be seats located in one stand. In each case, the number of seats can include those that have to be provided for the press and for club directors and committee members. The relevant figures are:

Grade A-C	X = 500	Y = 250
Grade D	X = 300	Y = 150
Grade E	X = 250	Y = 150
Grade F	X = 100	Y = 100
Grade G	X = 100	Y = 50
Grade H	No minimum seating specified	

There are further sections covering the provision of refreshments and toilet facilities for spectators before consideration is given to matters 'behind the scenes', including standards for dressing rooms for the players and officials, and the availability of adequate medical facilities both for participants and spectators.

Finally, those clubs that have reached the pinnacle of the non-League game are required to prepare for the possibility of promotion to the Football League, and there is a whole section in the Grade A document dedicated to the steps Conference National clubs need to take.

Early in the season, every Conference National club is sent instructions on how to carry out *'a self-assessment of its facilities having regard to The Football League's Membership Criteria'*. Each club must submit a completed self-assessment form to the Football League by 31 December. In addition, the Football League offers an advisory service to help clubs determine what improvements would be needed in the event of promotion. Those in contention for promotion as at 31 March are required to liaise with the Football Licensing Authority for guidance in a number of aspects of ground safety and, before Football League status can be confirmed, they will need to ensure that CCTV, emergency lighting, a control room, a monitoring system and automatic revolving turnstiles are all installed, and that the relevant Safety Certificates have been submitted to the Football League.

Complying with all these regulations can be a headache for clubs, who have to make some difficult decisions. The nearer a club moves to Conference status, the more stringent the regulations become, and clubs like Forest Green, an established Conference National side who decided to plan ahead by building a new stadium to Football League standards in 2006, can find themselves struggling to meet their financial commitments.

Not only that, but over the years there have also been some controversial FA decisions and rulings connected with ground grading, and it's easy to see why the subject arouses such passion in the non-League game.

In the summer of 2009, Northern Premier club Newcastle Blue Star became one of the more unfortunate victims of ground grading. Between 1999 and 2004, the club had secured grants from the Football Stadia Improvement Fund (FSIF) to carry out work on the Wheatsheaf Sports Ground, their home since 1970.

The FSIF grants were legitimately secured and correctly used, but in 2007, when the club was selected for the newly formed Northern Premier League Division One North, the facilities offered by the Wheatsheaf were deemed inadequate for the new league. Newcastle Blue Star promptly

relocated to the nearby Kingston Park Stadium, home to Rugby Union side Newcastle Falcons. As a result of the move, the FSIF demanded full repayment of the £61,000 the club had received for redevelopment of the Wheatsheaf, with the unfortunate consequence that the club folded prior to the start of the 2009-10 season. With Blue Star's decision coming after the Northern league AGM, the Northern Premier League was one team short of its normal complement of 22 clubs for the season.

King's Lynn were another side to fall foul of the regulations in 2009, although here the circumstances were slightly different. The club, promoted to the Conference North at the end of the 2007-08 season, were relegated again at the end of the 2008-09 season by the FA, the decision based on the fact that the club had failed to begin the work required to bring the Walks Stadium up to Conference North standards.

It was a controversial decision, hotly contested by the club, who had committed to carry out the required work but had been prevented from doing so because the improvements were to be funded by the local council, and their involvement had meant the ground couldn't be closed during the season. Despite the council's pledge to carry out the work prior to the 2009-10 season, and representations from both club and council members, the Linnets were unable to persuade the FA to relax the 1 April deadline, and suffered a compulsory relegation despite finishing three places above the drop zone. They went out of business in late 2009, though a re-formed club, Lynn FC, was launched in 2010 in their stead.

Clubs have been denied promotion on the failure of their grounds to achieve the relevant grading, but Conference history was made when Cambridge City, who finished fourth in Conference South in 2007-08, started the following season back in the Southern League Premier Division.

City's Milton Road home failed to earn the FA's Ground Grading Category B rating required of all Blue Square sides owing to a lack of terracing behind both goals and inadequate turnstile facilities. Clubs throughout non-

League were handed a deadline of 31 March to get their facilities up to scratch, although City had the added concern of fighting a legal battle with their landlords Ross River.

The Lilywhites won the right to remain at Milton Road until 2010 only the previous autumn, and the club argued that the court action left them with no time or money to improve the ground. A judgment delivered in September 2007 found that City had been the victims of bribery and fraudulent misrepresentation in a deal done by outgoing directors to sell the Milton Road ground. The Court restored the club's previous lease, which runs until 2010, and their right to half of future development profits. 'We made the case that legal action left us in the position that we were unable to confirm until the end of the court case that we would definitely be at Milton Road,' said director Rab Crangle, part of a new fans-based board. Nevertheless City were demoted, and this decision ended 22 consecutive seasons in the second tier of non-League football and resulted in only the third relegation in the club's history. (A groundshare with Newmarket is scheduled to begin in 2011-12, a further year having been negotiated at Milton Road.)

Macclesfield Town fans had every right to feel hard done by in 1995 when their side was refused entry to the Football League after finishing as Conference champions. The alleged problem was that their Moss Rose ground was not up to Football League standards, but just a couple of years earlier the FA had been perfectly happy to allow the then homeless Chester City to play their League games at Moss Rose while the Deva Stadium was under construction.

But, like it or not, ground grading is a fact of life at almost every level in the game. It may have come under attack from a variety of quarters over the years, but in the long term the improvement of facilities can surely only be a good thing for the fans. Clubs have to strike a balance between investing in players and investing in the infrastructure, but this has been part of the game for some time, and they should be used to the idea by now. That's not to say it's an easy balance to strike, but there's little point in a club spending money on players who can earn promotion if there's nothing left in the kitty to bring the ground up to the required standard once they've achieved it.

BRINGING IN THE MONEY

With the ever-present need to balance the books, non-League clubs have come up with some novel methods

Director For A Day

In 2009, AFC Telford United offered their fans the chance to be chairman for a day. A payment of £300 was promised to grant the following:

- Meeting and greeting opposition officials on arrival
- Seat in the directors' box
- Parking in a private bay
- Name in the match programme
- Matchday hospitality
  Meeting players and officials at a post-match presentation.

Weymouth's 100 Saviours

Weymouth fans and businesses pulled together in September 2009 to save the club from administration, raising £50,000 via the 'Terras Saviour 100' scheme after the board set a 10-day deadline to raise the cash. The campaign's profile was boosted when former manager Steve Claridge made a sensational playing return, though his comeback was spoilt by the 5-1 loss at home to Bromley.

Said Terras then chairman Ian Ridley: 'This is quite overwhelming. Everyone should be incredibly proud of what they have achieved, both those who have donated and those who have administered the scheme. There are those who think Weymouth FC should just exist in some minor form or even be quietly allowed to die. This shows just how many people out there will not let that happen while there is breath in their bodies. We will now do our utmost to ensure that we do not find ourselves in such a serious position again.' (The club survived, just, but without Ridley.)

A Place On The Board

Eastbourne Borough offered fans the chance to shape the destiny of the club, a £5,000 donation buying a place on the club's board for the 2009-10 season. Four directorships are up for grabs at the Conference National club and those who take up the deal will have full voting rights at board meetings. 'Obviously it is a way of raising funds,' Borough chairman Len Smith explained, 'but we are also hoping to get new people involved who can bring with them some fresh ideas. There is a quite a bit of kudos in being a director of a football club and you don't get offers like this at the likes of Chelsea or Manchester United.'

The package includes £500-worth of shares in the Community Interest Company, which oversees the running of the football club as well as Langney Sports and facilities like the indoor bowls club. Other perks are a seat in the directors' box for all home games, travel on the team coach for up to ten away games and two overnight stays at the team hotel.

Hendon Go Pop

Ryman Premier League side Hendon have benefited from a pop star's patronage in much the same way as nearby Watford. Instead of Elton John they have Saint Etienne indie-pop mastermind Bob Stanley who, after growing up in Surrey 'watching Redhill, Dorking and Leatherhead in their glory years', adopted Hendon as his local club when moving nearer London. In 2006 Saint Etienne made a 15-minute documentary film called *Monty The Lamb*, directed by Paul Kelly and depicting a day in the life of North London non-Leaguers Hendon, seen through the eyes of their club mascot, carpet fitter Dave Garner.

Then in 2009, with the supporters' trust-run club facing hard times amidst the recession, the band made the launch of their latest recording, 'Foxbase Beta', at London's trendy Social venue a fundraiser for the club. 'I was thinking of what I could do to raise some money,' said Stanley. 'I'm not sure it will be much, but hopefully it will keep the club going for a bit and pay the rent.'

Needs Must

Some non-League clubs, ever mindful of the need to raise revenue throughout the year and not just on home-game Saturdays, have businesses attached to their grounds.

For many years Bishop's Stortford FC provided secure, convenient car parking for travellers using nearby Stansted Airport, under whose flight path games are played. Essex neighbours Thurrock, known as Purfleet until 2003, have always been run as a business in conjunction with the nearby Thurrock Hotel. In fact their changing rooms used to be the hotel itself. Corporate patrons are allowed to use the banqueting suite once a year as part of their sponsorship package.

Staines Town play at the Wheatsheaf Park ground which was rebuilt to house a health and fitness club, the Thames Club, in a two-storey steel frame, brick-clad stand. The property also provides the club with changing facilities. Bizarrely the Thames Club was owned by Championship club Sheffield United, who sold it in 2008 in order to focus their leisure operations in the South Yorkshire area. Staines Town continued to lease their facilities from the health club as before.

BRINGING IN THE FANS...
...AND LOOKING AFTER THEM

Alfreton

When Alfreton crashed to a 3-0 defeat to Redditch in the Conference North early in the 2009-10 season they could point to a number of excuses: traffic problems, three players missing through injury and suspension and three more players sick on the coach, which arrived only half an hour before kick-off. But the players were disappointed at their display, so clubbed together and repaid the travelling supporters' entrance fee. Striker Liam Hearn admitted, 'The fans spend a lot of money following us, and our performance was awful – it was just a bad day all round.'

Boston United

When the rate of Value Added Tax was reduced from 17.5 per cent to 15 per cent in 2008, Boston United made the decision that the reduction in admission prices (6p on a child's £3 ticket and 18p on an adult's) was likely to make for long queues at the turnstiles if they were to give fans a refund on entry. They decided instead to give season ticket holders vouchers to be traded in for three free cups of tea over the course of the season – a stylish and refreshing solution.

Cambridge United

The crowd witnessing the clash between Cambridge United and Conference rivals Oxford United on the football field in January 2009 was swelled by 1,200 tickets given to the former city's university. In turn, the university made tickets available to staff for just £3 each, the cash from ticket sales going towards their 800th anniversary charity Camfed dedicated to fighting poverty and HIV/AIDS in rural Africa.

Crawley Town

Fans are well known for bemoaning the lack of support for their club, but few have done what Gavin Green did in 2009 – make a promotional film to encourage floating voters and put it on an internet social networking site!

Called *The Other Red Devils* as a not-so-subtle dig at Manchester United and their 'nationwide following', it is a 30-minute fly-on-the-wall documentary which roams from the usually forbidden confines of the dressing room to the manager's office. It took six months to put together and, said Green, was intended 'to raise the club's profile in the local area. The idea was to do something no one else was doing and to get people interested in the club again.' It can be seen at www.facebook.com/crawleytown.

Dorchester

With an average gate of less than 500 out of a population of 18,000, Conference South Dorchester were struggling in October 2007 when owner Eddie Mitchell promised fans that if 1,000 people turned up to the match against Bromley he would give every one of them their money back. 'I finally made the decision after I watched us play Eastleigh in the first round of the Setanta Shield. We went 2-0 down and came back to win 3-2, but I just felt totally despondent because the crowd was so low – there could only have been about 200. I just wanted to see if it was possible.'

The gesture would have cost between £5,000 and £6,000 but the magic number was not reached. 'Saying that, we got 619 which was still the fifth highest attendance in the league and I'm very thankful to the supporters who turned out. The extra few hundred certainly made it feel better in there and I know the players could sense it on the pitch.' Mitchell finally admitted defeat and moved on to AFC Bournemouth in 2009.

SPONSORSHIP

Some little-known facts about non-League sponsors and their links with the grass-roots game

Blue Square

When the current Conference was formed as the Alliance Premier League it was not sponsored. Carmakers GM Vauxhall were first to get involved, and it became the Nationwide Conference in 2004-05 before Blue Square, a bookmaker, took over the sponsorship of all three divisions in 2007 in a three-year deal.

The sponsorship deal, which was renewed for a further three years in 2010, covers the naming rights to the leagues, sponsorship of perimeter boards, corner flags, patches and match officials. Martin Belsham, Blue Square CEO, said at the time: 'In excess of 60 teams will benefit from our investment which will see monies filtered down through all three tiers. It will also allow us to connect to fans that have supported their clubs through thick and thin, and we will be looking at new ways to interact directly with them.'

In addition, Blue Square supported a number of new initiatives including Manager and Player of the Month awards. The Blue Square judging panel included Paul Parker, the former England and Manchester United defender, whose experience in the non-League game included a stint managing Welling.

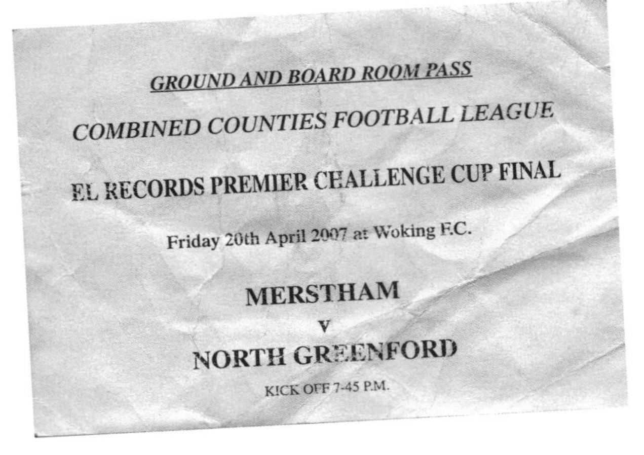
GROUND AND BOARD ROOM PASS
COMBINED COUNTIES FOOTBALL LEAGUE
EL RECORDS PREMIER CHALLENGE CUP FINAL
Friday 20th April 2007 at Woking F.C.
MERSTHAM
v
NORTH GREENFORD
KICK OFF 7-45 P.M.

Ryman

High-street stationery firm Ryman, controlled by Theo Paphitis of *Dragons' Den* fame, are well known in their own right. They have sponsored the Isthmian League since 1997 – two years after Paphitis took control – and follow in some illustrious footsteps. Despite its long history and traditional nature, the Isthmian was the first league to have sponsorship, having been selected by tobacco firm Rothmans, who had been active in other sporting sectors including cricket. (Tony Williams was a prime mover in this.) They sponsored the Isthmian League from 1974 to 1977, offering clubs prize money in relation to their finishing position in the table. This money was reduced for bookings, so encouraging fair play. The sponsors that succeeded Rothmans are: Michael Lawrie (1977-78), Berger (1978-82), Servowarm (1982-85), Vauxhall-Opel (1985-90), Vauxhall (1990-91), Diadora (1991-95), ICIS (1995-97) and Ryman (1997-present).

UniBond

Glue and household product manufacturers UniBond, sponsor of the Northern Premier League, are a subsidiary of Henkel AG & Co, an international company headquartered in Düsseldorf, Germany. Not the most interesting of stories, perhaps – 'Henkel develops products for a broad range of applications' states its website – but one of its products inspired a notable terrace song in late 2009.

A chant sung by Marine fans to the tune of 'When The Saints Go Marching In' offered free promotion for UniBond's anti-mould bath sealant product and became the BBC's Chant of the Week:

'The UniBond it has no nails
The UniBond it has no nails
And its anti-mould bath sealant
Is very good, it never fails.'

The Northern Premier League continued their association of adhesives in 2010 when Evo-Stik were announced as their new sponsors in succession to UniBond.

Cherry Red

Cherry Red Records are active in the football sponsorship field and lend their name to the Combined Counties League, having previously sponsored the Hellenic League. Their EL Records and Lemon Recordings offshoots are the sponsors of the CCL Premier Challenge Cup and Division One Cup respectively.

Cherry Red chairman Iain McNay is also chairman of AFC Wimbledon's holding company. They have been a corporate sponsor of the club since it was started, while his company have naming rights to the Kingsmeadow Stadium ground of AFC Wimbledon. Finally, Cherry Red lead the market in football-related music, with the most complete catalogue of soccer-related songs extant.

Zamaretto

In a remarkable break with conventional modern sporting practice, the Southern League was the last major non-League organisation to resist renaming for a sponsor. After a two-season spell with British Gas as its sponsor, it began 2009-10 as the Zamaretto League, this being a brand of exotic liqueur made by InterContinental Brands (ICB) Ltd. Ken Turner, League Chairman, commented: 'We are delighted that ICB has chosen to support the Southern League. Partnerships like these are great news for the profile and future of the semi-professional game. We are already finding that we have quite a lot in common with ICB in that we are both enterprising, positive, forward-looking organisations.'

Skilltrainingltd

The Northern League sponsors are a relatively small concern who won the naming rights in a raffle! The 125-year-old league lost its lucrative deal with former Gretna backer, the late Brooks Mileson, in 2008 so then had the idea of raffling the league's naming rights for £250 per ticket and, after a great deal of work, this has proved successful. Ann and Alan Barkas, through their company skilltrainingltd, won the raffle, and we couldn't have had more enthusiastic sponsors than them throughout the season. They have been so impressed by what they've seen, we are delighted to have signed a sponsorship deal with them, that is worth five figures per season. They are very much a hands-on couple, they love going to Northern League games, and they are proud to be associated with the league. Therefore, we are delighted to agree a five-year sponsorship deal with their company.'

The husband and wife team, whose company specialises in training courses for 16-to-60-year-olds from three bases in County Durham, were chairman and committee member respectively of Easington Colliery in their Northern League days.

Sponsorship Nightmare

When former Northern League side Durham City found themselves playing for the first time in the NPL Premier Division in 2009-10, it opened up new commercial possibilities such as sponsorship by an international property company. But the sponsorship was cancelled after the club was told that it would not be able to move up to Conference North if it won promotion because it has a plastic pitch. As a consequence, all players were made available for transfer with immediate effect.

Club chairman Stuart Dawson said, 'To lose our major sponsor in the new season's infancy means we will not be able to continue to sustain the club's budgets that were set prior to the season commencing, and continue at the level of football we are currently in.' The pitch, which cost almost £1 million, was also vital in bringing in revenue, being used throughout the week for youth and community games.

UEFA allowed the recent Russia versus England international to be played on a similar surface, but Durham have had to play home FA Cup games at neighbouring grounds because of the plastic pitch. The only other plastic pitch in senior football was installed in 2005 at Woodley Sports FC, based in Stockport, Greater Manchester, who play in the NPL Division One North.

Dennis Strudwick, general manager of the Football Conference, said: 'We have a ruling that no matches can be played on artificial pitches without prior approval of the board, and the board hasn't approved artificial pitches yet.'

Durham City played on with a team of rookies and remained winless until March 2010 when they beat FC United of Manchester 2-1. To add insult to injury they were deducted six points for fielding a player under an assumed name.

SUPPORTER POWER

Supporters Trust

Supporters' trusts have become a valuable part of football life in the last few years and can mean the difference between a club's continued existence or descent into oblivion. The status of the club is no barrier to the involvement of such trusts. It is estimated that more than 85,000 fans have joined trusts.

The government-backed Supporters Direct was set up to assist supporters in the act of seeking ownership of their club and should always be consulted when fans seek to take matters into their own hands via a trust. A growing number of clubs have Supporters Direct to thank for their current state of good health.

Supporters Direct is an umbrella organisation set up originally by the UK Government (with cross-party support) to provide support and assistance for its member trusts to secure a greater level of accountability and deliver democratic representation within football clubs and within the game's governing structures. Existing as an Industrial and Provident Society, Supporters Direct is owned by its members and funded by the Football Stadia Improvement Fund – the partner organisation of the Football Foundation – and in Scotland by the Scottish Government. It provides advice to supporters' trusts on how to organise and acquire a collective shareholding in their football on a not-for-profit basis for re-investment. While Football League clubs are also included, the non-League sphere where clubs are in peril on a seemingly monthly basis is the one where it is most active.

Fans have formed more than 100 supporters' trusts across England, Wales and Scotland. A number of supporters' trusts hold equity within their football clubs and some have supporter representation within their boards.

Football League club Charlton were one of the first clubs to introduce an elected supporters' director. From 1991, voting was open to supporters who had contributed to the Valley

SUPPORTERS DIRECT

Its aim is to help people 'who wish to play a responsible part in the life of the football club they support' and it offers support, advice and information to groups of football supporters.

Supporters Direct exists to:

Promote and support the concept of democratic supporter ownership and representation through mutual, not-for-profit structures

Promote football clubs as civic and community institutions

Work to preserve the competitive values of league football in the UK and promote the health of the game as a whole.

In order to promote and achieve this, Supporters Direct works to bring about the following objectives:
The formation of supporters' trusts as IPSs to ensure democratic, transparent representative bodies for supporters at their clubs

The democratic representation of supporters' trusts on Football Club Boards

The ownership of shares in clubs by supporters' trusts and the pooling of individually held shares in a club under the influence of the trust.

To assist supporters' trusts in this, Supporters Direct will work to ensure:

The identification and dissemination of best practice between trusts

Increasing influence of Supporters Direct with the governing bodies

High profile for Supporters Direct and supporters' trusts within the media and cognate organisations.

Investment Plan (VIP) which had got the club back to their moribund ground. In 2001, the election was opened up to the wider supporter base, one vote being allocated to each adult season ticket holder.

It is estimated that supporters' trusts have helped save over a dozen clubs and have brought about £10 million of investment into the game. Trusts have mobilised supporters and the local community, convincing businesses and individuals to come up with money to rebuild clubs. Some trusts have given significant funds to help their clubs rebuild.

York City Supporters Club

York City Supporters' Trust turned fantasy football into reality by buying their football club in March 2003. York became one of a small handful of clubs owned by their supporters. But in the end the trust found running a Conference club with no money was an uphill struggle and the experiment ended after three years.

In December 2001 chairman Douglas Craig had announced the club, founded in 1922 and still in the League, was for sale. If a buyer was not found by the end of January 2002 the club would offer its resignation to the Football League and York City would cease to exist at the end of the 2001-02 season. Several parties showed interest in the club, but the buyer was the Cheshire-based owner of the B and Q Racing Team, John Batchelor. Batchelor promised a new stadium and Premiership football for York, but it was all to end in tears less than a year later.

In just two seasons (1999-2001) the club had lost £2.5m. Crucially, ownership of the ground had been hived off to another company, Bootham Crescent Holdings. The owners of the ground then announced their intention to sell the ground for housing development and resign from the Football League. An estimated value for the ground for development was £4m.

In late December 2001 the local newspaper

(the *Evening Press*) helped to kick off the 'Save City Campaign' and arranged a meeting of a small group of fans. This swelled to a total membership of over 1,700, making them one of the best supported trusts in the country – the figure is even more impressive relative to average home support in recent years of around 2,500.

When York went into administration the trust were the only serious bidders. Preparing a cash flow forecast using sensible cost and income structures, they had to raise £200,000 within three weeks and fundraising began in a panic.

The first full season the trust presided over, 2003-04, led to relegation from the League and, despite a wage budget the third highest in the Conference, they failed to bounce back at the first attempt. The difficulties of running a Conference club on a shoestring became onerous and in 2006 trust members voted by three to one to accept a takeover offer from managing director Jason McGill. His company, JM Packaging, offered to invest a substantial sum in return for a majority shareholding. Although the deal was accepted, there was still a minority of fans against the deal.

Rushden & Diamonds fans came to the same conclusion in November 2006. Having had the running of the club passed over to them in 2005 by founder Max Griggs, their supporters' trust was unable to halt the slide out of the League and voted to yield ownership to former Peterborough vice-chairman Keith Cousins a few months into their return to the Conference. The trust had successfully reduced the inherited annual operating losses of £1.5m, but as chair of the Rushden and Diamonds Society, Paul Hadjuk, admitted, 'I think everyone is aware that running a football club requires more financial backing than the trust could afford to commit.'

Myfootballclub

Owning a football club is a dream well beyond the resources of most supporters. Until, that is, a website was launched in 2007 with the revolutionary aim of recruiting 50,000 fans to do just that. The idea was for people to pay £35 in a bid to raise £1.4m to take over a club, with each member an equal partner. Members would have a vote on transfers as well as player selection and all major decisions affecting the club.

The concept behind MyFootballClub was that of sportswriter Will Brooks, son of actor Ray. In return for an annual subscription, members would participate in every decision of a soon-to-be-bought football club – including, it was said, picking the team!

'I've created a vehicle that will pool fans' opinions, passion and wealth and turn fantasy football into reality,' said Brooks. 'I've always had the notion of a group of fans putting money into a club and not taking it out – it is a potent force for good as most owners look at clubs as a way of making money.'

Brooks acknowledged the scheme could encounter teething problems, particularly with regard to members picking the team. He stated: 'Before members voted on team selection the head coach would provide a briefing on the previous week's game, the next opponents and potential players and formations he suggests. 'Then the owners would vote and the head coach would have to follow their decision, although I think the owners would probably follow the head coach's advice. The head coach would know that this is a club with a difference – where the owners have their say – and, in many ways, the pressure will be taken off him because of this.'

Brooks expected the day-to-day running of the business to go on normally, with members voting on only the most important decisions.

MyFC had an initial target figure of more than 50,000 registrations and in July 2007 opened talks with a number of clubs from lower leagues while collecting payment from registrants. The club that was chosen in November 2007 – and indeed agreed to the takeover – was Conference National outfit Ebbsfleet United, the former Gravesend & Northfleet. As had been predicted, most of the member participation was approving transfers, it being agreed that team matters would be left to the manager, Liam Daish.

Daish wrote to the members thanking them for their support and, while sounding some understandable notes of caution, noted that the MyFC cash had enabled the club to improve their training facilities and equipment. When fans did come close to voting for team selection (albeit less than 1 per cent of the total membership participated) Ebbsfleet's Chief Executive David Davis said: 'If that is what the members want, then we have to do it. Liam has always said he hopes it never happens but if it does we have to deal with it.'

But even though the club won the FA Trophy – 26,000 Fleet fans old and new packing Wembley to watch them defeat Torquay United 1-0 – little effect was seen on home attendances, 'owners' failing to turn their cyber interest into physical presence. Perhaps that was not surprising with members living in over 80 countries. The cash from MyFC had given Ebbsfleet a much-needed financial boost, meaning they could push for honours. But much of the credit had to go to Liam Daish and his team, most of whom were already at the club when MyFC took over.

The summer of 2008 saw MyFC members and Fleet fans join forces to raise the £20,000 needed to sign Michael Gash from Cambridge City. At the end of August, MyFC members voted to sell young striker John Akinde to Bristol City for £150,000, the first time fans had voted in a major transfer deal. Then, in January, the fans voted to buy Darius Charles from Brentford for £25,000. This was democracy in action.

The acid test of the concept was always going to be the take-up rate of the second season and there was an inevitable drop-off of support. This could have been because team-picking promises remained unfulfilled, or people were unhappy that a non-League club was selected instead of a higher-profile outfit. But, whatever the reason, the result was inevitably destabilising for the football club.

The club's payroll was slashed and a squad of full-time players decimated as many saw their futures elsewhere. Reversion to a part-time basis was considered, while a 'Friends of the Fleet' initiative was launched by grass-roots fans, raising £2,000-plus a month towards the playing budget. Chief executive John Moules was happy that the club was debt free. 'The rules of MyFC state that we can only spend what we earn, so it's impossible to overstretch by having things that we can't afford.'

By the end of August 2009 membership had fallen to 9,087 but while the club's weekly budget had risen, they were in the relegation zone of Conference National. (They were relegated at the end of the season after eight years in the Conference.) If the end of the 2009-10 season were to see MyFC unable to sustain their investment, they have said that they will pass control to the supporters' trust. In the end the association between MyFC and Ebbsfleet continued into another season.

CLUB PROFILES

THE CONFERENCE NATIONAL (BLUE SQUARE PREMIER) CLUBS

AFC WIMBLEDON

Nickname – The Dons/The Wombles/ The Crazy Gang
Official Club Website – www.afcwimbledon.co.uk

The Cherry Red Records Fans' Stadium – Kingsmeadow
(Capacity 4,722 [1,265 seated])
Jack Goodchild Way
422a Kingston Road
Kingston Upon Thames
Surrey
KT1 3PB

AFC Wimbledon was formed by a group of disgruntled supporters from Wimbledon Football Club who objected strongly to their club being relocated to Milton Keynes. The new club came into being just days after the Football League's controversial decision to sanction the move was made in May 2002, and an inaugural squad was hurriedly assembled from players who attended a series of trials held on Wimbledon Common the following month.

Playing in the blue and yellow colours associated with Wimbledon FC, and having claimed as their own the former club's nicknames of the Dons or the Crazy Gang, AFC have climbed the non-League ladder at a rapid pace. After two seasons in the Premier Division of the Combined Counties League, they gained promotion to the Isthmian League First Division, completing their league campaign undefeated. The following season saw them secure a second successive promotion that took them into the Isthmian League Premier Division, where the success story continued. Although they were unsuccessful in the play-offs in 2005-06 and 2006-07, AFC finished as champions in 2007-08 to secure promotion to the Conference South, and in 2008-09 were

again almost unstoppable on their way to a second successive championship and elevation to the Blue Square Premier League.

Along the way, AFC Wimbledon secured a place in the record books, holding the all-time English record for the most consecutive unbeaten league games by any senior football club. They remained unbeaten for 78 league matches between 22 February 2003 (a 2-0 defeat at home to Withdean 2000) and 4 December 2004 (a 2-0 defeat at Cray Wanderers).

ALTRINCHAM

Nickname – The Robins
Official Club Website – www.altrinchamfc.co.uk

Moss Lane (Capacity 6.085 [1,154 seated])
Altrincham
Cheshire
WA15 8AP

Founded in 1891 as Broadheath FC, Altrincham are, perhaps, better known for their exploits in the FA Cup than for their achievements in other competitions, although their two FA Trophy wins, in 1978 and 1986, and their appearance in the 1982 final, should not be overlooked. Their FA Cup victims have included Crewe, Blackpool (twice), Sheffield United, Rotherham, Scunthorpe and Birmingham City, but their finest hour was undoubtedly a 1-1 draw with Everton at Goodison Park in 1975, before losing 2-0 in a replay at Old Trafford.

Founder members of the Manchester League in 1893, Broadheath changed their name to Altrincham FC in 1903, and played their football in the same competition until the First World War. When hostilities ended, Altrincham were one of the clubs that started the new Cheshire League in 1919, and were later in at the start of both the Northern Premier League in 1968 and the Alliance Premier League 11 years later.

Success in the latter was immediate – Altrincham finished each of the first two Alliance Premier League seasons as champions, but failed to gain Football League status via the voting system that was then in place. They remained contenders for much of the eighties, but began to struggle in the decade that followed, and their survival in the top flight of non-League football in recent seasons since their 2005 ascent has been due almost entirely to the misfortunes suffered by those around them. In 2009-10 they finished a creditable 14th.

BARROW

Nickname – The Bluebirds
Official Club Website – http://barrowafc.com/

Holker Street Stadium (Capacity 4,256 [1,000 seated])
Wilkie Road
Barrow-in-Furness
Cumbria
LA14 5UW

Founded in September 1901, Barrow were a Football League team between 1921 and 1972, being founder members of Division Three (North) after 20 years spent in the Lancashire Combination. It has to be said that they made few waves during their 50 years of Football League tenure, their biggest success being promotion from Division Four at the end of the 1966-67 season. Euphoria was, however, short-lived – after finishing a very creditable eighth in their first season in Division Three, they then endured two difficult seasons that ended with relegation in 1970, and the following year they slumped to the bottom of Division Four. After a similarly dismal 1971-72 season, Barrow found themselves voted out of the Football League in favour of Hereford United, then riding high after their sensational FA Cup win over Newcastle United.

Since then, Barrow have had a somewhat chequered existence, from being founder members of the Alliance Premier League in 1979 to being expelled from the Conference 20 years later due to financial irregularities. Winning the FA Trophy in 1990 was clearly a highlight of their non-League history, but this may well have been eclipsed by the spectacular run-in that saw them into the Conference National via the play-offs in 2008. Two years later they won the FA Trophy again, turning round a single-goal deficit to beat Stevenage 2-1 at Wembley in a bad-tempered game that ended ten versus nine.

BATH CITY

Nickname – City (occasionally, and unofficially, The Romans)
Official Club Website – www.bathcityfc.com

Twerton Park (Capacity 8,800 [1,000+ seated])
Twerton
Bath
BA2 1DB

Bath City started life as Bath AFC in 1889, but it would be almost 20 years before they embarked on a life in league football, joining the Western League Division Two in 1908. After the First World War, Bath switched to the Southern League, where they played until the outbreak of the Second.

By this time, the club had been in existence for 50 years without making much of an impact, but the decision to maintain a programme of competitive football during the war brought with it some big changes, and Bath were accepted into the Football League's temporary Division Two Northern Section, playing alongside big-name clubs like Liverpool, Everton and Manchester United. What's more, they finished as champions, giving them the unique achievement of becoming the only semi-professional side ever to lift a Football League trophy.

After the war, Bath were forced to return to the Southern League, picking up where they had left off. In the late fifties and early sixties the club enjoyed a relatively successful period that saw them finish as champions in 1960 and runners-up the following season, but this was short-lived and in the years that followed the club bounced up and down between the Southern League's Premier Division and Division One.

The late seventies saw another renaissance. A second Southern League title in 1978 gave their bid to join the Football League added impetus, but they fell just short of securing enough votes and instead became founder members of the new Alliance Premier League.

Since then, they have twice been relegated back to the Southern League, spending a single season at the lower level at the end of the eighties, and enduring a rather longer spell there from 1997. The arrival of manager John Relish in 2005 signalled the start of a revival, and the club only narrowly missed out on promotion at the end of his first season in charge, but they made no mistake in his second term, finishing as champions to claim a place in Conference South. Mid-table finishes in each of their first two seasons preceded Bath's play-off final against Woking in 2010 after a fourth-place finish. They finished the season in style and were promoted at last.

CAMBRIDGE UNITED

Nickname – The U's
Official Club Website – www.cambridge-united.co.uk

Cambridge United Football Club Limited
(Capacity 9,617 [4,376 seated])
The R Costings Abbey Stadium
Newmarket Road
Cambridge
CB5 8LN

The amber and black colours of Cambridge United have been a permanent fixture since the club's formation as Abbey United as long ago as 1912. (A club called Cambridge United played in the city between 1909 and 1915, but has no connection with the club that exists today.) Abbey United played in local amateur competitions for many years and, on the way to joining the Football League in 1970, also played in the United Counties League, the Eastern Counties League and the Southern League.

They turned professional in 1949, changing their name to Cambridge United two years later, and by the early sixties could be found plying their trade in the Southern League's Premier Division. Two consecutive championships helped to secure their election to the Football League in 1970, when they replaced Bradford Park Avenue.

In 35 years as a Football League club, Cambridge United had mixed fortunes. Among the highlights were two spells in Division Two (second tier): the first between 1978 and 1984 and the second between 1991 and 1993. In 1992, they finished fifth, securing a place in the play-offs, but missed the chance to become founder members of the new Premier League after losing to Leicester City. Spirits were also lifted by two impressive FA Cup runs in 1989-90 and 1990-91, when they reached the last eight while still in Division Four, but thereafter successes were few and far between, and the financial difficulties that affected the club in the wake of the Football League's failed deals with ITV Digital and NTL saw the club go into administration and drop out of the Football League in 2005.

After an indifferent start to life in the Conference, United were soon pressing for an early return to the League, featuring in the play-offs in both 2008 and 2009.

CRAWLEY TOWN

Nickname – The Red Devils
Official Club Website – www.crawleytownfc.net

Broadfield Stadium (Capacity 4,996 [1,150 seated])
Brighton Road
Crawley
West Sussex
RH11 9RX

Founded in 1896, Crawley spent their early years in the Mid-Sussex League, Sussex County League and Metropolitan League, turning professional in 1962. The following year they joined the Southern League First Division. Apart from a single season in the Premier Division in 1969-70, they stayed in the Southern League First Division (in its various incarnations) until promoted in 1984, then spent the next 20 years in the Premier Division.

During this time, they won various regional cup competitions, including the Sussex Professional Cup, the Sussex Senior Cup and the Sussex Floodlight Cup, the latter on four occasions in the nineties including three successive seasons in 1991-93.

After almost 50 years at Town Mead, Crawley moved to their current home in 1997, but the financial problems the club experienced shortly afterwards resulted in a period of administration in 1999. Having weathered the storm, Crawley re-established themselves, and in 2003-04 they were convincing winners of the

Southern League Premier Division, gaining a place in the Conference that they have maintained despite some serious setbacks. Not only have they seen the departure of both valuable players and popular members of the management team, they have also survived a second period of administration and points deductions for both financial issues and fielding an unregistered player. More happily a recent takeover has steadied the ship and offered hope of a brighter future.

DARLINGTON

Nickname – The Quakers, Darlo
Official Club Website – www.darlingtonfc.net

Northern Echo Darlington Arena (Capacity 25,000 [restricted to 10,000])
Neasham Road
Darlington
Co Durham
DL2 1DL

Though a League club for the major proportion of their history, Darlington are no strangers to the Conference. They were relegated to it in 1989 despite ex-England and Aston Villa man Brian Little being brought in as manager to save them. They bounced back under him and achieved promotions in successive seasons, but his departure to Leicester stalled progress.

Since then, a pair of play-off finals which failed to see them leave the Third Division were followed by the after-effects of former chairman George Reynolds' overreaching ambitions, which included a ground they have struggled to even half-fill. Managers and players came and went on a revolving door basis, and money problems plagued them.

In February 2009, Darlington went into administration for the second time in two years, triggering an automatic 10-point deduction without which they would have again reached the play-offs, but the inevitable end-of-season fire sale preceded a last, disastrous League season which saw managers Colin Todd, Steve Staunton and Simon Davey in turn unable to halt the decline after seven of the first nine games were lost.

Darlington fans deserve a period of consolidation at least but, with the Conference at its most competitive, may not get it.

EASTBOURNE BOROUGH

Nickname – The Sports
Official Club Website – www.eastbourneboroughfc.co.uk

Priory Lane (Capacity 4,151 [542 seated])
Langney Sports Club
Priory Lane
Eastbourne
East Sussex
BN23 7QH

A club with a relatively short history, Eastbourne Borough were known as Langney Sports Club until 2001, a change of name prompted by the recognition that very few people had any idea where Langney was.

Langney Sports Club had itself started under another name, Langney FC, in 1964, but adopted the longer name four years later when the club was affiliated with the Langney Community Association. In 1983, they became founder members of the Sussex County League Division Three, and the club also began playing home games at Priory Lane. Langney quickly found their feet, and two promotions in successive years saw them into the Sussex County League's top flight, where they finished outside the top four only twice in 13 seasons and enjoyed FA Cup success against several more senior sides.

In 2000, they achieved promotion to the Southern League Eastern Division, adopting their current name the following year. To ensure continuity, however, Eastbourne Borough were careful to retain the old club's badge, colours and the 'Sports' nickname.

Progressing through the Southern League Premier Division, Eastbourne enjoyed an excellent 2007-08 season in the Conference South, finishing in second place behind Lewes and securing a place in the Conference National via the play-offs. The newly promoted club found things difficult at first and struggled in the lower reaches of the division, but eventually attained respectability after the introduction of new players.

FLEETWOOD TOWN

Nickname – The Fishermen, The Fleet, Cod Army
Official Club Website – www.fleetwoodtownfc.com

Highbury Stadium (Capacity 3,663)
Fleetwood
Lancashire
FY7 6TX

The current Fleetwood Town FC was established in 1997, but can trace its history back to 1908 via two earlier clubs that have represented the town. The first of these, known simply as Fleetwood FC, was established in 1908 and played for many years in the Lancashire Combination, winning the league title in 1924.

After almost 60 years in the same league, Fleetwood became founder members of the Northern Premier League in 1968, performing reasonably well in their first few seasons in the new competition before suffering a decline that ultimately led to the club folding after the Inland Revenue issued a winding-up order in 1976.

The following year Fleetwood Town FC was launched, with many of those who were at the earlier club helping to start the new one. Starting life in the Cheshire League, the reformed club was an immediate success, becoming founder members of the North West Counties League Division Two in 1982, and gaining promotion to Division One two years later. Losing FA Vase finalists in 1985, Fleetwood Town became founder members of the Northern Premier League Division One in 1987, winning the championship in the inaugural season. It was an auspicious start, and early indications were that the club would do well, but a rapid decline in the mid-nineties, fuelled by financial instability, led to the sudden collapse of the second club, which folded in 1996.

Reformed the following year as Fleetwood Wanderers, the club was allocated a place in the North West Counties Football League, although a sponsorship deal saw them renamed Fleetwood Freeport FC before a ball was kicked. The club was renamed Fleetwood Town after the sponsorship deal ended in 2002, since when three promotions in four years have seen them rise through the Northern Premier League to Conference North. They finished second in 2010, nine places above their nearest challengers, and justifiably won promotion via the play-offs.

FOREST GREEN ROVERS

Nickname – The Rovers
Official Club Website – www.forestgreenroversfc.com

The New Lawn (Capacity 5,140 [2,500 seated])
Nympsfield Road
Forest Green
Nailsworth
GL6 0ET

Hailing from Gloucestershire, Forest Green Rovers were originally known as Nailsworth & Forest Green when formed in 1889, and from 1894 they played their football in the Mid-Gloucester League. After the MGL folded in 1902, the club moved to the newly formed Stroud & District League, where they played for over 30 years. Over the years, they also competed in the Gloucestershire Northern Senior League, the Gloucestershire County League and the Hellenic League.

Forest Green Rovers enjoyed their best-ever season in 1982, finishing as champions of the Hellenic League and winning the FA Vase. They started the following season as members of the Southern League Midland Division, but struggled to find form and went into a gradual decline. In an attempt to revitalise the club, it was renamed Stroud FC in 1989, but the move alienated many long-standing fans and the decision was reversed three years later.

Things improved steadily from then on, and by 1998 Forest Green found themselves in the Conference after back-to-back promotions through the Southern League's Southern and Premier divisions. They were losing finalists in

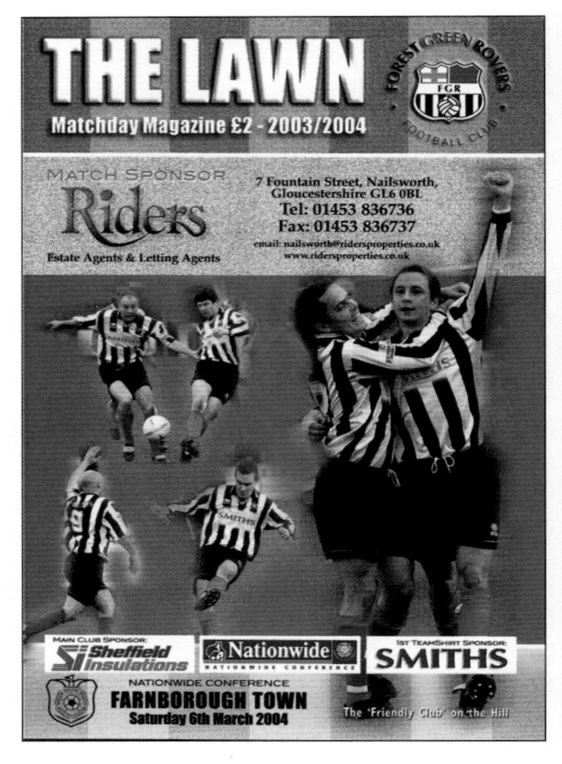

the FA Trophy in both 1999 and 2001, giving them the distinction of becoming the first club to have reached the final of both the FA Vase and the FA Trophy.

In 2006, Forest Green moved to their current home from the Lawn, where they had played from the club's foundation over a century earlier. Recent seasons have been something of a disappointment after the success of the late nineties, and relegation from Conference National in 2010 was only avoided when Salisbury were expelled.

GATESHEAD

Nickname – The Tynesiders, The Head
Official Club Website – www.gateshead-fc.com

Gateshead International Stadium
(Capacity 11,800 [all seated])
Neilson Road
Gateshead

Tyne and Wear
NE10 0EF

The history of Gateshead FC is confusing to say the least, and over the years there have been at least three clubs operating under the name. The first came into being in 1930, when South Shields FC, then members of the Football League's Division Three (North), moved to the town and changed their name to Gateshead AFC. The renamed club played in the Football League until 1960, when they failed to gain re-election. The club then played in a number of regional leagues, including the Northern Premier, before disbanding in 1973.

Amazingly, history then repeated itself. A reformed South Shields FC, then playing in the Northern Premier League, relocated to the Gateshead International Stadium in 1974 and became Gateshead United FC, although this was a short-lived endeavour, and the club went out of business just three years later.

A new Gateshead FC was formed to take their place, and it is this incarnation that has endured to this day. After winning promotion to the Alliance Premier League in 1983, the club enjoyed mixed fortunes, having been relegated and promoted several times since. Gateshead fans have had relatively little to shout about over the years, but after two successive promotions their club now find themselves one step away from reclaiming a Football League place for the town. With new investment and plans for a move to a purpose-built stadium in the next few years, Gateshead FC's future is looking brighter than it has for many years.

GRIMSBY TOWN

Nickname – The Mariners
Official Club Website – www.grimsby-townfc.co.uk

Blundell Park (Capacity 9,456 [all seated])
Cleethorpes
DN35 7PY

The descent of Grimsby Town on the last day of the 2010 season brought another big name into non-League football but ended a 99-year unbroken spell in the League structure for the Cleethorpes-based club. They were previously the most successful of the three professional league clubs in historic Lincolnshire, being the only one to play top-flight football (albeit most recently in 1939). They are also the only club of the three to reach an FA Cup semi-final.

The Mariners went on to win four and draw one of the last six games going into the last game of the 2009-10 season, but were defeated 3-0 by League new boys Burton Albion to relegate them from the Football League for the first time for 99 years.

Grimsby have consistently punched above their weight in footballing terms, helped by a string of promising young managers. What effect becoming non-League will have on them has yet to become apparent – and while it seems unlikely that their hardcore support will desert them, they will do well to compete among the shoal of ex-League heavyweights currently swimming in the Conference.

HAYES & YEADING UNITED

Nickname – United (Hayes FC – the Missioners; Yeading FC – the 'Ding)
Official Club Website – www.hyufc.net

Church Road (Capacity 4,730 [500 seated])
Church Road
Hayes
Middlesex
UB3 2LE
(Due to be demolished – the club will go to The Warren [ex-Yeading FC])

The result of a merger of the Hayes and Yeading clubs, the newly formed team had a modest start to life in Conference South in 2007-8, but their second season of existence proved to be highly successful, culminating in promotion to the Conference National via the play-offs.

Hayes FC had existed for almost a century before the merger, having started life as Botwell Mission, a youth team started by Emily Shackle, the daughter of a wealthy local landowner, in 1909. They took their name from a local mission church built in memory of Emily's grandfather, and the club nickname, the Missioners, survived the change of name to Hayes FC that accompanied their acceptance into the Athenian League in 1929.

Hayes played steadily over the years without making too many ripples, surviving a particularly lean spell in the sixties to establish themselves as Isthmian League stalwarts by the end of the decade that followed. The highlight was, perhaps, their run in the 1972-73 FA Cup competition, in which they disposed of Football League side Bristol Rovers in the first round before bowing out to Reading.

In the meantime, Yeading FC, who also started life as a youth side, were busy climbing the non-League ladder, moving up through the Middlesex League, the Spartan League and the Isthmian League and winning the FA Vase for good measure in 1990.

In 1992 the two sides became rivals on the field for the first time in the Isthmian Premier Division, but in 1996 Hayes won the championship and with it promotion to the top flight of non-League football. It would be almost ten years before they would resume their rivalry in the newly formed Conference South in 2005, but by this time both clubs were in decline, and the merger was seen as the only way either of them could ensure a long-term future at the level they were playing at.

HISTON

Nickname – The Stutes
Official Club Website – www.histonfc.co.uk

The Glassworld Stadium (still referred to by many as Bridge Road) (Capacity 3,800 [1,700 seated])
Bridge Road
Impington
Cambridgeshire
CB24 9PH

Histon FC can trace their origins back to 1903 and the foundation of the Histon Institute by John Chivers, then chairman of the largest local employer, jam-maker Chivers & Sons. Histon Institute FC started up the following year, playing their games on a field donated for the purpose by the company. The field was initially covered in roses, a fact commemorated to this day in the club's badge.

Histon Institute played for many years in the Cambridgeshire Football League before becoming members of the Delphian League in 1960, but by 1963 the Delphian League had disbanded, and the club joined the Athenian League. In 1965, they moved on again, joining the Eastern Counties League and shortening

their name to Histon FC at the same time.

At the end of the 1999-2000 season, Histon won promotion to the Southern League Eastern Division, where they spent the next three seasons consolidating their position. Another promotion followed in 2004, when they moved up again to the Southern League Premier Division, but few could have predicted that they would finish the season as champions, securing a place in the Conference South for 2005-06. Another season of consolidation followed, but in 2006-07 Histon romped home to finish a staggering 19 points clear at the top of the table to achieve their fourth promotion in seven years and claim a place in the Conference National.

Finishing seventh in their first season of top-flight non-League football was an impressive enough start, but they did even better in 2008-09 by making it into the play-offs, where they lost to eventual winners Torquay in the semi-finals. But boardroom unrest saw the departure of chairman Gareth Baldwin and long-serving manager Steve Fallon during the 2009-10 season.

KETTERING TOWN

Nickname – The Poppies
Official Club Website – www.ketteringtownfc.co.uk

The A-Line Arena (still referred to by many as Rockingham Road) (Capacity 6,264 [1,747 seated])
Kettering
Northants
NN16 9AW

A club with a long and distinguished history, Kettering Town are probably better known for their exploits in the FA Cup than in the world of non-League football, but over the years they have amassed a considerable amount of silverware, including 12 league championship trophies and no fewer than 28 victories in the Northants Senior Cup.

Formed as long ago as 1872, Kettering Town turned professional in 1891 and played in a number of different leagues before becoming founder members of the Alliance Premier League in 1979, although things might have been very different had their bid to join the Football League in 1974 been successful. The club maintained its position in non-League's top flight for 22 years until they suffered relegation to the Southern League Premier in 2001.

A period of uncertainty followed, with promotion in 2002, another relegation in 2003 and then five turbulent years during which consistency proved elusive, a situation not helped by a series of managerial comings and goings that included Paul Gascoigne's famous 39-day spell in charge.

Kettering narrowly missed out on promotion in 2006-07, but the following season saw them win the Conference North title and reclaim their position among the non-League elite. In 2008-09, Kettering once again swept aside League opposition in the FA Cup, beating Lincoln and Notts County on the way to losing a fourth-round tie against Fulham. Their league form was similarly impressive, and Kettering ended the 2009-10 campaign just one place outside the play-offs.

KIDDERMINSTER HARRIERS

Nickname – The Harriers
Official Club Website – www.harriers.co.uk

Aggborough Stadium (Capacity 6,238 [3,140 seated])
Hoo Road
Kidderminster
DY10 1NB

Kidderminster Harriers have their origins in an athletics club of the same name founded in 1877, but by 1886 they had switched to football and three years later joined the newly formed Birmingham & District League. The following year, they amalgamated with local rivals Kidderminster Olympic, after which they continued to play in the Birmingham League until 1939, winning the championship in 1938 (without losing a game) and again in the final pre-war campaign. They moved to the Southern League for the 1939-40 season, but the outbreak of war brought an end to proceedings after only three games.

Immediately after the war, Kidderminster played in the Birmingham League before rejoining the Southern League in 1948. Three years later, the club made history by becoming the first in the country to host a floodlit FA Cup match, as well as the first floodlit fixtures in a number of local league and cup competitions.

Apart from a spell back in the Birmingham League (by then known as the West Midlands Regional League) between 1960 and 1972, Kidderminster played in the Southern League until 1983 when, after pushing for promotion for several seasons, they finally secured a place in the Alliance Premier League. This ushered in a 25-year period of unprecedented success for the club. They won the FA Trophy in 1987, and made two further appearances in the final in 1991 and 1997.

But the 1993-94 campaign will almost certainly be remembered as their most successful, with an FA Cup run that saw them beat Birmingham City at St Andrews and Preston North End at Aggborough before narrowly losing at home to Premiership side West Ham. At the end of the season, Kidderminster sat proudly at the top of the GM Vauxhall Conference, only to be denied entry to the Football League because the facilities at Aggborough were deemed inadequate.

When they finally achieved Football League status at the end of the 1999-2000 season, Harriers struggled to make headway and dropped back to the Conference in 2005. After three disappointing campaigns, Kidderminster looked to have turned the corner in 2008-09, finishing just outside the play-off positions. They did likewise in 2009-10.

LUTON TOWN

Nickname – The Hatters
Official Club Website – www.lutontown.co.uk

Kenilworth Road Stadium
(Capacity 10,226 [all seated])
1 Maple Road
Luton
Bedfordshire
LU4 8AW

It is hard to imagine that, just over 20 years ago, Luton Town were riding high in the top flight of the English game, enjoying lengthy runs in domestic cup competitions and holding their own, week in, week out, against the best teams in the country. They reached the semi-finals of the FA Cup in 1985 and 1988, the final of the League Cup in 1988 (when they beat Arsenal 3-2 to secure their last major honour) and again in 1989, and finished the 1986-87 season seventh in Division One, their best-ever placing. Their eventual exit from the Football League in 2009 had as much to do with events off the field of play as on it, after the Football League imposed a 30-point penalty for a combination of financial irregularities and circumstances surrounding a period in administration, but the club had been in decline for a number of years.

Formed in 1885, Luton Town played three seasons in Division Two at the end of the 19th century, but were playing in the Southern League in 1920 when the Football League absorbed it to form the new Division Three. Their League career was something of a roller-coaster ride, with promotion to Division To in 1937 and Division One in 1955 followed by a rapid descent to Division Four within ten years. By 1971, they were back in Division Two, and spent the next 20 years in one or other of the top two divisions.

It has been downhill almost all the way since 1992, when Luton suffered the curious fate of

being relegated from Division One to Division One with the introduction of the Premiership. Further relegations in 1996 and 2001 saw them back in the League's basement, and although they enjoyed a brief renaissance in the middle of the decade, the club's financial difficulties and a series of managerial changes all contributed to their spectacular fall from grace, with three successive relegations leaving them as a non-League club for the first time in 90 years. They lost in the play-offs in 2010, condemning them to at least one more non-League season.

MANSFIELD TOWN

Nickname – The Stags
Official Club Website – www.mansfieldtown.net

Field Mill (Capacity 10,000 [all seated])
Quarry Lane
MansfieNottinghamshire
NG18 5DA

Another former Football League side adapting to life in the Conference, Mansfield Town can trace their origins, like so many clubs, back to a church side. Mansfield Wesleyans started playing in 1897 and joined the Mansfield & District Amateur League five years later. In 1906, the club found themselves disowned by the church and banned from using the title 'Wesleyan' after turning professional, so for the next few years they were known as Mansfield Wesley.

In 1910, the club became Mansfield Town, and in 1919 they took over the lease of Field Mill, former home of Mansfield Mechanics, when the previous tenants failed to renew. After pressing hard for election to the Football League's Division Three (North) in the twenties, Mansfield changed tack and applied to join Division Three (South) in 1931, figuring that they would stand a better chance of support from northern clubs. The ploy worked, and Mansfield replaced Newport County for the start of the 1931-32 season.

Their League career was spent almost entirely in the lower divisions, a single season in Division Two in the late seventies being the only highlight. Off the field, things were rather more interesting, with allegations of financial irregularities in the early fifties leading to several former club officials and players being banned from the game, while the celebrations that followed the club's promotion in 1963 were seriously dampened by an investigation into match-fixing associated with a betting scam. Described by one newspaper as 'the football scandal of the century', the investigation led to the imprisonment of three Mansfield players and seven from other clubs.

In more recent years, Mansfield fans have had little to cheer about, the only highlights being the Freight Rover Trophy win in 1987 and promotion to Division Two (third tier) in 2002. Their loss of Football League status in 2008 followed several dismal years in its lowest division, but the arrival of manager David Holdsworth seemed to offer hopes of a more stable future.

NEWPORT COUNTY

Nickname – The Exiles, The Ironsides
Official Club Website – www.newport-county.co.uk

Newport Stadium (Capacity 4,300 [1,100 seated])
Langland Way
Newport
NP19 4PT

Although the name of Newport County has been familiar to football fans for almost a century, the current club is a relative newcomer, formed after the previous incarnation was wound up in 1989. Initially known as Newport AFC, the new club was renamed Newport County AFC in 1999, reflecting their ambition to regain the Football League place their predecessors had lost a year before their collapse.

Formed in 1912, the original club played briefly in the Southern League before joining the new Football League Division Three in 1920. Apart from a return to non-League football for a single season in 1931-32, they remained there until the Second World War, finishing as champions in 1939. When League football resumed in 1946, Newport began life as a Division Two sde with high hopes, but their only season in the second tier was to be a bitter disappointment, and they finished six points adrift at the bottom of the table.

Thereafter, they divided their time between the third and fourth tiers, although there were some highlights – in 1980, Newport won the Welsh Cup and earned a place in the European Cup Winners' Cup, reaching the quarter-finals thanks to goals from a young John Aldridge, and in 1982-83 they narrowly missed out on a return to Division Two. By the mid-eighties, however, they were struggling again and two successive relegations saw them drop out of the Football League in 1988. By this time, Newport were also in serious financial difficulty, and before they could complete their first season as a Conference side, the club was officially wound up in February 1989.

Shortly afterwards, Newport AFC was formed, and the new club was given a place in the Hellenic League for the 1989-90 season. Forced by football politics to play their 'home' games in the Gloucestershire town of Moreton-in-Marsh, Newport became known as the Exiles. They won promotion to the Southern League at the first attempt and played the following two seasons at Newport County's old home ground, Somerton Park.

Further political wrangling saw them back in Gloucester for the 1992-93 season and forced to take legal action to prevent them from being forced out of the English Football Pyramid. In a landmark High Court judgment, the new club won not only the right to remain in the English game but also to return home to Newport, where they resumed the fight to bring League football back to the town at the newly built Newport Stadium in 1994. Via promotion to the Southern League Premier Division in 1995, earning a place in the new Conference South in 2004 and Conference National in 2010 under manager Dean Holdsworth, the Exiles are now just one step away from achieving their stated aim.

RUSHDEN & DIAMONDS

Nickname – Diamonds
Official Club Website – www.thediamondsfc.com

Nene Park (Capacity 6,441 [4,641 seated])
Irthlingborough
Northants
NN9 5QF

Rushden & Diamonds came into existence in 1992 as a result of the merger of two existing sides, Rushden Town and Irthlingborough Diamonds. Rushden Town had been formed as long ago as 1889, playing their football for many years in the Midlands and Northamptonshire Leagues until joining the United Counties League. There, they continued a largely unremarkable career until they were elected to the Southern League Midland Division in 1983. In 1991, Rushden were promoted to the Southern League Premier Division, and the future looked bright. However, the club suffered a serious blow at the end of their first season in the higher division when their ground was declared not to be of the required standard (despite the improvements that had been made), and they were relegated again despite finishing in fourth place.

Irthlingborough Diamonds were a rather younger club, formed as a youth side in 1946. They achieved seniorstatus and joined the United Counties League where they enjoyed some success, finishing as champions in 1971. In the early eighties, Irthlingborough also did well in the FA Vase, but went into decline thereafter and found themselves in dire need of a financial boost by the end of the decade.

The search for sponsorship led them to approach a local businessman, Max Griggs, who suggested the merger with Rushden as a way for both clubs to move forward. Despite some opposition from both sides the plan was agreed, with the new club playing at Irthlingborough's ground, Nene Park. The merger ushered in a period of great success, culminating in 2001 with a Conference championship and promotion to Football League Division Three.

Rushden & Diamonds announced their arrival by reaching the play-offs in their first League season, but had to wait another year before securing promotion as champions. However, life at the higher level placed great pressure on the Northamptonshire club and bythe conclusion of the 2005-06 campaign they were back in the Conference.

SOUTHPORT

Nickname – The Sandgrounders
Official Club Website – www.southportfc.net

Haig Avenue (Capacity 4,923 [1,184 seated])
Southport
Lancashire
PR8 6JZ

Formed in 1881, Southport FC played in a variety of local leagues prior to becoming founder members of the Central League in 1911. In 1918, an association with the Vulcan Motor Company led to the club playing for a single season as Southport Vulcan, the first example of a club changing their name as part of a sponsorship deal.

League football came to Haig Avenue in 1921 when Southport were one of the founder members of the new Football League Division Three (North), and ten years later they became the first club from that division to reach the sixth round of the FA Cup, although the celebrations were less enthusiastic after the Sandgrounders suffered a 9-1 defeat a the hands of Everton. The following season, Southport enjoyed another lengthy run in the competition, eventually losing to Newcastle United in a fourth-round replay.

Despite these occasional bouts of excitement in the FA Cup, Southport's Football League career was largely unremarkable, with two promotions out of the basement division each being followed by a rapid return. By the mid-seventies the club was struggling to compete, and a dismal 1977-78 season ended with a failure to secure re-election. Southport spent the next 15 years in the Northern Premier League, turning down an invitation to join the Alliance Premier League when it was formed in 1979 on financial grounds. In 1993, Southport were easy winners of the NPL title and moved up to the Conference, ushering in a successful spell that saw them perform well in the league and reach the final of the FA Trophy in 1997.

A slump in form saw them relegated back to the NPL in 2003, but the following year they were invited to join the new Conference North and in 2005 they became its first champions. Relegated again after two seasons in the Conference National, Southport regained top-flight status in 2010.

TAMWORTH

Nickname – The Lambs
Official Club Website – www.thelambs.co.uk

The Lamb Ground (Capacity 4,065 [518 seated])
Kettlebrook
Tamworth
Staffordshire
B77 1AA

Tamworth FC were formed in 1933 after local side Tamworth Castle FC folded. Early games

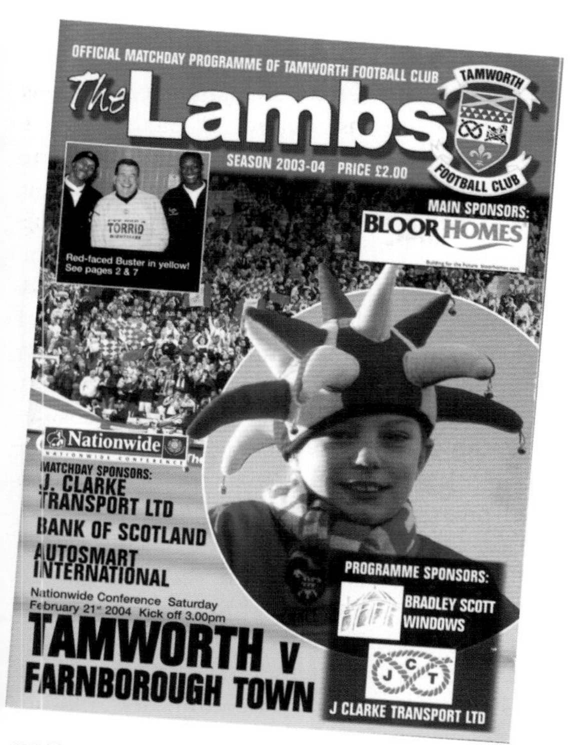

were played on a field next to a local public house, but thew club moved to their present ground, The Lamb, within a year. For many years, Tamworth played their football in local leagues, notably the Birmingham Combination and the Birmingham & District League, with only moderate success. The highlights of this lengthy period of the club's history were Birmingham League championships in 1964 and 1966, and occasional success in local cup competitions.

In 1972, Tamworth were promoted to the Southern League, but their stay was relatively short because of falling attendances and the consequent financial struggle, and they soon found themselves back in the Birmingham & District League (by this time known as the West Midlands Regional League).

Promoted again as champions at the end of the 1987-88 season, Tamworth fared rather better during their second spell in the Southern League, winning the FA Vase a year later and securing a Conference place in 1993. Ten years later, they stepped up to the Conference National, but struggled to compete and only the resignation of Canvey Island in 2006 saved them from relegation. A year later, they were not so lucky and slipped back to the Conference North, but in 2009 they bounced back as champions with high hopes for the future.

WREXHAM

Nickname – The Red Dragons
Official Club Website – www.wrexhamafc.co.uk

The Racecourse Ground (Capacity 15,500 [10,500 seated])
Mold Road
Wrexham
LL11 2AH

One of the oldest football clubs in the UK, having been founded in 1872, Wrexham's stay in the Football League lasted from 1921, when they became one of the initial members of Third Division (North), until 2008 after a period when the goings-on behind the scenes overshadowed much that was happening on the pitch. All twenty-two members of the playing staff were told by manager Brian Little that they were no longer required at the club after relegation to the Conference. This was a sad episode for a club proud of their lengthy stay in the Football League, during which they made the quarter-finals of the FA Cup three times and a similar stage of the League Cup twice.

In the early days, Wrexham played mainly friendly matches, their competitive football restricted to the Welsh Cup in which they have enjoyed numerous successes over the years. After playing in the Football Combination and the Birmingham & District League, Wrexham began their Football League career in the new Division Three (North), narrowly missing out on promotion twice in the years leading up to the Second World War.

The club went into decline at the end of the fifties, and by 1966 they were at rock bottom, finishing at the foot of the League's basement division. Fortunes improved under John Neal in the early seventies, with promotion to Division Three and a Welsh Cup victory that brought European football to Wrexham for the first time. Better was to come, as Wrexham enjoyed lengthy runs in the domestic cup competitions, and even an appearance in the last eight of the European Cup Winners' Cup in 1976, and they ended the decade as a Division Two side.

However, their star quickly faded, and by the start of the 1983-84 season Wrexham were back in Division Four after two consecutive relegations. In January 1992 they sensationally knocked reigning League champions Arsenal out of the FA Cup. But between then and their exit from the Football League in 2008, Wrexham gave their fans little to cheer about. Two mediocre seasons in the Conference, the second under Welsh international Dean Saunders, will need to be improved upon to restore their fortunes.

YORK CITY

Nickname – The Minstermen
Official Club Website – www.ycfc.net

Kitkat Crescent (formerly Bootham Crescent)
(Capacity 9,196 [3,409 seated])
Bootham Crescent
York
YO30 7AQ

Formed in 1922, York City joined the Football League in 1929, taking over from Ashington in Division Three (North). They made a good start, finishing sixth in their debut season, but for some time thereafter their existence was largely unremarkable, although an appearance in FA Cup semi-finals in 1955 and the League Cup quarter-finals seven years later gave fans something to shout about. When the Football League was reorganised to create the new Division Three and Division Four in 1958, York City found themselves as founder members of the new basement division.

Their subsequent League career was far more eventful – with six promotions, six relegations and no fewer than six applications for re-election along the way. They enjoyed two seasons in the old Division Two (second tier), the first, in 1974-75, including the unlikely scenario of League games against Manchester United, then enduring a rare season out of the top flight.

Successive relegations saw them back in Division Four by 1977, but seven years later they secured promotion in a remarkable season that saw them score 96 goals and amass 101 points (becoming the first League club to top 100 points in a season) in their 46 games. Further relegations and promotions followed, but York's life in the Footall League finally came to an end in 2004, after several years languishing in the lower reaches of its bottom tier. A losing appearance in the final of the FA Trophy in 2009 was followed by a return visit to Wembley in the 2010 promotion play-offs.

The Conference North (Blue Square North) Clubs

AFC TELFORD UNITED

Nickname – The Bucks, The Lilywhites
Official Club Website – www.telfordutd.co.uk

New Bucks Head Stadium
(Capacity 6,300 [2,200 seated])
Watling Street
Wellington
Telford
Shropshire
TF1 2TU

AFC Telford United rose from the ashes of the town's previous club, Telford United, who were forced into liquidation after the collapse of chairman and club owner Andrew Shaw's business empire left them with severe financial problems. Despite the fans' best efforts, which saw over £50,000 raised in short order in an effort to bale their club out, debts stood at around £4 million and United were wound up in May 2004.

It was a sad end to a club with more than 130 years of history and a proud record of FA Cup giant-killing. Formed in 1872 as the Wellington Parish Church Institute side, they were known as Wellington Town by 1879, and competed under that name in the Shropshire, Birmingham & District, Cheshire and Southern Leagues until 1969, when they changed name again and became Telford United.

In the seventies and eighties, United enjoyed considerable success in the FA Trophy and the FA Cup where they overcame Football League opposition on a number of occasions. In 1985, they defeated Lincoln City, Preston North End, Bradford City and Darlington on the way to a fifth-round tie in front of over 47,000 spectators against then League champions Everton at Goodison Park.

Thereafter, the club went into something of a decline, but by 2003 there were signs of a renaissance, cruelly cut short by events off the field of play. On the day that Telford United ceased to exist, the supporters' trust that had been set up to try and save the club announced the formation of AFC Telford United. Adopting the Latin motto *numquam obliviscere* (meaning 'never forget'), the new club was granted a place in the Northern Premier League Division One at the beginning of the 2004-05 season.

Two promotions in three years saw them into Conference North, where they finished in a play-off position in each of their first two seasons. In 2009, they lost narrowly to Gateshead in the play-off final, but despite a mid-table 2010 finish it seems only a matter of time before they are back in non-League's top flight.

ALFRETON TOWN

Nickname – The Reds
Official Club Website – www.alfretontownfc.com

The Impact Arena
(Capacity 3,600 [1,500 seated])
North Street
Alfreton
Derbyshire
DE55 7FZ

Alfreton Town came into existence in 1959 as a result of a merger between two earlier clubs, Alfreton United and Alfreton Miners' Welfare. Starting life in the Central Alliance North Division One, the new club moved to the Midlands Counties league in 1961, where they spent their first few years comfortably if unspectacularly.

Towards the end of the sixties, Alfreton began to make an impression, and in 1970 they won the first of their three Midland League championships. During the seventies, they also achieved three consecutive victories in the

Midland League Cup, being awarded the trophy permanently in recognition of the feat. In 1982, they were founder members of the Northern Counties East League (formed through the merger of the Midland League and the Yorkshire Leage), from which they progressed to the Northern Premier League in 1988.

After several years of struggle, Alfreton enjoyed a purple patch that saw them promoted to the Northern Premier League's Premier Division in 1996, but life at the higher level proved too much, and successive relegations saw them back in the Northern Counties East League by 1999. Since then they have rarely looked back, performing well in league and cup competitions and becoming the first non-League side to win the prestigious FIFA Fair Play Award in 2001. Successive championship wins in 2002 and 2003 saw them return to the NPL Premier Division where they finished fourth in their first season to earn a place in the new Conference North for 2004-05.

After several seasons of rebuilding both on and off the field of play, Alfreton enjoyed their best-ever campaign in 2008-09, finishing third in Conference North and only narrowly losing the play-off semi-final. They also reached the second round of the FA Cup for the first time in their history, and with the established management team of Nicky Law and assistant Russ O'Neill in place for a third season, the club reaped the benefits of much-needed stability when they finished third and reached the play-off final.

BLYTH SPARTANS AFC

Nickname – Spartans
Official Club Website – www.blythspartansafc.co.uk

Croft Park (Capacity 4,435 [563 seated])
Blyth
Northumberland
NE24 3JE

Founded in September 1899, Blyth Spartans played only friendly matches for a while before joining the Northumberland League in 1901 and winning it in their first season. Two more championships led to a move to the Northern Alliance in 1907, where further success prompted the club to go semi-professional in 1913 and move to the North Eastern League, where they would remain until the competition folded in 1958.

Honours were rather less frequent during this period, Spartans having to contend with a far higher standard of opposition than in their earlier years, but along the way fans could celebrate a league championship in 1937 and wins in the league's cup competition in 1950 and 1955.

After the demise of the North Eastern League, there was an unsettled period that saw Blyth spend time in the Midland League and the Northern Counties League, each of which failed, before a return to the revived North Eastern League in 1962. The revival was short-lived and the North Eastern League closed for good two years later, at which point, without a semi-pro league place, Blyth returned to the amateur game and joined the Northern League.

Between 1964 and 1994, when the club were promoted to the Northern Premier League, Blyth won the Northern League championship on ten occasions, and finished as runners-up on five more. Their first season in the Northern Premier League exceeded all expectations, bringing promotion to the Premier Division, where they stayed until 2006, when they won the league championship and stepped up to Conference North.

Blyths FA Cup record is amongst the best of all non-League sides, with 32 first-round,15 second-round, and four third-round appearances, but their most memorable run saw them through to the fifth round in 1977-78, where they lost to Wrexham after a replay. After several lean years, they returned to giant-killing ways in 2008, when they beat Football League sides Shrewsbury and AFC Bournemouth on the way to a third-round meeting with Premiership side Blackburn Rovers, who were relieved to escape from Croft Park with a 1-0 win under their belts.

BOSTON UNITED

Nickname – Pilgrims
Official Club Website – www.bufc.co.uk

York Street (Capacity 6,643 [5,711 seated])
Boston
Lincolnshire
Lincolnshire PE21 6JN

Formed in 1933, Boston United spent the first 35 years of their existence fairly quietly in a variety of regional leagues, including the Midland League and the Southern League, the highlight of this period coming in January 1956 with a third-round FA Cup tie against Tottenham Hotspur at White Hart Lane. The Pilgrims lost 4-0, but the match attracted a crowd of more than 46,000, of whom over 10,000 were travelling fans.

Boston were in at the start of both the Northern Premier League in 1968 and the Alliance Premier League 11 years later, and the club made their only appearance at Wembley so far in the 1985 FA Trophy final, losing 2-1 to Wealdstone. In 2000, having meanwhile been relegated to the Northern Premier League then transferred to the Southern League, they won promotion bac to the Conference.

Two years later, Boston fans were celebrating promotion to the Football League but, as related elsewhere, their five-year spell in the League was shrouded in controversy. In 2007, the club lost League status on the final day of the season, taking a two-division drop to the Conference North for financial reasons. May 2008 brought another FA-imposed relegation, but Boston won promotion back to the Conference North in 2010.

CORBY TOWN

Nickname – The Steelmen
Official Club Website – www.corbytown.net

Rockingham Triangle Stadium (Capacity 3,000 [960 seated])
Rockingham Road
Corby
Northants
NN17 2AE

In the years leading up to the Second World War, Corby was represented in the United Counties League by the steelworks side, Stewarts & Lloyds. With the town growing rapidly in the late forties, an independent football club seemed appropriate, and so Corby Town was formed in 1948. Links with the earlier club and local industry are recognised in Corby's nickname, the Steelmen.

Between 1948 and 1952 they played in the

UCL, finishing as champions in each of their last two seasons, then moved to the Midland League. In 1958, they joined the Southern League, where they would stay for the next half-century, experiencing everything from the joy of winning the Premier Division title in 1965 to the despair of propping up the league on a number of occasions. During this time, their geographical location saw them compete in Southern League Division One (North), Division One (West), Division One (East), Southern Division and Midland Division, but in 2009 they left all this behind when a Premier Division championship ushered in a new era in the club's history with promotion to Conference North. Sixth place in their first season was quite an achievement.

Their record in cup competitions is generally unspectacular, but older Corby fans still cherish the memory of the club's only giant-killing act, when they knocked Luton Town out of the FA Cup in a second-round replay at Kenilwoth Road in December 1965.

DROYLSDEN

Nickname – The Bloods
Official Club Website – www.droylsdenfc.com

Butchers Arms Ground (Capacity 3,500 [500 seated])
Market Street
Droylsden
Manchester
M43 7AW

Droylsden have a history stretching back to the early years of the 20th century, when a football club was formed at the instigation of Butchers Arms landlord Joseph Cropper to play on a field adjacent to the pub. The club's early years are a story of local league football, friendly matches and, it seems, instability, since there is evidence that the club disbanded and reformed on several occasions prior to the outbreak of the First World War.

After the war, however, things were on a more stable footing, with Droylsden now the only football club operating in the village. They joined the Manchester League, settled on the current club colours of red and white and acquired their unusual nickname, thought to derive from the name of their home ground, the Butchers Arms.

The twenties were relatively quiet, but the arrival of the legendary Ernest 'Gilly' Gillibrand, a prolific goalscorer who netted 275 times for the club in just four seasons, led to league championships in 1931 and 1933 and, ultimately, to a successful application to join the Lancashire Combination in 1936. The following year they also became a nursery club for Manchester City.

During the Second World War, Droylsden enjoyed some success in the Cheshire League, but the immediate post-war period was alean time, including a period in exile after the Butchers Arms lease was sold to local rivals Belle Vue FC, who added insult to injury by renaming themselves Droylsden United. The Bloods, meanwhile, returned to the Lancashire Combination in 1948, playing their home games at Moorside Trotting Stadium. Four years later Droylsden returned to their former home after the local council acquired the Butchers Arms and, with the two bitter rivals both struggling to attract enough supporters in what was a small town, brokered a merger between the two clubs.

Droylsden continued in the Lancashire Combination until 1968, then joined the Cheshire League, where they enjoyed a successful spell in the late seventies. The eighties were something of an anticlimax, but by 1990 they had battled their way up to the Northern Premier League Premier Division, where they stayed for most of the time until they were invited to join the new Conference North in 2004. After two near-misses, Droylsden won promotion to the top flight of non-League football for the first time in their history in

2007, but joy was short-lived and they were back in Conference North after a single campaign. They ended 2009-10 in fifth place and in the play-offs.

EASTWOOD TOWN

Nickname – The Badgers
Official Club Website – www.eastwoodtownfc.co.uk

Coronation Park (Capacity 2,500 [650 seated])
Chewton Street
Eastwood
Nottinghamshire
NG16 3HB

Formed in 1953, the current Eastwood Town has no connection with an earlier club of the same name that existed briefly in the early twenties. Like its earlier namesake, however, the current club also started life as an amateur side in the Nottinghamshire Alliance, where they won the championship once and finished as runners-up on six occasions before enjoying similar success in the Central Alliance and East Midlands Regional League.

After turning professional in 1971 the Badgers joined the Midlands League, moving from there to the Northern Counties East League and then the Northern Premier League, but after 16 years in the NPL, Eastwood Town were relegated for the first time in their history, spending the 2003-04 season in the Northern Counties East League. Bouncing back at the first attempt, they clearly learned from the experience, and recent seasons have seen the club grow in confidence. Promotion to the NPL Premier Division in 2007 was followed by a year of consolidation before another successful campaign saw them into the Conference for the first time in 2009.

The Badgers have also enjoyed considerable success in local cup competitions, their 2008 victory in the County Senior Cup completing their second hat-trick of wins in the tournament and bringing their total number of victories to 13 in just over 30 years. In the same season, they also lifted the NPL Challenge Cup for the first time in their history, and carried their winning ways into the following season's FA Cup, were they reached the third round after beating Wrexham, Brackley Town and Wycombe Wanderers. The FA Cup run, promotion to the Conference, victory in the Peter Swales Memorial Shield and a fourth successive appearance in the Nottingham Senior Cup final all ensured that the 2008-09 season will live long in Badgers' fans' memories.

GAINSBOROUGH TRINITY

Nickname – Trinity, The Holy Blues, The Recreationalists
Official Club Website – www.gainsboroughtrinity.com

The Northolme Stadium (Capacity 4,304 [504 seated])
North Street
Gainsborough
Lincolnshire
DN21 2QW

Formed as Trinity Recreationalists in 1873, Gainsborough Trinity are one of the oldest clubs in the country, and can even boast a lengthy spell as a Football League side, but that ended almost a century ago and for much of the time since then they have enjoyed a relatively stable existence as a non-League side.

Trinity first played competitively in the Midland League, of which they were founder members in 1889. Their Football League career began in 1896 when they were elected to Division Two, where they spent the next 16 years without ever seriously challenging for promotion. During their final seasons in the League they struggled to compete, and it was no surprise when they were voted out in 1912, making way for Lincoln City.

They made an immediate return to the Midland League and remained there for the next 50 years, but their FA Cup performances ensured that their profile was maintained, and it is probably as a giant-killing side that they remain best known. Between 1927 and 1939 Trinity made no fewer than eight appearances in the second round proper, recording victories against three Football League sides in the process: Crewe Alexandra in 1928 and 1931, Port Vale in 1937 and Gateshead in 1938. Their last win over League opposition came in 1946, when the victims were Mansfield Town.

The 1927-28 season also brought the first of Trinity's three Midland League championships, the others following in 1949 and 1967. In 1969, they became founder members of the Northern Premier League, where they would spend the next 35 years in relative obscurity. There were no further championships, and no more giant-killing – the next big event in Trinity's history came in 2004, when they finished high enough in the league to earn a place in the new Conference North, where they remain to this day. Things may change in the near future, however, since new chairman Peter Swann has recently become the club's majority shareholder and his investment has allowed the club to bring in a number of former Football League players to bolster the squad. The arrival of former Aston Villa boss Brian Little is a measure of the club's new-found ambition.

Trinity claim to be one of the few English clubs never to have experienced a relegation, their exit from the Football League being via the ballot box rather than a recognised promotion and relegation process. They also provide another example of football's innate symmetry, being the first and last opponents of Middlesbrough Ironopolis.

GLOUCESTER CITY

Nickname – The Tigers
Official Club Website – www.gloucestercityafc.com

The Corinium Stadium (Capacity 4,500 [all seated])
Kingshill Lane
Cirencester
Gloucestershire
GL7 1HS
(Groundshare with Cirencester Town)

Another club with a lengthy history, Gloucester City came into being in 1883, and began to play competitive football a few years later after being founder members of the Gloucester & District League. Like many clubs, Gloucester City disbanded during the early months of the First World War, but didn't reform once hostilities had ceased. Instead, many of the players who had been with City before the war joined Gloucester YMCA, but by 1925 the club had been renamed Gloucester City and helped to form the new Northern Senior league.

City turned professional in 1935 and joined the Birmingham Combination, moving to a new home ground, Longlevens, at the same time. Four years later, the outbreak of war again interrupted English football, but this time the game was seen as a morale booster and City were one of many clubs who played in regionalised leagues throughout the conflict. They played in the Southern League West section, starting an association with the Southern league that would last for 70 years, ending only with the club's promotion to Conference North at the end of the 2008-09 season.

From 1964, City played at the Horton Road Stadium, close to Gloucester city centre, but moved again in 1986 to Meadow Park, in Hempstead. Two years later, the arrival of former Aston Villa player Brian Godfrey as manger sparked a major revival at the club, and in 1989

City were promoted to the Southern League Premier Division.

After narrowly missing out on promotion to the Conference in 1991, City had an up-and-down existence aggravated by frequent changes of manager and a rapid turnover of players, although they again came close to winning promotion in the mid-nineties before suffering relegation in 2000. By 2004 they were back in the Premier Division, and five years later the dream of a place in the Conference became reality after City won a play-off final against Farnborough – ironically the side who had so narrowly beaten them to the punch in 1991.

This achievement is all the more remarkable considering that Meadow Lane has twice been overwhelmed by floods in recent years when the River Severn has burst its banks, once in the winter of 2000 and again in July 2007, putting an enormous financial strain on the club. City have since taken the decision to look for a new home, ground sharing in the meantime with Forest Green Rovers in 2007-08, and Cirencester Town since August 2008.

GUISELEY

Nickname – The Lions
Official Club Website –
www.pitchero.com/clubs/guiseley/

Nethermoor Park (Capacity 3,000 [300 seated])
Otley Road
Guiseley
West Yorks
LS20 8BT

Guiseley AFC are a club that have constantly flirted with silverware and cup finals, but until recently have never managed to break through the glass ceiling to the higher echelons of non-League football.

They were founded in 1909, and the West Yorkshire club only had to wait four years to pick up their first League trophy. Four more followed in various local leagues in the first half of the 20th century. Arguably Guiseley's most successful period came in the 1960s, when they notched up an astonishing nine out of a possible ten Wharfedale & District FA Challenge Cup victories.

They joined the now-defunct second division of the Yorkshire Football League in 1968, suffering relegation to the third tier two years later Bouncing back at the first time of asking, they won the second division in 1974 but couldn't win the top title, finishing runners-up in both 1980 and '82.

When the league was merged with the Midland League that year, Guiseley became founder members of the new Northern Counties East League. A Wembley appearance in 1991 saw them draw with Gresley Rovers in the FA Vase Final; they won the replay at Bramall Lane. A second consecutive final appearance in '92 saw them lose their trophy to Wimborne Town. A six-year spell in the Northern Premier League Premier Division from 1994 to 2000 preceded relegation to the First Division. Guiseley returned in 2004 for another six years, this time exiting the league from the right end and gaining promotion to the Conference North for the 2010-11 season.

HARROGATE TOWN

Nickname – The Sulphurites, Town
Official Club Website –
www.harrogatetown.com

Wetherby Road (Capacity 3,800 [500 seated])
Harrogate
West Yorkshire
HG2 7RY

Harrogate AFC was formed in 1914, but the outbreak of war effectively put the club on hold before it had played a competitive fixture. After the war the club was reformed, and joined the West Riding League for the 1919-20 season.

The next few years saw the club play in a succession of league competitions, often moving on after a single season, before a period of relative stability saw them spend five years in the Northern League before disbanding.

Following a three-year hiatus the club was revived in 1935 under a new name, Harrogate Hotspurs, but after the Second World War, they renamed themselves Harrogate Town and entered a period of relative stability, spending the next 35 years in the West Yorkshire and Yorkshire Leagues.

1982 saw a move to the new Northern Counties East Football League, where they stayed for five years before being invited to join another new competition, the Northern Premier League Division One. Despite ambitions to climb up the new football Pyramid, Harrogate often struggled, and only narrowly avoided relegation on a couple of occasions. However, their fortunes had revived sufficiently for them to be far enough up the table in 2004 to allow them a place in the newly created Conference North.

For the majority of their existence, Harrogate have hardly set the world alight, their Yorkshire League championship way back in 1927 being a rare highlight. However, their recent form has generally been encouraging, their appearance in the play-offs in 2006 being followed by a near-miss in 2007 and two top 10 finshes in the seasons since then.

The 2009-10 season brought a decline on the pitch after the departure of manager Neil Aspin, and they were fortunate to escape relegation when Northwich Victoria lost their Conference North place.

HINCKLEY UNITED

Nickname – The Knitters
Official Club Website – www.hinckleyunited.com

Greene King Stadium – De Montfort Park
(Capacity 4,329 [1,600 seated])
Leicester Road
Hinckley
Leicestershire
LE10 3

Hinckley United are a young club, having been formed in 1997 by the merger of local rivals Hinckley Town and Hinckley Athletic. Although the stated aim of the merger was to improve the standard of football in the town, the success of the new club has exceeded all expectations.

United took over Hinckley Town's place in the Southern League Western Division and quickly established themselves. In 2000-01 they won the Western Division championship, and spent the following season consolidting their new place in the Southern League Premier Division, but that didn't prevent them from enjoying a lengthy FA Cup run that extended as far as the second round proper, where they lost 2-0 at home to Football League Division Three high-fliers Cheltenham Town.

During the next two seasons United maintained the momentum, finishing mid-table in 2003 and sixth in 2004, earning them a place in the new Conference North. Their first season as a Conference side was distinguished by another excellent FA Cup run that again took them into the second round, but this time included a victory over League opposition, with Torquay United suffering a 2-0 reverse at Middlefield Lane. United took Brentford to a replay in the second round, before losing 2-1 at Griffin Park.

Since then, United have generally finished mid-table, although the 2006-07 season is worthy of special mention. In September, the club was rocked by the loss of centre-half Matt Gadsby, who collapsed and died during a mach against Harrogate Town. In the months that followed, the side showed tremendous character by battling their way into the play-offs, and came close to achieving promotion in memory of their team-mate, losing 4-3 to Farsley Celtic in a scintillating final.

HYDE

Nickname – The Tigers
Official Club Website – www.hydefc.co.uk

Ewen Fields (Capacity 4,100 [850 seated])
Grange Road
Hyde
Cheshire
SK14 2SB

The story of Hyde United (renamed Hyde in June 2010) starts in 1919, when the club was formed to represent the town in the wake of the collapse of Hyde FC, best known for the famous FA Cup tie in which they suffered a 26-0 defeat at the hands of the mighty Preston North End, a score that remains the heaviest defeat in FA Cup history.

To all intents and purposes, Hyde United were a continuation of the earlier club, who had played their home games at Ewen Fields until the land had been turned over to allotments in the First World War. It is believed that the club styled itself Hyde United rather than Hyde FC to avoid liability for the earlier incarnation's debts, but in all other respects it simply picked up where the old club had left off.

United started life in the Manchester League, winning the championship on five occasions before moving on to the Cheshire County League in 1930. After the Second World War, Hyde United enjoyed their best-ever spell, the Cheshire Senior Cup win in 1946 being the first of many successes in the decade that followed, including two consecutive wins in the Cheshire League Cup and two successive league championships followed by three successive runners-up spots.

The Tigers were founder members of the Northern Premier League in 1968, but resigned two seasons later and returned to the Cheshire League. There they remained until 1982, when a championship win earned them a return to the NPL and ushered in another successful period in the club's history, including two League Cup wins and a victory in the Cheshire Senior Cup. In the nineties, Hyde enjoyed some good runs in the FA Trophy and won several local cup competitions, but towards the end of the decade there were signs that things were not going well, and in 2003 they were relegated to Division One.

Under new manager Steve Waywell, Hyde not only bounced back at the first attempt but won the NPL Premier Division title under controversial circumstances in 2005 to earn a place in Conference North. In each of their first three seasons at the higher level things went well and United fnished mid-table, but in 2008-09 they finished in 20th position and would have been relegated had it not been for the compulsory demotion suffered by King's Lynn for not having met ground grading requirements.

United's future was in the balance after the club was wound up in September 2009 with tax debts of around £120,000. A concerted effort to raise funds in the days following the winding-up order led to a review a week later, at which the original decision was reversed. They finished the season 15th, ten points above the relegation zone, but have now changed name, and their colours from red to blue.

ILKESTON TOWN

Nickname – The Reds, Ilson, The Robins
Official Club Website – www.ilkeston-townfc.co.uk

The New Manor Ground (Capacity 3,500 [306 seated])
Awsworth Road
Ilkeston
Derbyshire
DE7 8JF

The current Ilkeston Town FC came into being in 1945, and has no connection with any of the clubs that represented the town in the years before the Second World War. Senior football had been played in Ilkeston since 1882, but Ilkeston Mechanics, Ilkeston United, Ilkeston Wanderers and an earlier Ilkeston Town had all gone to the wall by 1937, and the new club was formed to fill the gap.

After two years in the Nottinghamshire & Derbyshire Senior League the Reds joined the newly reformed Central Alliance, where they soon became dominant. They won the first of four successive league titles in 1952, adding the Derbyshire Senior Cup for good measure, and remained amongst the best teams in the league until moving to the Midland League in 1961. Athough the standard in the Midland League was higher, Ilkeston continued to impress, winning the championship in 1968.

The next few years were difficult, however. The formation of the Northern Premier League, also in 1968, led to a drop in quality in the Midland League, and attendances suffered. The renaissance of local League side Derby County also affected gates, and by the early seventies Ilkeston were feeling the pinch.

A move to the Southern League in 1971 proved disastrous after the side struggled and attendances fell even further, and by 1973 they had returned to the Midland League in an attempt to steady the ship. The Reds survived, but there was little for fans to cheer throughout the seventies and eighties. When local businessman Paul Millership took control of the club in 1989, things began to change. Over the next ten years, Ilkeston moved to a new stadium, made some crucial signings and worked their way up to the Southern League Premier Division, although promotion to the Conference eluded them.

In 2004, Ilkeston suffered a setback when the restructuring of non-League football saw them transferred to the Northern Premier League Division One, but they secured promotion to the Premier Division at the first attempt and survived a difficult 2007-08 season to win a place in Conference North via the play-offs in 2009. An eighth-place finish in 2010 was praiseworthy.

NUNEATON TOWN

Nickname – The Boro'
Official Club Website – www.nuneatontownfc.com

Liberty Way (Capacity 4,350 [250 seated])
Attleborough Fields Industrial Estate
Nuneaton
CV11 6RR

Nuneaton Town, in its various guises, is a club renowned for defying adversity. The club has gone out of existence twice since its foundation as Nuneaton St Nicholas in 1889, but on both occasions has risen from the ashes to continue to battle for the ultimate goal of League football.

Nuneaton Borough had the longest spell representing the town, from 1937 until 2008. Known as the 'Boro', they were founder members of the Conference National in 1979, and finished second in 1984 and '85, though the club were not elected to the Football League on either occasion.

It would prove to be a rare period of on-pitch success for the Midlands club, which struggled throughout most of the nineties before reaching the Conference again in 1999. Relegation in 2003 preceded Borough's biggest moment three years later – a 1-1 draw with Premier League Middlesbrough at Manor Park in the FA Cup third round.

Nuneaton Borough went into liquidation in 2008 after financial difficulties and was consequently relegated two divisions. Renamed Nuneaton Town, the club wasted no time in righting the perceived wrong, clinching promotion from the Southern League Division One Midlands in 2008-09.

The club impressively sealed back-to-back promotions in 2010 with a second consecutive play-off final victory, this time against Chippenham Town. Just two years after folding, Nuneaton were back where their predecessor left off, and looking to continue their momentum up the leagues.

REDDITCH UNITED

Nickname – The Reds
Official Club Website – www.redditchutdfc.co.uk

Valley Stadium (Capacity 5,000 [400 seated])
Bromsgrove Road
Redditch
B97 4RN

One of the older Midlands clubs, Redditch United can trace their history back to 1891 and the foundation of Redditch Town FC, who joined the Birmingham Combination for the 1891-92 season and remained there for the next 80 years.

Their lengthy stay in the Birmingham Combination was mostly unremarkable, occasional success in regional cup competitions giving the fans something to cheer during the long periods between the club's championship seasons. The early thirties proved relatively rewarding, with victories in the Worcestershire Senior Cup and the Birmingham Senior Cup in successive seasons and a league championship in 1933.

There was another brief flowering in the mid-fifties, with championship wins in 1953 and 1955, but nothing further of note until the club switched to the Southern League in 1971. After a solid start, Redditch were soon pushing for promotion, narrowly missing out in 1975, but finishing as champions the following season to secure a place in the Premier Division. Their first season at the higher level started well, but their challenge for a second successive championship ultimately faded, and the next few years proved to be a difficult period.

Although they were founder members of the Alliance Premier League in 1979, Redditch were relegated at the end of the inaugural season. Preparations for the Alliance Premier League had placed a considerable strain on the club's finances and they struggled badly in the years that followed, only narrowly avoiding liquidation.

For the next 20 years, Redditch had an up-and-down existence in the Southern League, but the club's fortunes were revived at the start of the new millennium and United began the climb back up the football Pyramid. Promotion to the Southern League Premier Division and selection for the new Conference North in successive seasons brought fans some much-needed cheer, although United have certainly not found life in the Conference easy. Three points separated them from relegation in 2010, and this may indeed have been their fate had Farsley Celtic not folded.

SOLIHULL MOORS

Nickname – The Moors
Official Club Website – www.solihullmoorsfc.co.uk

Damson Park (Capacity 3,050 [280 seated])
Damson Parkway
Solihull
West Midlands
B91 2PP

New kids on the block Solihull Moors were formed in 2007 from a merger of two local rivals, Solihull Borough and Moor Green, the new club taking Moor Green's place in Conference North at the start of the 2007-08 season.

Formed in 1901, Moor Green spent their first 20 years playing friendly matches and local cup competitions before joining the Birmingham AFA in 1922. In 1936 they moved to the Central Amateur League, making an immediate impression by winning the league championship in each of their first three seasons. After the Second World War the club joined the Birmingham Combination but, as an amateur side in a mostly professional league, struggled to make any headway. By 1966 they had moved to the Midland Combination League, where they stayed until 1983. Their championship win in 1981 was a factor in their successful application to join the Southern League two years later, but things really began to happen for the club in the late eighties after the arrival of legendary Moors manager Bob Faulkner.

Faulkner spent 21 years in charge, overseeing a period during which the Moors achieved promotion to the Southern League Premier Division, enjoyed considerable success in local cup competitions and eventually became founder members of the new Conference North in 2004. The inaugural Conference North season was to prove to be a traumatic one, both on and off the pitch. The Moors narrowly avoided an immediate relegation, but two arson attacks at their Moorlands Stadium led to them becoming tenants at Solihull Borough's nearby Damson Park, and indirectly to the merger that took place two years later.

Solihull Borough was formed in 1953, progressing through local leagues before joining the Midland Combination in 1969. They spent 22 seasons in the Combination, 20 of them in the Premier Division, their finish as runners-up in 1991 earning them promotion to the Southern League. As they would be again 15 years later, Solihull Borough and Moor Green were ground sharing at the time, but on this occasion the arrangement had been put in place after Borough's plans to relocate in the wake of selling their Widney Lane ground had fallen through.

Solihull remained in the Southern League from then until the 2007 merger, dividing their time between the Premier Division and the lower levels and enjoying several long runs in the FA Trophy.

Solihull Moors have made a rather tentative start to their career, finishing just above the drop zone in each of their first three seasons. With attendances falling short of expectations, it remains to be seen whether the merger will ultimately prove to be a success.

STAFFORD RANGERS

Nickname – Rangers
Official Club Website – www.staffordrangersfc.co.uk

Marston Road (Capacity 3,000 [426 seated])
Marston Road
Stafford
ST16 3BX

Formed around 1876, Stafford Rangers spent their early years playing friendly matches and taking part in cup competitions before spending time in both the Shropshire League and the Birmingham League. In 1896, they moved to their present home at Marston Road and started a four-season spell in the North Staffordshire League, but in 1900 they returned to the Birmingham League where they spent the vast majority of the next 40 years. The late twenties proved to be a particularly successful period, with a league championship, two runners-up spots and two third place finishes in five memorable seasons, but in the decade that followed financial problems led to a desperate struggle for survival.

After the Second World War, Rangers spent half a dozen seasons in the Birmingham Combination before switching to the Cheshire League, where they stayed with varying degrees of success until finishing as runners-up in 1969 and stepping up to the Northern Premier League.

The seventies saw Rangers' most successful period to date, with a Northern Premier League championship, FA Trophy and Cheshire Senior Cup treble in 1972, a lengthy FA Cup run in 1974-75 and a second FA Trophy final appearance the following year. Three years later, they were back again, this time taking the silverware back to Marston Road after a 2-0 win over Kettering Town.

In 1979, Rangers were amongst the founder members of the Alliance Premier League, but a drop in form saw them relegated after just four seasons, and although they bounced back to the Conference two years later, the late eighties and nineties were mostly difficult times for the club. Managers came and went, success proved elusive, and by 1996 Rangers found themselves in the Southern League Midland Division after two successive relegations.

A period of rebuilding followed, with promotion in 2000 and a good finish in 2004 taking the club into the new Conference North, and another promotion in 2006 seeing them back in non-League's top flight. However, 2008 was a difficult year for the club, relegation at the end of the 2007-08 season being followed by financial meltdown towards the end of the year, but Rangers survived and remained hopeful of a brighter future.

STALYBRIDGE CELTIC

Nickname – Celtic
Official Club Website – www.stalybridgeceltic.co.uk

Bower Fold (Capacity 6,500 [1,350 seated])
Mottram Road
Stalybridge
Cheshire
SK15 2RT

Stalybridge Celtic are another club currently plying their trade in Conference North who can lay claim to have spent time in the Football League, although if you'd blinked you'd have missed their brief sojourn in Division Three (North), which lasted just two seasons in the early twenties.

Celtic's formation is usually quoted as 1909, although there is evidence to suggest that the club may already have been operating three years earlier. Prior to their brief flirtation with the Football League, Celtic played in a number of regional competitions, including the Lancashire & Cheshire Amateur League, the Lancashire Combination and the Central League, spending the last season before the First World War in the Southern League, a move designed to improve the club's standing.

After the war, Stalybridge resumed their playing career as a Central League side, becoming a Football League club with the creation of the new Division Three (North) in 1921. They got off to a good start, but resigned from the League after just two seasons, fearful that gate receipts would be insufficient to sustain a League career. Rather than risk bankruptcy, Celtic returned to the Cheshire League, playing there without particular distinction or disgrace for almost 60 years. Their tenure was ended only by the amalgamation of the Cheshire League and the Lancashire Combination in 1982, making Celtic a founder member of the resultant North West Counties League.

Champions in 1984 and 1987, Celtic progressed to the Northern Premier League, where they stayed until winning the title in 1992 and moving up again, this time to the Football Conference. Further relegations and promotions followed, the club achieving a return to the Conference when the new North and South divisions were instituted in 2004. Since then, they have remained in Conference North but their first season in the new division was almost their last, Celtic clawing their way back from what looked like certain relegation to finish just above the drop zone. Things have since improved, and Celtic have fairly consistently featured amongst the promotion hopefuls in recent seasons.

VAUXHALL MOTORS

Nickname – The Motormen
Official Club Website – www.vmfc.com

Motassist Arena (Capacity 4,722 [1,265 seated])
Rivacre Road
Hooton
Ellesmere Port
South Wirral
CH66 1NJ

Formed in 1963, shortly after the new car plant was opened in Ellesmere Port, Vauxhall Motors started life in the Ellesmere Port League and the Wirral Combination, but quickly progressed to the West Cheshire League, starting the 1965-66 season in Division Two. By the end of the sixties they had been promoted to Division One, but progress slowed dramatically thereafter, and for the next fifteen years there were few real highlights.

The most dramatic developments during this period concerned the club's facilities. Early games were played at Hooton Park, which lay inside the car-plant complex, but in the late seventies plans were laid to move to a new location, and the Vauxhall Motors Sports and social Club purchased the current Rivacre Road site in 1980. Over the next seven years, the site was developed into a modern sports complex, and the new facilities were opened in time for the start fo the 1987-88 season.

By this time, the club's fortunes had improved, and the Motormen had clinched their first West Cheshire League championship in 1986, following this with a victory in the Wirral Senior Cup and a successful application to join the North West Counties League Division Two at the end of the following season.

With a new stadium, and under a new name, Vauxhall GM made a solid start in the NWCL, finishing mid-table in their first season before cruising to the championship in their second, but after two seasons at the higher level the club committee decided to withdraw from the NWCL and return to the West Cheshire League.

By 1995 they were back in the NWCL, winning Division Two at the first attempt. After several successful campaigns and some impressive performances in both the FA Vase and several regional cup competitions, the Motormen finished as NWCL Division One champions in 2000, then finished as runners-up in their first season in the Northern Premier League Division One to secure a place in the NPL Premier Division for 2001-02.

Their meteoric rise continued unabated as they finished as runners-up in their first NPL Premier Division campaign, then made headlines in 2002-03 by beating Queens Park Rangers in the first round of the FA Cup. Unsurprisingly, Vauxhall Motors were amongst the clubs invited to join Conference North in 2004, but since then they have enjoyed mixed fortunes, avoiding relegation at the end of the 2007-08 season only because of the liquidation of Nuneaton Borough and the expulsion of Boston United. Their mid-table finish in 2009 was followed by a reprieve from relegation in 2010; fans will hope for better.

WORCESTER CITY

Nickname – The Loyals, The Royals, City, The Dragons, The Faithfuls, The Blues
Official Club Website – www.worcestercityfc.co.uk

St George's Lane (Capacity 4,749 [1,223 seated])
Worcester
WR1 1QT

Worcester City FC was formed in 1902 in the wake of the liquidation of another local club, Berwick Rangers. Taking over Rangers' fixture list in the Birmingham League, City went on to enjoy considerable success in their early years, winning the Worcester Cup every year from 1908 to 1914 and recording two Birmingham League titles, one in the final peacetime season before the First World War, the other in 1925.

After leaving the Birmingham League in 1938, Worcester City joined the Southern League, where they remained until the formation of the Alliance Premier League in 1979. Their only Southern League championship came in 1940 in one of the regionalised competitions organised during the Second World War, but the club came to national attention in January 1959 after a 2-1 victory over Liverpool, then in the Second Division, in the third round of the FA Cup.

Worcester's stay in non-League's top flight lasted just six years, although their relegation at the end of the 1984-85 season came as something of a shock, the side having been high in the table in the weeks leading up to Christmas. Back in the Southern League, City spent the next 19 years in a fruitless quest to win the championship and regain their Conference status, but in the end a return to the Conference came with non-League reorganisation in 2004, when Worcester became founder members of Conference North.

In 2008, Worcester became the first club to have played in both Conference North and Conference South, being transferred from one to the other to balance the numbers after no southern teams were relegated from Conference National. (This will be reversed in 2010-11.)

City have played at St George's Lane since 1905, but there are plans to move to a new 6,000-capacity purpose-built stadium at Nunnery Way, which lies to the southeast of the city. It remains to be seen whether the fact that the sale of St George's Lane in a depressed property market is likely to bring in far less money than was originally hoped will affect plans for the new development.

WORKINGTON

Nickname – The Reds
Official Club Website – www.workingtonafc.com

Borough Park (Capacity 3,101 [500 seated])
Workington
Cumbria
CA14 2DT

Formed in 1884, Workington AFC were founder members of the Cumberland Association League, where they played until moving to the Cumberland Senior League in 1894. The years leading up to the First World War saw Workington play in a number of regional competitions, including the Lancashire League, the Lancashire Combination and the North Eastern League, but the club experienced increasing financial difficulties and went into voluntary liquidation in 1911.

In 1921, Workington AFC were revived, and made a successful application to rejoin the North Eastern League for the 1921-22 season. Fans had little to cheer for the remainder of the twenties, and the thirties started just as quietly, but by the middle of the decade a free-scoring Reds side were beginning to taste success, lifting the NEL Challenge Cup in 1935 and 1937. They also reached the fourth round of the FA Cup in 1934. During this period, the club recorded a 15-1 victory over Walker Celtic and a 16-1 win against Chopwell Institute, scoring more than 100 league goals on no fewer than eight occasions, including a total of 147 in the 1933-34 campaign. Surprisingly, Workington never finished as league champions, their best effort being runners-up in 1938-39.

In 1951, Workington were elected to replace New Brighton in the Football League, taking their place in Division Three (North). Their League career started badly, the club finishing bottom of the table, and there was little improvement in the second season. Under the legendary Bill Shankly, things improved briefly in the mid-fifties, but when the League was reorganised in 1958, Workington found themselves in the new Division Four.

In the mid-sixties, Workington enjoyed a brief spell in Division Three, reaching the dizzy heights of fifth place in 1966, but relegation the following season marked the beginning of a terminal decline, and in 1977 they were voted out of the League in favour of Wimbledon.

Workington resumed their non-League career in the Northern Premier League, but seemed to lose momentum and by 1998 had suffered two further relegations to find themselves in the North West Counties League. This marked the low point for the club, who made an immediate return to the NPL and have since worked their way back up to Conference North, where they reached the play-offs in 2007, but otherwise maintained mid-table respectability.

The Conference South (Blue Square South) Clubs

BASINGSTOKE TOWN

Nickname – The Dragons or The 'Stoke
Official Club Website – www.basingstoketown.net

The Camrose (Capacity 6,000 [650 seated])
Western Way
Basingstoke
Hampshire
RG22 6EZ

Formed in 1896 through the merger of two local sides, Aldworth United and Basingstoke Albion, Basingstoke Town began their competitive career in the Hampshire League, winning the championship in 1912 and 1920. After that, things were quiet for more than 40 years, the club's next honours coming during a purple patch in the late sixties when the Dragons finished either as champions or runners-up every season between 1965-66 and 1970-71, winning a league championship and Hampshire Senior Cup double in 1970-71 without sustaining a league defeat.

Stepping up to the Southern League for the 1971-72 season, Basingstoke started well and finished just above mid-table in their first season, during which they also reached the first round of the FA Cup for the first time in their history. In 1984-85, they remained unbeaten at home in a campaign that brought their only Southern League championship, the club moving on to the Isthmian League Premier Division three years later.

Life in the Isthmian League was less to the Dragons' liking. They suffered relegation at the end of a miserable first season, and despite bouncing back at the first attempt, struggled for several years thereafter. Another relegation and promotion followed in the mid-nineties, although fans could take some comfort in a pair of Hampshire Senior Cup wins during the same period.

Plagued by inconsistency, Basingstoke reached the final of the Isthmian League Cup in 1998, held on to their Premier League status by a whisker in 2000, and finished third in the table in 2001.

The pattern continued until 2004, when Basingstoke unexpectedly secured a place in the new Conference South. Having spent all season battling to achieve a league placing high enough to qualify for the new division, the Dragons agonisingly finished 14th, one spot too low, but were handed a lifeline when Hendon decided not to take up the place they had earned. After a bright start, Basingstoke have generally found life in the Conference difficult, although there have been some good runs in the Hampshire Senior Cup and FA Trophy to cheer the fans.

BISHOP'S STORTFORD

Nickname – The Bishops, The Blues
Official Club Website – www.bsfc.co.uk

Woodside Park (Capacity 4,000 [298 seated])
Dunmow Road
Bishop's Stortford
Hertfordshire
CM23 5RG

Another club with a long history in non-League football, Bishop's Stortford can trace their origin back very precisely to a meeting held in the town's Chequers Hotel on 28 January 1874. Founder members of the Hertford Football Association in 1885, the Bishops embarked on a career in league football in the final years of the 19th century, passing through numerous local competitions in the years that followed. They would frequently compete in more than one league at a time, and achieved two 'doubles', winning the Saffron Walden & District League and the Stansted & District League titles in 1912-13, and the East Hertfordshire League and the Stansted & District League in 1919-20.

From 1929, the Bishops played in the Spartan League, moving to the newly formed Delphian

League in 1951 and winning the occasional championship along the way. In 1963, they reached the quarter-finals of the FA Trophy, losing 1-0 away to eventual winners Wimbledon, a first sign of the success the club would enjoy later in the decade.

By now members of the Athenian League, Bishop's Stortford were runners-up in Division Two, champions of Division One and runners-up in the Premier Division in successive seasons, and made a successful application to join the prestigious Isthmian League for the 1971-72 season. An FA Amateur Cup win in 1974 proved to be the highlight of the next few years, during which the Bishops lifted a number of other trophies and did well in the league.

Thereafter, the club enjoyed mixed fortunes, experiencing several relegations and promotions over the next 25 years. There were also some notable cup runs, including the 1981 FA Trophy win that made the club the first to lift both the FA Amateur Cup and the FA Trophy, and a thrilling journey in the 1982-83 FA Cup that came to an end in the third round where the Bishops held Middlesbrough to a draw before losing the replay.

Having weathered a traumatic move to their new home at Woodside Park in 1999, Bishop's Stortford secured a return to the Isthmian League Premier Division in 2002 and finished high enough in the league the following season to claim a place in the new Conference South. Unfortunately they have struggled most seasons, and parted company with long-serving manager and ex-Arsenal player Martin Hayes in 2008.

BOREHAM WOOD

Nickname – The Wood
Official Club Website – www.webteams.co.uk/borehamwoodfc

Meadow Park (Capacity 4,502 [500 seated])
Broughinge Road
Borehamwood
Hertfordshire
WD6 5AL

Hertfordshire-based Boreham Wood FC, whose ground is only a few hundred yards from Elstree film studios, was founded as Boreham Rovers in 1948 before merging with the unusually-named Royal Retournez in 1966. (Note that while the place name Borehamwood is one word, the club, uniquely, is two.) The club played in local leagues before winning two promotions in five years to exit the now-defunct Athenian League in 1974.

The club's reward was a place in the Isthmian League. They didn't take long to adapt, securing promotion to the Premier Division in the 1976-77 season. But it wasn't until 1996 that Boreham Wood began to make waves in the non-League system, and the FA Cup.

Progression to the second round saw a plum away tie at nearby Division Two club Luton, though it brought a 2-1 defeat. The following season they secured second place in the Isthmian Premier, narrowly missing out on promotion to the Conference. They reached the FA Cup second round for the second consecutive year, this time losing to Cheltenham at Meadow Park, before drawing Luton again in 1998, this time losing 3-2 in the first round.

A brief sojourn in the Southern League saw them win the Division One East title before yet more league restructuring saw them back in the Isthmian League.

Boreham Wood reached the second tier of non-League football in 2010 when they won the Isthmian Premier play-off final against Kingstonian at their own Meadow Park. Their reward was a place in the Conference South for the first time in their 62-year history, led by former Arsenal stalwart Ian Allinson.

BRAINTREE TOWN

Nickname – The Iron
Official Club Website – www.braintreetownfc.org.uk

Cressing Road (Capacity 4,151 [553 seated])
Clockhouse Way
Braintree
Essex
CM7 3RD

The name of Braintree Town has appeared in footballing records only since 1981, but the club itself has a far longer history, having been formed as the works team of the Crittall Window Company in 1898. Crittall was, at one point, amongst the leading window manufacturers in the country, famous for making the iron window frames so characteristic of both commercial and domestic buildings of the twenties and thirties. This gave rise to the club's unusual nickname.

Initially known as Manor Works FC, the club was immediately accepted into the North Essex League, competing there under that name until 1921, when they became Crittall Athletic FC. In 1935, Crittall became founder members of the Eastern Counties League, topping the table at the end of the 1936-37 season. After switching to the Essex County League for the 1937-38 campaign, Crittall were back in the ECL for the final season before the Second World War.

When football resumed six years later, it did so without Crittall Athletic, who appear to have been inactive until applying to rejoin the ECL for the 1952-53 season, but their return was short-lived and after the club resigned from the league in 1955 there seems to have been another lengthy period of inactivity.

In 1964, Crittall Athletic reappeared in the Greater London League, where they played for two seasons before moving to the Metropolitan League. Four years later there was another move, this time back to the ECL, but by this time the club had changed name again, and competed as Braintree & Crittall Athletic until links with Crittall ended in 1981 and the current name was adopted. Under their new identity, the club enjoyed a period of enormous success, finishing as ECL champions twice and runners-up four times before stepping up to the Southern League in 1991.

Braintree continued their nomadic habit in 1996, transferring to the Isthmian League, where three promotions in five years took them from Division Three to the Premier Division by 2002. Winning the Premier Division title four years later secured promotion to Conference South, where the Iron initially maintained the momentum and featured in the play-offs in each of their first two seasons in the league. A disappointing 2008-09 campaign saw them finish in the bottom half of the table, but fans were encouraged by a more impressive seventh place in 2009-10.

BROMLEY

Nickname – The Ravens, The Lilywhites
Official Club Website –
http://bromleyfootballclub.co.uk/0910/

The Courage Stadium (Capacity 5,000 [1,300 seated])
Hayes Lane
Bromley
Kent
BR2 9EF

Bromley FC was founded in 1892, playing friendlies against local sides for a year or so before joining the South London League for the 1893-94 season. The next 20 years saw them ply their trade in a bewildering selection of local competitions, including the Southern, London, Kent and Spartan Leagues, a championship win in the latter in 1908 prompting a move to the Isthmian League, where they took the title in each of their first two seasons. The club also won the FA Amateur Cup in 1911, further proof of their status as one of the south's leading amateur sides of the time.

After the First World War, Bromley joined the Athenian League, where they added to their tally of league championships in 1923. A second Amateur Cup win followed in 1938, but otherwise the period leading up to the Second World War was relatively quiet.

When football restarted in 1946, Bromley initially picked up where they had left off in the Athenian League, achieving a double in 1949 when they lifted the FA Amateur Cup to go with their Athenian League championship trophy. That year's Amateur Cup final was the first in the competition's history to be held at Wembley, where a crowd of 96,000 saw Bromley beat Romford by a single goal.

In 1952, Bromley made an impressive return to the Isthmian League, finishing as runners-up in their first season before winning the title in their second. After winning the championship again in 1961, Bromley went into a sharp decline, and recorded only two top-half finishes in the period leading up to their relegation in 1975.

The next 30 years saw the club dividing their time between Isthmian League Division One and the Premier Division, with several promotions and relegations along the way. Managers came and went as the club struggled to achieve stability, and in more recent years the day-to-day running of the team has often been handled by committee. But the 2006-07 season finally brought success when Bromley won promotion to Conference South via the play-offs. They have retained their status with few alarms since.

CHELMSFORD CITY

Nickname – The Clarets
Official Club Website –
www.chelmsfordcityfc.com/html/home.htm

Melbourne Park (Capacity 3,000 [1,300 seated])
Salerno Way
Chelmsford
Essex
CM1 2EH

An amateur Chelmsford City FC was formed in 1878 and moved to the New Writtle Street ground in 1922, but the club fell on hard times and folded in 1938. The present club was formed immediately afterwards as a professional side, taking over at New Writtle Street, and are thus effectively a continuation of their earlier namesake.

The new club made an immediate start in the Southern League and finished in a creditable tenth place in their debut season. Not only that, but they announced their arrival in no uncertain terms by reaching that year's FA Cup fourth round, having knocked out Darlington and Southampton on the way to a 6-0 defeat at the hands of Division One side Birmingham City.

After the Second World War, Chelmsford remained in the Southern League, winning the championship and Southern League Cup 'double' in 1946. Thereafter, Chelmsford's fortunes declined and the next decade or so proved difficult for the club both on and off the field, another League Cup win in 1960 providing the only highlight of the period.

After a brief renaissance in the late sixties, including championships in 1968 and 1972 and a lengthy run in the 1972-73 FA Cup that ended in a third-round defeat at the hands of Ipswich Town, Chelmsford suffered another decline and their first-ever relegation in 1977. Two years later, the introduction of the Alliance Premier League put them back in the Southern League Premier Division, where, apart from a single season in Division One, they would stay until 1997.

During the late nineties, the Clarets struggled to remain solvent, suffering the indignity of having the New Writtle Street ground sold from under them by the Official Receiver in 1997, a blow made worse by the relegation they suffered the same year. The club kept going, ground-sharing arrangements with Maldon Town and later Billericay Town providing them with somewhere to play until their current Melbourne Park stadium was ready in 2006. In the meantime, Chelmsford struggled to return to the Southern League Premier Division, being denied in 1998 because Billericay Town's New Lodge ground was not of the required standard, but succeeding three years later after the required improvements had been made.

In 2004, the reorganisation of the non-League game saw Chelmsford move to the Isthmian League, from where they gained promotion to Conference South in 2008, enjoying an excellent first season in which they reached the play-offs. They did so again in 2010.

DARTFORD

Nickname – The Darts
Official Club Website – www.dartfordfc.co.uk

Princes Park (Capacity 4,100 [642 seated])
Grassbanks
Darenth Road
Dartford
DA1 1RT

Dartford FC nearly went out of business in 1992, losing their Watling Street Stadium in the process. But the club survived 14 nomadic years to triumphantly return to a stadium of their own in 2006 and head back in the right direction.

Formed in 1888, Dartford had won the Southern League twice, and the Kent Senior Cup on four occasions by the end of the Second World War. All six trophies came in the thirties under the leadership of inspirational Scottish manager Bill Collier.

The immediate post-war period was spent in the Southern League; indeed, as of 2006, Dartford had spent more seasons in the league than any other club. A title victory in 1974 brought hope of election to the Football League, though unfortunately this did not occur.

The eighties saw the Darts again reach the top level of the non-league game; they had two stints in the Conference National in 1982-83 and from 1984-86. A trophy-laden period under Peter Taylor followed; the former Tottenham winger led them to two Kent Senior Cups, two Southern

League Championships and two Southern League Cups.

In 1988 Dartford would open their Watling Street home to Maidstone United as they entered the Football League. When United went bust in 1992 the repair costs were borne by the Darts, who were forced to sell their home and groundhop for nearly 15 years.

Tenures at Erith & Belvedere's Park View ground, Purfleet's Ship Lane, and Gravesend & Northfleet's Stonebridge Road home preceded Dartford's move to their present home, Princes Park, in 2006. There, two promotions in three seasons saw them reach the Conference South in 2010. Financially stable once more, Dartford will be hoping to push on from there.

DORCHESTER TOWN

Nickname – The Magpies
Official Club Website – www.dorchestertownfc.co.uk

The Avenue Stadium (Capacity 5,009 [710 seated])
Weymouth Avenue
Dorchester
Dorset
DT1 2RY

Formed in 1880, Dorchester Town were founder members of the Dorset League in 1896 but made little impact in the competition for more than 40 years before their championship win in 1938.

After the Second World War, Dorchester switched to the Western League in 1947, starting in Division Two. They won promotion three years later, the precursor to one of the club's more successful periods during which they won the Western League championship in 1955, lifted the Dorset Senior Cup for the first time, and enjoyed a number of successful FA Cup runs. The 1953-54 competition saw them reach the second round, where they lost to eventual semi-finalists York City, and there were other memorable matches against League opposition, including Port Vale, Plymouth Argyle, Queens Park Rangers and Norwich City to keep fans entertained.

There were no more championships, but the Magpies won the Dorset Senior Cup on four more occasions prior to their move to the Southern League in 1972, where they played in Division One (South) until the introduction of the Alliance Premier League in 1979, whereupon they were placed in the new Southern Division. After winning the league the following year, Dorchester entered an uncertain period that ended with the club in financial disarray and relegated at the end of the 1983-84 season. Remarkably, after almost dropping out of the league completely the following year, Dorchester staged a brilliant recovery, coming back to win the championship in 1987 and reclaim a place amongst the Southern League elite.

Since then, fans have been treated to a roller-coaster ride, with the Magpies alternately flirting with relegation and challenging for honours. At the end of the nineties, the side suffered a loss of form and a subsequent relegation to the Southern League Eastern Division in 2001, but they bounced back, winning the Southern League Cup for the first time in 2002 and regaining their place in the Premier Division the year after.

DOVER ATHLETIC

Nickname – The Whites
Official Club Website – http://doverathletic.com

Crabble Stadium (Capacity 6,500 [1,000 seated])
Lewisham Road
River
Dover
Kent
CT17 0JB

Failing football clubs feature prominently in non-League history, but it is doubtful whether they feature more prominently in any town's history than Dover. The current club is the sixth to represent the town since the 1890s, and was formed in 1983 after Dover FC folded under the weight of massive debts.

Dover Athletic took their predecessors' place in the Southern League, starting out with an initial squad composed mainly of reserve players from the old club. Predictably, they struggled to compete at first, but gradually gained momentum after Chris Kinnear replaced Steve McRae as manager in 1985 and the squad was strengthened. Promoted in 1988, the Whites went on to win the Southern League championship in 1990, but were prevented from taking their place in the Conference because their ground was not up to standard. Having made the required changes, a second title win in 1993 allowed them to make the step up.

Despite finishing eighth in their first Conference season, Dover soon began to struggle and, in the wake of Kinnear's dismissal during the 1994-95 season, went into a downward spiral. A succession of managers failed to stop the rot, and in 1996 Dover survived as a Conference side only because of a technicality that prevented Boston United from taking their place.

Between 1997 and 2001, the Whites did rather better under Bill Williams, but the club was losing money, and debts were mounting up. In 2002, the club weathered the resignation of the entire Board of Directors, a takeover by a supporters' trust and relegation from the Conference. A further relegation, another financial crisis and several more managers followed before a takeover by a consortium headed by former director Jim Parmenter in 2005 saved the club from extinction and put them on a firm financial footing for the first time in years.

Successive promotions in 2008 and 2009 have continued the recovery, and former Gillingham manager Andy Hessenthaler maintained the momentum in Conference South by taking the Whites to the play-offs at the first time of asking, before leaving.

EASTLEIGH

Nickname – The Spitfires
Official Club Website – www.eastleigh-fc.co.uk

Silverlake Stadium (Capacity 3,000 [380 seated])
Ten Acres
Stoneham Lane
Eastleigh
Hampshire
SO50 9HT

The current Eastleigh Football Club came into being in 1980, but the club can trace its origins back to 1946 and the formation of the junior side, Swaythling Athletic. Starting out in the Southampton Junior League, the new club quickly progressed to the Southampton Senior League (West) and from there, in 1950, to the Hampshire League. In 1952, they won the Division Three (West) championship and lifted the Hampshire Intermediate Cup.

By 1956, Swaythling were playing in Hampshire League Division One, where they remained for almost 30 years, but honours were thin on the ground during this period and their time in the league was mostly unremarkable, with few highs or lows. In 1957, Swaythling moved to Eastleigh's current home at Ten Acres, gradually developing the site throughout the sixties and seventies to create one of Hampshire's best grounds, a fact recognised by its use for regional cup finals and representative matches.

In 1980, the club changed their name to Eastleigh FC, and six years later became founder members of the Wessex League, but the lack of honours continued, and in 17 years of Wessex League football Eastleigh managed only one top three finish, coming in the 2002-03 championship season that brought a promotion to the Southern League.

Their first Southern League season was a success, the club finishing in fourth place and thus, after the restructuring of the non-League system, starting the 2004-05 season in the Isthmian League Premier Division. Here, the success story continued, with Eastleigh finishing in third place and winning the play-offs to secure promotion to Conference South.

In 2005-06, the Spitfires almost made the play-offs again, and with one eye on the real possibility of yet another promotion, Eastleigh FC became a limited company and began to invest in the improvements necessary for admission to Conference National. The 2006-07 season proved disappointing, but Eastleigh have been pushing for promotion ever since, finishing two points short of the play-offs in 2008 and losing out to Hayes & Yeading in the play-off semis in 2009.

EBBSFLEET UNITED

Nickname – The Fleet
Official Club Website – www.ebbsfleetunited.co.uk

Stonebridge Road (Capacity 4,098 [500 seated])
Northfleet
Gravesend
Kent
DA11 9GN

Known as Gravesend & Northfleet until a change of name in 2007, Ebbsfleet United is a club that can trace its roots back to Victorian times. Gravesend & Northfleet themselves came into being in 1946 as a result of the merger of two local clubs, Gravesend United and Northfleet United, both of whom had been active since the 1890s. The new club played unspectacularly in the Southern League until the mid-seventies, their championship win in 1958 and an FA Cup run that ended after a fourth-round replay against Sunderland in 1963 the only real highlights of their first 30 years.

Solid performances after promotion to the Southern League Premier Division led to Gravesend & Northfleet becoming founder members of the Alliance Premier League in 1979, and, after a disappointing period in the eighties and early nineties, they found themselves starting the new millennium back in non-League football's top flight. In 2007, two important decisions affecting the club's future were made – the first was the change of name, but the second was far more radical. Towards the end of the year it was announced that the club would be taken over by MyFootballClub, an internet-based group in which members pay a subscription in order to have a share in the club and a say in how it is run, including team selection.

The new owners had something to cheer about within a very short period, as Ebbsfleet triumphed over Torquay United at Wembley to lift the FA Trophy, but the 2008-09 season was an anticlimax and an unexpected decline in MyFC membership combined with relegation in 2010 to leave the club facing an uncertain future.

FARNBOROUGH

Nickname – The Boro'
Official Club Website – www.farnboroughfc.co.uk

Cherrywood Road (Capacity 4,200 [627 seated])
Farnborough
Hampshire
GU14 8UD

Farnborough Town, formed in 1967 and a Conference side for many seasons, went into liquidation in May 2007 and were expelled from the Conference South. The newly formed Farnborough FC dropped two divisions and began the 2007-08 season in the Southern Football League Division One South and West. Their mission was simply to get back where they started, and promotion into Conference South in 2010 was mission accomplished.

Farnborough Town had enjoyed brief fame in the 1990s and early 2000s through their exploits

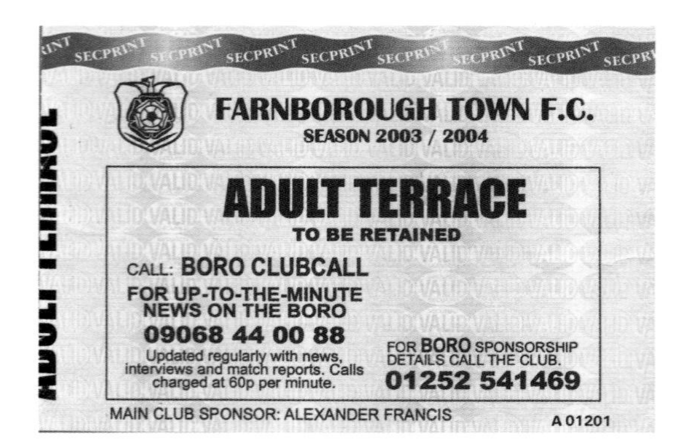

in the FA Cup. They held Premier League West Ham to a draw at Upton Park in 1991 before losing the replay, and in 2003 they drew then-Premier League Champions Arsenal in the fourth round, losing 5-1 at Highbury in a game controversially switched from their own ground; FA Cup rules now forbade such moves.

Retaining their Cherrywood Road home, Farnborough FC began their new existence away to Godalming Town under the leadership of joint managers Andy Clement and Steve Moss. A 3-3 draw was the beginning of a season that would see them storm to the league title with three games to spare.

Farnborough's first season in the Southern Football League Premier Division under new manager Francis Vines saw them almost achieve back-to-back promotions; they missed out on the top spot by a point after leading for much of the season. Their misery was compounded as they lost to Gloucester City in the play-off final at Cherrywood.

There would be no such problems the next season as Farnborough, now under former Lewes manager Steve King, captured the title with games to spare.

Just three years after their re-formation, Farnborough had returned where their predecessors had left off. With rebuilding of their ground under way, fans will be hoping for even greater things as they fight to emerge from the shadow of League neighbours Aldershot.

HAMPTON & RICHMOND BOROUGH

Nickname – The Beavers, Hampton
Official Club Website – www.hamptonfc.net

The Beveree Stadium (Capacity 3,350 [362 seated])
Beaver Close
Hampton
Middlesex
TW12 2BX

Although their name might suggest that they are the result of a merger, Hampton & Richmond Borough are nothing of the sort, having been known as Hampton FC for more than 70 years before deciding on a change of name in an attempt to broaden their fan base within the area.

Formed in 1921, Hampton spent their early days in the Kingston & District and South West Middlesex Leagues, winning the former twice in the early thirties but never managing to repeat the achievement in the latter despite 26 attempts. In 1959, they stepped up to senior football and joined the Surrey Senior League, their 1964 championship win earning them promotion to the Spartan League and ushering in a period of unprecedented success. Hampton finished in the top four in each of their seven Spartan League campaigns, winning the title in 1965, 1966, 1967 and 1970 and finishing as runners-up in 1968.

In 1971 they were elected to the Athenian League Second Division, where they came close to achieving promotion in their debut season before finishing as runners-up in 1973. They started the following campaign in the newly introduced Isthmian League Division One, having already made a succesful application to join.

All good things come to an end, and after 17 years in the Isthmian League's second tier, Hampton suffered their first ever relegation in 1990. To add insult to injury, when the Isthmian League was reorganised at the end of the following campaign, Hampton found themselves consigned to the new Division Three, the Isthmian League's fourth tier, marking their low point to date. However, after a stroke of good fortune, the Beavers spent only one season at this level, inishing just below the automatic promotion slots, but being elected at the Isthmian League's AGM to fill a vacancy that had arisen in Division Two.

Promotions in 1996 and 1998 took them back to the league's top flight, where they stayed for all but one of the next nine seasons, changing their name to Hampton & Richmond Borough in 1999. In 2007, having come close to a play-off spot in 2005 and been losing finalists in the 2006 play-offs, the Beavers finished as league champions and moved up to Conference South, where they started strongly and reached the play-off final in each of their first two seasons under long-serving Alan Devonshire.

HAVANT & WATERLOOVILLE

Nickname – The Hawks
Official Club Website – www.havantandwaterloovillefc.co.uk

West Leigh Park (Capacity 5,250 [526 seated])
Martin Road
Havant
Hampshire
PO9 5TH

Another relatively new name in the football record books, Havant & Waterlooville came into being in 1998, the result of a merger between Havant Town and Waterlooville. Both were long-established clubs, the older by a matter of 20 years or so being Havant Town, who were formed in 1883 and spent much of their competitive career in the Portsmouth Football League.

In 1969, Havant Town merged with local Sunday League side Leigh Park and adopted a new name, Havant & Leigh Park. The merged club clearly meant business, winning the Portsmouth League championship in their first season to secure promotion to Hampshire League Division Four, the rapidly climbing the Hampshire League ladder with three promotions in seven seasons to stake a place in Division One for the 1977-78 campaign.

With their league status threatening to outstrip the facilities at their Front Lawn ground, the club began to look for a new home, buying land in nearby Leigh Park for the purpose. The resulting West Leigh Park Stadium opened in 1982, at which point the club became Havant Town. Founder members of the Wessex League in 1986, Town finished as runners-up on three occasions prior to winning the championship, and with it promotion to the Southern League, in 1991.

Waterlooville were formed in 1905, and immediately joined the Waterlooville & District League, where they played for a number of years without any great distinction. Shortly before the

Second World War, Waterlooville transferred to the Portsmouth League, winning the Division Three title in their first season. In the years immediately following the war, they won the Division Two campionship, spent a few years consolidating their new position and then claimed the Division One title for three consecutive seasons. Waterlooville played in the Hampshire League between 1953 and 1971, then moved to the Southern League for the remainder of the time before the merger.

The merged club enjoyed immediate success, winning the Southern League Southern Division in their debut season. After five seasons in the Southern League Premier Division, the Hawks finished well enough in 2004 to earn a place in the new Conference South, where they have remained since.

Despite their short history, Havant & Waterlooville have a higher profile than many of the clubs at the same level because of their FA Cup exploits, their progress to the fourth round in 2007-08 being of particular note. They have made several other appearances in the first round proper, and seem to enjoy cup competitions in general, reaching the FA Trophy semi-finals in 2003, and the quarter-finals in 2009. The Hawks had to fight to hold on to their place in the Conference in 2008-09 but finished just one place short of the play-offs in 2010.

LEWES

Nickname – The Rooks
Official Club Website – www.lewesfc.com

The Dripping Pan (Capacity 3,000 [600 seated])
Mountfield Road
Lewes
East Sussex
BN7 2XD

Lewes FC were formed at a meeting in the Royal Oak pub in September 1885, and for the first few years of their existence played in light green shirts chosen to reflect the atmosphere of the nearby South Downs, but by 1893 they had switched to the red and black colours worn ever since. Before the First World War, Lewes played in the Mid Sussex League, winning the championship twice before football was abandoned for the duration in 1915.

In 1920, the club became founder members of the Sussex County League, finishing as runners-up on four occasions before finally winning the league championship in 1965. The same season saw them lift the Sussex RUR Cup and the Sussex Senior Cup, a dramatic urnaround for a club whose only other success during their Sussex County League days had been an earlier Sussex RUR Cup win.

The Rooks began the following season in the Athenian League, where they progressed quickly, winning the Division Two title in 1968 and promotion to the Premier Division as Division One champions two years later. A move to the newly expanded Isthmian League followed in 1977 and at first it seemed that the success story would continue. Promotion to Division One came in 1980, but there was no further progress and by the early nineties Lewes were struggling. A quick-fire sequence of relegations and promotions left them in the Isthmian League's basement division by 1994, where they languished for a number of disappointing seasons.

The arrival of manager Jimmy Quinn during the 1998-99 season prompted a revival, and Lewes had soon achieved two consecutive promotions, taking them to the Isthmian League Division One South. Under his successor, Steve King, the Rooks won the Division One South championship in 2004 and stepped up to Conference South, where they settled in quickly and finished in fourth position in each of their first two seasons. However, facilities at the club's famous Dripping Pan ground were deemed inadequate for participation in the play-offs, and it wasn't until

Lewes topped the table at the end of the 2008 season that they were able to move up to Conference National.

The board's controversial decision not to renew King's contract for 2008-09 proved devastating. The appointment of the inexperienced Kevin Keehan as King's successor and the break-up of the championship-winning side during the summer led to a disastrous season and, ultimately, relegation. Financial difficulties only compounded the Rooks' problems, but they retained their Conference South status by a single place in 2010.

MAIDENHEAD UNITED

Nickname – The Magpies
Official Club Website – ww.maidenheadunitedfc.co.uk

York Road (Capacity 3,000 [450 seated])
Maidenhead
Berkshire
SL6 1SQ

The oldest of all the Conference clubs, and one of the oldest in the country, Maidenhead United have almost 140 years of continuous history going back to the formation of Maidenhead Football Club in October 1870. In February 1871, the club played their first game at York Road, a ground that had been used for cricket matches since the late 18th century. Maidenhead play there to this day, giving York Road a place in the record books as the oldest continually used football ground in the world.

In 1871, Midenhead were one of the 15 clubs that entered the first FA Cup competition, and they were also in at the beginning of the Berkshire & Buckinghamshire Cup in 1878 and the FA Amateur Cup in 1893. As founder members of the Southern League in 1894 Maidenhead played alongside some of the best teams in the region, but it was soon clear that they were finding it hard to compete and they dropped back to local league competitions.

Meanwhile, the town acquired another club with the formation of Maidenhead Norfolkians in 1884. After playing in a number of other local leagues, the Norfolkians joined Maidenhead in the Great Western Suburban League, where the two remained as local rivals until the outbreak of the First World War.

When football resumed in 1919 the two clubs merged as Maidenhead Town, adopting the now familiar black and white striped kit and winning the Great Western Suburban League at the first attempt. The following year, they changed their name to Maidenhead United, and in 1922 moved to the Spartan League, where they won the championship three times before the Second World War intervened. An FA Amateur Cup semi-final appearance in 1936 was another highlight of the period.

In 1946, United resumed in the Corinthian League, enjoying a particularly successful six-year spell in the late fifties and early sixties that saw them finish as champions three times, runners-up twice, and make three appearances in the FA Cup first round proper. In 1963, they switched to the Athenian League and ten years later moved on again, to the Isthmian League, but were never able to repeat their earlier successes. By the late eighties they had not only suffered relegation for the first time in their history but were also in financial difficulties.

By 1991, they had regained their place in the Isthmian League Division One, but made little headway until former West Ham and England midfielder Alan Devonshire was brought in as manager in 1996. Under Devonshire, the Magpies gained promotion to the Premier Division in 2000, and under his successor, John Dreyer, finished high enough in 2004 to claim a place in Conference South. Since then, they have survived a spell back in the Southern League and a period of financial struggle, but now seem established in Conference South.

ST ALBANS CITY

Nickname – The Saints
Official Club Website – www.sacfc.co.uk

St Albans City Football Club (Capacity 4,500 [900 seated])
Clarence Park
York Road
St Albans
Hertfordshire
AL1 4PL

Formed in 1908, St Albans City FC have no connection with the earlier St Albans FC, active between 1881 and 1904. City's early years were spent in the Hertfordshire County and Spartan Leagues, but a switch to the Athenian League after the First World War ushered in the club's most successful period. Two league championships in three seasons earned them election to the Isthmian League, where they went one better, winning the title at the first attempt and repeating the feat twice more before the end of the twenties. The decade also saw the club's best performances in the FA Amateur Cup, although they never appeared in the final despite reaching the semi-finals on three occasions.

City remained in the Athenian League until 2003, but the championship trophy never again made its way to Clarence Park. When an extra division was introduced in 1973, St Albans achieved the unwanted distinction of becoming one of the first two clubs to be relegated within the Athenian League, and a further relegation in 1985 marked the low point in the club's history.

Looking for inspiration, City brought in former player John Mitchell as manager. A remarkable transformation ensued, with the club winning two promotions in three years to regain their place in the Isthmian League's top flight. The improvement continued, and the 1992-93 season saw them finish as Premier Division runners-up, but they were denied promotion because Clarence Park fell short of Conference standards.

Having survived serious financial problems that almost led to the closure of the club in the early part of the new millennium, St Albans found themselves well enough placed to compete in the 2004 play-offs for a slot in the new Conference South. Victories over Heybridge Swifts and Bedford Town saw them home and dry, and in 2006 they put their earlier play-off experience to good use in winning promotion to Conference National.

City found life at the higher level difficult, and immediately dropped back to Conference South. Since then, there has been a rapid turnover of both players and managers, but there were signs of an upturn in the club's fortunes in 2008-09, with a place in the play-offs a distinct possibility in the latter part of the season. The summer of 2009, however, brought further financial uncertainty for the club and a mid-table finish in 2010 was commendable under the circumstances.

STAINES TOWN

Nickname – The Swans, The Wheatsheafers, The Massive
Official Club Website – www.stainesmassive.co.uk

Wheatsheaf Park (Capacity 3,000 [300 seated])
Wheatsheaf Lane
Staines
Middlesex
TW18 2PD

A team from the town's St Peter's Institute competed in the 1879-80 FA Cup, but the appearance of Staines Town in 1892 is generally regarded as the starting point of the club that exists today. Soon afterwards, Staines Town and St Peter's Institute merged, and the club went on to win local honours as both Staines FC and Staines Albany.

Several more changes of name followed, but by the early thirts the club had suffered a serious decline, and it folded in 1935. Accounts vary as to what happened next, some suggesting that a new club, Staines Vale, appeared just before the Second World War, others that it was formed towards the end of the war, but a club of that name certainly competed in the Great Western Suburban League, and later the Great Western Combination, in the immediate post-war period.

As Staines Town, they were founder members of the Hellenic League in 1953, then moved to the Spartan League in 1958, the Athenian League in 1971, and the Isthmian League two years later. Between then and 2009, the Swans bounced up and down between the Isthmian League's Premier Division and Division One, promotions in 1974, 1989 and 1996 being negated by a demotion because of a ground grading decision in 1984, and relegation in 1993 and 1997.

Wheatsheaf Lane underwent major rebuilding works during 2001 and 2002, during which time the club ground-shared with Walton & Hersham and later Egham Town before returning home in February 2003. When the football Pyramid was reorganised at the end of the 2003-04 season, Staines secured a place in the Isthmian League Premier Division for 2004-05.

The next three seasons saw the Swans blow hot and cold, but the 2007-08 season saw them reach the second round of the FA Cup for the first time ever after a memorable first-round victory over Stockport County, and then go on to the Premier League play-offs, where they lost in the fnal to AFC Wimbledon. But they made no mistake in 2008-09, beating south London sides Sutton United and Carshalton Athletic to claim a place in the Conference for the first time in their history.

THURROCK

Nickname – The Fleet
Official Club Website – www.thurrockfc.webs.com

Ship Lane (Capacity 3,500 [500 seated])
Aveley
Essex
RM19 1YN

Formed in 1985 as Purfleet FC, Thurrock changed to their current name in 2003, a year before they became members of the new Conference South.

Purfleet started life in the Essex Senior League Reserve Division, playing their early games on a pitch that was part of the Thurrock Hotel complex and had dressing rooms in the main hotel building. It was a set-up that restricted them to junior-level football, but the provision of a new dressing room block during their debut season allowed them to apply for senior status, and they started the following season in the Senior Division.

With an eye to future advancement, further improvements to the ground were made early in 1988, including a new grandstand and the erection of floodlights. Purfleet then put in an application to join the Isthmian League, the success of which would depend on their finishing in the top three of their league. Having won the Senior League championship, they started the next season in the Isthmian League's Division Two North.

By 1994, two promotions in three years had taken them to the Premier Division, a remarkable achievement for a club that had been playng at the junior level just nine years earlier. For the next eight years Purfleet played at the same level with varying degrees of success, but generally finished in the upper reaches of the table. Local cup competitions provided more excitement, although the Fleet had a habit of falling at the final hurdle.

At the end of the 2002-03 season, the name of the club was changed to Thurrock in the belief that having a name that represented a wider geographical area, that of the borough in whic Purfleet lies, would attract more fans. Regardless of whether there were more paying customers, the change of name seemed to bring good fortune,

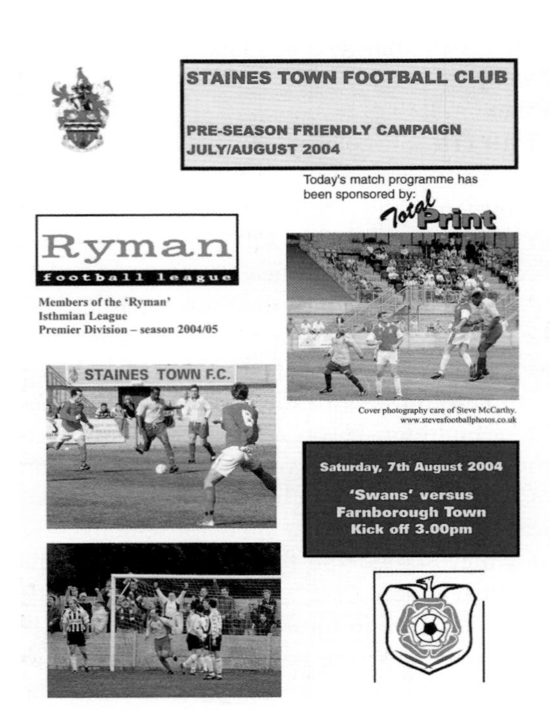

and at the end of their first season the club finished third in the league and earned a place in the new Conference South. For good measure, the Essex Senior Cup and the Isthmian League Cup also found their way into the trophy cabinet.

After reaching the play-offs in their first season, Thurrock have found life in the Conference something of a stuggle, finishing just above the drop zone in 2006-07 and escaping relegation in 2008-09 only because Team Bath resigned from the league. The following season saw them overperform under manager Hakan Hayrettin, threatening a play-off finish before subsiding to 10th.

WELLING UNITED

Nickname – The Wings
Official Club Website – www.wellingunited.com

Park View Road (Capacity 4,500 [1,000 seated])
Welling, Kent
DA16 1SY

Welling United started life as an Under 15 Sunday side back in 1963, but just over 20 years later they were squaring up to the country's best non-League teams in the Football Conference.

In their earliest days, Welling United played their football on pitches at a local sports ground in nearby Butterfly Lane, Eltham. As the club grew, they switched from Sunday to Saturday football, joined the Spartan League and in 1977, with future development in mind, took over the Park View Road ground that had been home to defunct Southern League side Bexley United. The following year, the Wings joined the Athenian League, and in 1981 they moved on again, stepping up to the Southern League's Southern Division, but the Southern League was reorganised for the following season, and Welling found themselves allocated to the newly reintroduced Premier Division.

Three seasons of consolidation followed, but 1985-86 proved to be an astonishing campaign in which the Wings swept everything before them and finished as Premier Division champions by a staggering 23 points. Promotion to the Football Conference completed a remarkable ascent of the non-League ladder that had started in earnest just eight years earlier.

Although they stayed in the Conference for 14 years, Welling often found life there a struggle and only twice finished in the top half of the table. In their first few years as a Conference side, Wings fans could console themselves with a series of respectable runs in the FA Cup, their side making six consecutive appearances in the first round proper starting in 1986-87. The best run came in 1988-89, when Welling beat Bromsgrove Rovers and Bath City to set up a third-round tie at home to Division Two side Blackburn Rovers, who sneaked a 1-0 win. The Wings finally lost their Conference place on the last day of the 1999-2000 season, returning to the Southern League until 2004, when the Pyramid was reorganised and Welling started the following season in the new Conference South.

The first season was something of a struggle, and the club had another brush with relegation in 2007-08, but 2008-09 proved to be a far better season, and a ninth-place finish for manager Andy Ford in 2010 was a step towards taking Welling back into non-League's top flight.

WESTON-SUPER-MARE

Nickname – The Seagulls
Official Club Website – westonsupermareafc.co.uk

Woodspring Stadium (Capacity 3,500 [350 seated])
Winterstoke Road
Weston-Super-Mare
North Somerset
BS24 9AA

The exact year in which Weston-super-Mare FC came into being is uncertain, although it is known that a club of that name played in a local competition in the 1887-88 season, and thus 1887 is generally accepted as the correct date. Weston started out played in local league and cup competitions, their first recorded success coming in 1911, when they won the Weston Charity Cup. When the First World War brought football to an end in 1915, Weston were playing in the Bristol Charity League, but like so many clubs at that time, they disbanded for the duration.

During the inter-war years, Weston continued as they had before, the occasional regional cup win providing the highlights in an otherwise humdrum existence in local leagues.

Although organised football continued to be played during the Second World War, Weston once again disbanded, remaining inactive until 1948, when players in the former Weston Aircraft side suggested at their AGM that a club bearing the town's name should be formed.

The new club started life in the Western League's Division Two, where they stayed until the division was disbanded in 1960 and they became one of four former Division Two sides voted into Division One.

In the mid Seventies, the Seagulls enjoyed their most successful spell to date, finishing as runners-up in the league and recording a League Cup and five Western Senior Cup wins in a seven-year period. In 1983 they moved to their current ground at Woodspring Park, and in 1989 they achieved their first-ever promotion, finishing as Western League champions to win a place in the Southern League's Midland Division.

The Nineties proved a frustrating time for Seagulls supporters, with their club pushing for promotion at the start of the decade and struggling to avoid relegation by the end, but things were gradually turned round, and in 2003 Weston finished as runners-up in the Western Division to Merthyr Tydfil and won promotion to the Premier Division. The following season saw them win a place in Conference South, as well as reaching the Second Round of the FA Cup for the first time in their history, and the Fourth Round of the FA Trophy.

Weston proudly claim never to have suffered a relegation, although the 2006-07 season almost brought an end to that when they finished 21st out of 22 and were only saved from the drop by the demise of Farnborough Town and the merger of Hayes and Yeading. The following season also saw them finish in the relegation places, but they were saved yet again by the compulsory demotion of Cambridge City. The slight improvement shown in 2008-09 was not maintained and they stayed up again on a technicality, thanks to Salisbury's demise and neighbours Forest Green's Conference reprieve.

WOKING

Nickname – The Cards
Official Club Website – www.wokingfc.co.uk

Kingfield Stadium (Capacity 6,036 [2,500 seated])
Kingfield
Woking
Surrey
GU22 9AA

Formed in 1889, Woking FC joined the West Surrey League six years later and won the league title at the first attempt, but that early momentum wasn't maintained and the club spent the next few years in relative obscurity. In 1907-08, however, they came to national attention after they enjoyed a lengthy run in the FA Cup, battling through five qualifying rounds to make an appearance in the first round proper, where they played First Division side Bolton Wanderers.

In 1911, Woking joined the Isthmian League, where they would maintain a presence in the top division for more than 70 years. Their best season was 1956-57 when they finished as runners-up to Wycombe Wanderers, and the strength of the side at this time was emphasised by an appearance in the FA Amateur Cup final the following year, where the Cards beat Ilford 3-0 to lift the trophy.

During the sixties and seventies Woking kept plugging away in the league without any great success, but by the early eighties they were in decline and the club's first-ever relegation came in 1983. A further disaster in 1985 saw them drop to Isthmian League Division Two South, but the arrival of former player Geoff Chapple as manager during the second relegation season proved to be a turning point.

Chapple guided Woking to promotion in 1987 and again in 1990, taking them back to the Isthmian League's top flight, and then masterminded the club's memorable FA Cup run of 1990-91, which began in the fourth qualifying round and saw them beat Conference sides Bath City, Kidderminster Harriers and Merthyr Tydfil on their way to a third-round victory over Second Division West Bromwich

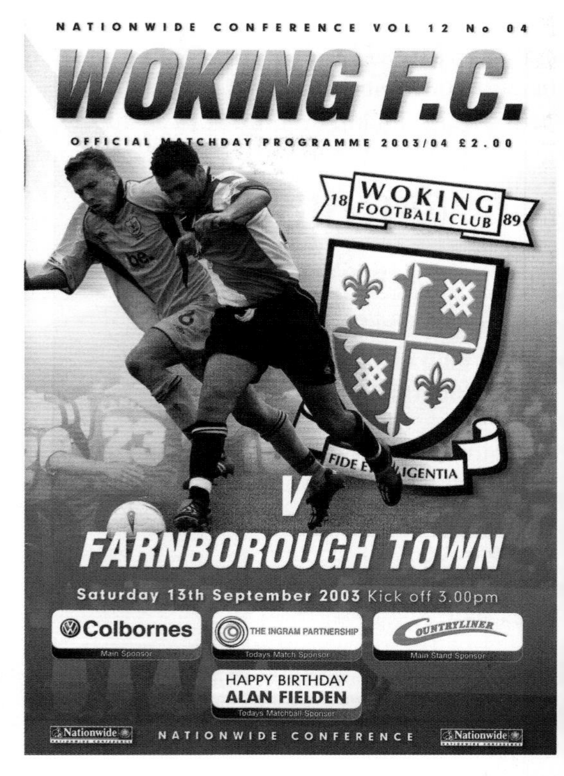

Albion. In the fourth round, they gave Division One stalwarts Everton a scare, losing by the only goal of the game.

The following year saw them promoted to the Football Conference, where the success story continued. Woking won the FA Trophy in 1994, became only the second club to retain it in 1995, and came back again to lift it for a third time in 1997. In the league, the Cards managed five successive top five finishes, including being runners-up in 1995 and 1996. In the FA Cup, Woking achieved victories over Millwall, then Division Two leaders, and Cambridge United, then flying high in Division Three.

After Chapple moved on to Kingstonian in 1997, Woking's star faded and, in the seasons that followed, the club twice found themselves in very real danger of relegation. After a brief renaissance in 2004-05, Woking faded again, suffering relegation to Conference South at the end of the 2008-09 campaign. Manager Graham Baker, elevated from youth-team coach, took them to the play-offs, offering hope for the future.

THE AFCS

With money pulling the strings, fans up and down the country have attempted to take back control of the game they love. Whether by forming new clubs, trying to take over old ones, starting again from the bottom when their club has gone bust, or forming a supporters' trust as a lifebelt in case the worst should happen, their ventures are to be commended.

The histories of AFC Telford United and AFC Wimbledon have been covered elsewhere in this book, but it is worth mentioning FC United Of Manchester, a club that sprang out of objections by Manchester United fans to the takeover at Old Trafford by American magnate Malcolm Glazer and his family. As with the residents of Old Trafford, they can justifiably claim support all over the world.

The club has enjoyed a successful start to life from its formation in 2005, winning the Second Division of the North West Counties Football League in its first season and bagging the First ivision title in 2006-07. This has meant elevation to the Northern Premier League First Division, surely beyond everybody's wildest expectations in such a short space of time. Games are played at Bury's Gigg Lane ground, boasting a capacity of close to 12,000, and pull in healthy crowds for non-League football.

This democratically-run club has many ambitions for the forthcoming years, including elevation to Conference North, the building of a new stadium in the Greater Manchester area and the formation of a women's team.

Dorchester Town – A Curious Tale

In the summer of 2009 two footballers aged 18 and 21 became England's youngest owners of a football club. Brothers Tom and Josh Mitchell ran non-League Dorchester Town after their father gave them the club. The pair were handed control of the club after their father and former chairman Eddie moved to AFC Bournemouth.

Tom insisted that playing was his main priority and the boardroom dealings would be left to brother Josh, telling the *Dorset Evening Echo*: 'It is an exciting development but although the club will now be in mine and my brother's name my main interest is still playing football. As for the other side of it, it will be Josh who will be more involved in the boardroom than me. I won't do much on that side at all.'

There were fears that Dorchester and Bournemouth could both be expelled from the FA Cup had Tom and Josh stayed on at board level as it is against FA rules. Poole-based estate agent Tony Newman, who had originally been lined up for the role, had also been adjudged to have been a close associate of Mitchell. Rules would not allow any individual or their associates to have a controlling interest in more than one football club.

So former vice-chairman Shaun Hearn was unveiled as the new majority shareholder of Dorchester Town in September 2009, and the Mitchells reverted to player status.

FORMER LEAGUE TEAMS NOW IN NON-LEAGUE FOOTBALL

As we've already seen, a number of the clubs now plying their trade in non-League football have spent time playing with the big boys, and here we take a closer look at their past achievements and failures. We also include Merthyr and Bootle, who are not directly associated with their famous forebears.

Ashington

Ashington is a small town in Northumberland, a former mining community whose chief claim to footballing fame is as the birthplace of Bobby and Jackie Charlton. But in the twenties, Ashington boasted a Football League club, one of the founder members of the new Division Three (North) that came into being in 1921.

Ashington FC was formed in 1883, and played in the Northern Alliance, the East Northumberland League and the North Eastern League for various periods before the Football League came knocking. They made an encouraging start, finishing mid-table in four of their first five seasons, but thereafter they gradually lost momentum, finishing sixth in 1927, 18th in 1928, and bottom of the table in 1929. Having failed to gain re-election – York Ciy took their place – Ashington dropped out of sight, playing few, if any, matches in the 1929-30 season.

The club relaunched in time for the 1930-31 campaign, for which they rejoined the North Eastern League, where they remained until becoming founder members of the ill-fated Midland League in 1958. After the Midland League collapsed in 1960, Ashington played in a number of local league competitions until joining the Northern League in 1970, where they remain to this day.

AFC Darwen

AFC Darwen was formed immediately after the 134-year-old Darwen FC was finally wound up in May 2009, and may thus be regarded as a logical continuation of the former club.

Formed in 1870, Darwen FC played rugby and cricket for the first five years, switching to Association Football in 1875. Although their League career was brief, lasting just seven years, they have left their mark on the game in a number of ways, some more desirable than others.

In 1878-79, Darwen became the first northern side to achieve any success in the FA Cup, reaching the quarter-finals. In the process, they opened up the debate about professionalism in the game when they fielded Fergus Suter and James Love, believed to be the first paid players to appear in the English game. In 1881, they reached the semi-finals after demolishing Romford 15-0 in the quarter-finals, a record score unlikely ever to be broken.

Their League career in the newly expanded Division One in 1891 did not start well – they finished with just 11 points from their 26 matches, and on their way to becoming the first club relegated to the new Division Two they suffered a 12-0 defeat at the hands of West Bromwich Albion, still the biggest ever top-flight defeat.

Before bowing out of the League at the end of the 1897-98 season, Darwen set a few more records. In 1896-97, they went the whole season without drawing a game, still a unique achievement for a League side. In their final season, they set the less impressive record of 18 straight defeats, conceding no fewer than 141 goals in their 34 games – another record!

Darwen then joined the Lancashire League, switching to the Lancashire Combination a few years later. There they stayed for more than 70 years, the highlight of the period being the 1931-32 FA Cup run that saw them beat League side Chester City in the second round and earn a third-round match against reigning League champions Arsenal. Darwen lost 11-1, but so impressed their hosts with their sporting attitude that they were presented with a set of the Gunners' famous red strip, adopting it as their own thereafter. In 1976 Darwen moved to the Cheshire County League and moved again, in 1982, to the North West Counties League, remaining there until their demise.

Barrow

Barrow AFC were founded in July 1901 and played at the Strawberry Ground, Roosecote and Ainslie Street before moving to their current home, Holker Street, in 1909. They spent some years in the Lancashire Combination prior to becoming one of the founder members of Football League Division Three (North) in 1921.

Their League form was hardly scintillating – they finished bottom of the table in four of their first ten League seasons, and it was not until 1931-32 that they managed to finish in the top half of the table. Having repeated the feat in each of the following two seasons, Barrow once more returned to a life spent almost exclusively in the lower reaches of the division until 1957-58 when they finished in 18th position, and thus found themselves consigned to the newly created Division Four.

The fans did have something to cheer during the following year, though, as Barrow made a rare appearance in the FA Cup third round where they gave a good account of themselves against Wolves, then the Football League champions. In 1967, there were more celebrations as Barrow won promotion to Division Three, but their finish in eighth position in their first season at the higher level was as good as it got, and two years later they were back in the League basement.

After two more dismal campaigns, Barrow were voted out of the Football League in 1972, and since then have divided their time between the Northern Premier League and the Football Conference, of which they were founder members in 1979. In recent years, Barrow have gone from the thrill of winning the FA Trophy in 1990 (repeated in 2010) to the despair of going into administration in the opening weeks of 1999, but seem to be on a better footing now, and are working hard to retain the place in the Conference National that they regained in 2008.

Bootle

Founder members of the Football Alliance in 1889, and Everton's main Merseyside rivals before the arrival of Liverpool, Bootle were FA Cup quarter-finalists in 1890 and founder members of the Football League Division Two in 1892. They finished eighth of the 12 clubs that played in that inaugural season, then dropped out of the League.

There seems to be no record of what happened next, but they faded from view, and appear to have folded almost immediately. Appropriately enough, their place in Division Two was taken by Liverpool. The current North West Counties League Premier Division club of the same name has no connection with its predecessors.

Boston United

Formed in 1933, Boston United worked their way up through the Midland and Southern Leagues to become founder members of both the Northern Premier League in 1968 and the Alliance Premier League in 1977. In 2000 they won promotion back to the then-renamed Conference and two years later exited as champions after their side had pipped Dagenham & Redbridge to the title on goal difference.

But the Pilgrims' five-year spell in the League both began and ended amid controversy. In their first season, manager Steve Evans and former chairman Pat Malkinson were charged with breaking Football Association rules concerning the registration of players. Both men received FA bans, and Boston were fined and docked four points, but Dagenham & Redbridge were incensed, arguing that the points deduction should have applied to the season in which the offences took place, and they had therefore been robbed of a place in the League.

In 2007, Boston lost their Football League status on the final day of the season, and were thus due to start 2007-08 in the Conference National. The club was in serious financial difficulties, and realising that going into administration after the season had ended would incur a 10-point penalty, entered into a Company Voluntary Arrangement ten minutes before the final whistle in their last game so that the points deduction would then be made in the 2006-07 season instead of the 2007-08 season. The plan backfired, though, because the terms of the CVA were such that FA rules stipulated a two-division drop, so Boston began the following season in Conference North. Failure to exit administration by May 2008 brought another FA-imposed relegation, and Boston played two seasons in the Northern Premier League Premier Division before returning to the Conference North in 2010.

Bradford Park Avenue

Although it is a rather more tenuous connection than in some similar cases, the current Bradford Park Avenue AFC can legitimately claim to be descended from an earlier incarnation of the club that had a lengthy, if unspectacular, Football League career.

The earlier club had roots that stretched back as far as the formation of the Bradford Football Club, which played Rugby Union with some distinction in the early years of the 20th century. In 1907, however, some of the players decided to switch to Association Football, continuing to play at the club's Horton Park Avenue headquarters. It was a move that split the club, with the rugby players electing to decamp and set up a new club, Bradford Northern (later the Bradford Bulls), and leave the soccer players to it.

Bradford Park Avenue joined the Football League a year later, replacing Lincoln City in Division Two. In 1914 they were promoted to Division One, where they finished in ninth position in their first campaign, the highest placing the club were ever to achieve. FA Cup quarter-final appearances in 1912-13 and 1919-20 were a reflection of the club's standing at the time.

Soon after the First World War, however, they suffered a dramatic loss of form, lasting just two more seasons in Division One before successive relegations saw them start the 1922-23 season in the new Division Three (North). Their fortunes improved thereafter, and between 1928 and 1950 they could be found in Division Two, even making a third appearance in the last eight of the FA Cup in 1945-46, but by the time the League was reorganised in 1958 the club had been in decline for several years, and they found themselves in Division Four.

In 1970, after finishing bottom of the League for three successive seasons, Bradford Park Avenue were voted out of the League in favour of Cambridge United. They were accepted into the Northern Premier League, but soon found themselves in dire financial straits and had to sell Park Avenue in 1973 in an attempt to stave off liquidation, entering into a ground sharing arrangement with Bradford City. It wasn't enough, and in May 1974, the club was wound up.

The current club is descended from the new Sunday League side that was formed in the immediate aftermath, which stepped up to senior level in 1988. They played in a variety of amateur leagues until 1995, when they joined the Northern Premier League. In 2004, they were founder members of Conference North, but suffered immediate relegation to the Northern Premier League, where they have remained since.

Cambridge United

Known as Abbey United from their formation as an amateur side in 1912 until deciding to adopt their current name in 1951, Cambridge United played in a number of different league competitions until being elected to replace Bradford Park Avenue in the Football League in 1970.

Promoted to Division Three in 1973, Cambridge struggled at the higher level and suffered immediate relegation back to the basement. Next time it was very different – United achieved two successive promotions in 1977 and 1978, and spent the next six seasons just one step from the top flight, but their fall from grace was as spectacular as their earlier elevation, and two successive relegations put them back in the bottom drawer for the 1985-86 season.

Remarkably, history repeated itself a few years later, promotion via the play-offs in 1990 being followed by the old Division Three championship the next year. Only defeat at the hands of Leicester City in the 1992 play-offs prevented Cambridge United from becoming the first team ever to go from the bottom division to the top in successive seasons.

Once again, they failed to consolidate, and by 1995 Cambridge United found themselves back in the League's basement division. Hopes were raised by a brief spell in Division Two (then the third tier) around the turn of the decade, but United struggled in the wake of the collapse of ITV Digital in 2002, and lost their battle for League survival in 2005. Relegation to the Conference National brought with it a period in administration, but the club have pulled through and after a modest start to their non-League career have recently been pushing hard to regain their Football League status.

Chester City

Chester FC had been in existence for almost 50 years before replacing Nelson in the Football League Division Three (North) in 1931. Their early years had been spent for the most part in the Lancashire Combination and the Cheshire League, and they had enjoyed considerable success in the latter in the years leading up to

their successful bid to join the big boys.

These were heady days for Chester fans, who saw their club make an immediate impression, finishing third in their first League campaign, a position they would attain on a total of three occasions in the seasons leading up to the Second World War. In 1935-36, a season which saw them record a resounding 12-0 League win over York City, they went one better, but with only the champions of each of the regional Division Three competitions being promoted to Division Two, Chester remained in the third tier.

A third-place finish in the first post-war season gave no indication of the decline that was to follow, but the fifties were particularly depressing for the Chester faithful, with the club finishing 92nd in the League on two occasions, unsurprisingly being consigned to the new Division Four when it was introduced in 1958. The sixties and early seventies were, in general, no better, but the club then enjoyed a minor renaissance, and with it the thrill of their first League promotion in 1975. But it certainly wasn't the start of anything big, and Chester enjoyed mixed fortunes at the higher level for seven seasons before dropping back to the basement.

On returning to Division Four in 1982, the club changed their name to Chester City and regrouped. Four years later, they repeated the earlier cycle, gaining promotion in 1986, spending seven seasons in the third tier, then dropping back down. Despite bouncing straight back in 1994, they were unable to maintain the momentum, and suffered an immediate relegation.

The late nineties saw a steady decline in Chester City's fortunes both on and off the field, and although they survived a period in administration at the close of the decade, the club lost their League status after almost 70 years at the end of the 1999-2000 season. Four years later, they were back as Conference champions, their first league title since their days in the Cheshire League, but a succession of managerial changes failed to achieve much in the way of success, and Chester City became the second club (after Halifax Town) to lose Football League status for a second time at the end of the 2008-09 season.

To add insult to injury, the club also entered administration for the second time in ten years, and finally collapsed in mid-season in 2009-10, their playing record being expunged.

Darlington

The present Darlington FC were founded in 1883. For many years they were one of the most successful amateur outfits in the north-east of England, and turned professional in 1908. Darlington were founder members of Division Three North in 1921. They played for many years at Feethams, a ground very close to the town centre, before moving to the 25,000-capacity arena they now call home.

In 2003 the then chairman, George Reynolds, who had great ambition for his club, moved them into a new stadium. Having undergone many name changes, this ground is now known as the Northern Echo Darlington Arena. It is the financial demands of running such a large stadium with crowds of just a few thousand that has contributed to the club's recent problems.

Darlington's League highpoint came as long ago as 1926 when they finished 15th in Division Two, then the second tier of English football. Returning to the Third, they twice survived re-election in the thirties but also, in 1934, enjoyed their first success in a nationally-organised cup competition, winning the Football League Third Division North Cup.

They began their second spell in the Conference in 2010 after a season during which three managers failed to turn round a disastrous start. If even a dent is to be made in the Northern Echo Darlington Arena's capacity – limited to 10,000 for normal games – then a good start to 2010-11 will be very important. Otherwise, the freefall could continue.

Durham City

Formed in the last days of the First World War, Durham City played two seasons of North Eastern League football before stepping up to the Football League as founder members of Division Three (North) in 1921. Their Football League career was short but far from sweet, and they failed to finish in the top half of the table in any of the seven seasons they spent there. Their application for re-election at the end of the 1927-28 campaign was unsuccessful, and they made way for Carlisle United.

After several years back in the North Eastern League, Durham folded in 1938, but in 1950 the club was revived, and began playing in the Wearside League. After two seasons the revitalised Durham City moved to the Northern League, where they stayed without causing many ripples for more than 40 years. In 1993-94, Durham City won the championship, but were unable to take up a place in the Northern Premier League because their new, purpose-built home, the Arnott Stadium, wasn't ready.

They had to wait 14 years for another chance, but their second championship win in 2008 saw them move up to the Northern Premier League Division One. They were clearly at home there, sweeping to a second successive championship to start the 2009-10 season as members of the NPL Premier Division. But this proved a step too far and, with sponsorship withdrawn due to their 'plastic pitch' being deemed unfit for Conference football (should it be achieved), they suffered a player exodus and a humiliating season.

ENTO Aberaman

Although the name of Aberaman never graced the Football League, ENTO Aberaman can trace their roots back to the dissolution of Aberdare Athletic FC, a Football League side for six seasons between 1921 and 1927.

Aberdare Athletic were founded in 1892 and spent their early years in relative obscurity apart from being Welsh Cup runners-up in consecutive years in 1904 (losing 3-0 to Druids) and 1905 (losing 3-0 again, this time to Wrexham). Their decision to join the Southern League's Welsh Section in 1920 proved to be a turning point, and, after a successful campaign, they were invited to become founder members of the new Football League Division Three for the 1921-22 season.

Aberdare did reasonably well, finishing mid-table in four of their first five seasons, but playing soccer in the rugby stronghold of south Wales meant that they struggled to bring in the crowds, and a disastrous dip in form in their last campaign saw them finish at the bottom of the table. The actual reason for their exit from the League remains something of a mystery, with some saying that they failed to secure re-election, and others that they didn't even try, but either way Aberdare's time as a League club was up and they made way for Torquay United.

The Aberaman connection came the following season, when Aberdare Athletic and Aberaman Athletic merged and rejoined the Southern League as Aberdare & Aberaman Athletic, but the alliance was short-lived, and the two sides parted company again after a single season. The Aberdare faction folded shortly afterwards, but Aberaman carried on, and ENTO Aberaman are their direct descendants.

FC Halifax Town

Like Newport County, the current FC Halifax Town can be regarded as a logical continuation of an earlier, similarly named club with Football League experience, hence their inclusion here. The revived club have been in existence for only a short time, and have been forced to renew their league career in the lower reaches of the football Pyramid, but their intentions are clear – to bring League football back to the Shay.

Halifax Town AFC were formed in 1911, and joined the Football League ten years later when the Third Division (North) came into being. Their League career was undistinguished, and was spent for the most part in the lowest tier of the Football League, either Division Three (North) or Division Four.

Their first spell outside the bottom drawer came in 1958 after finishing in an uncharacteristically high position in Division Three (North) and thereby earning a place in the new, national Division Three. Life at the next level proved difficult at times, and after five fairly mediocre seasons Halifax Town found themselves back in the League basement, but they bounced back in 1969, and two years later enjoyed a thrilling campaign that finished with the side in third position, just four points short of promotion to Division Two.

Unfortunately, that was as good as it got, and the 1976-77 season saw Halifax Town playing their football in Division Four again. Only once in the next 17 seasons did they finish above 15th in the table, a largely miserable existence that came to an inevitable conclusion with relegation to the Conference in 1993. In 1998, Halifax won the Conference National championship and League football returned to the Shay, giving their long-suffering fans something to celebrate for the first time in almost 30 years.

It proved to be a short-lived renaissance, and Halifax earned the unwanted distinction of being the first club to lose Football League status for a second time just four years later. By 2007, they were in deep financial difficulty and entered administration. Worse was to come, and Halifax were expelled from the Conference in 2008 after failing to get a Company Voluntary Arrangement finalised. With debts rumoured to be in the region of £2 million, the club was wound up, FC Halifax Town rising from the ashes and accepting the FA's offer of a place in the Northern Premier League Division One (North) for 2008-09. They left this as champions in 2010, heading upwards once more.

Gainsborough Trinity

Formed as Trinity Recreationalists by the vicar of Holy Trinity Church as long ago as 1873, they had changed their name to Gainsborough Trinity by the time they joined the Midland League in time for the 1889-90 season. Finishing a very creditable seventh in their debut season, Trinity went on to win the championship in their second term, and maintained high enough standards in the years that followed to be accepted into the Football League in 1896.

Gainsborough remained in the Football League for 16 years, but at no point did they manage to finish higher than sixth place, their usual end-of-season position being around two-thirds of the way down the table. Towards the end of their League career, Gainsborough struggled to compete, finishing in the bottom three in each of their last three seasons.

The axe fell in 1912, when they failed the re-election ballot and made way for local rivals Lincoln City. Returning to the Midland League, Gainsborough seemed far more at home, winning the league championship three times and enjoying the occasional victory over League opposition in the FA Cup. Founder members of the Northern Premier League in 1969, this long-established club now ply their trade in the Nationwide Conference North, having been allocated a place in the newly created league on the basis of their NPL Premier Division performance in 2003-04.

Gateshead/South Shields

Of all the towns and cities to be found in this section, Gateshead is undoubtedly the one with the most convoluted football history, several clubs having represented the town over the past 120 years.

Not much is known about the earliest of these, Gateshead NER FC, formed in 1889 and active in the Northern Alliance until 1903. More prominent were Gateshead Town FC, who played in the Northern Alliance from 1905 to 1911 when they joined the North East Counties League and turned professional. However, the club were not particularly successful, and did not resume playing after ceasing operations during the First World War.

A second Gateshead Town FC, who also played briefly in the Northern Alliance, had been founded as Close Works FC in 1919, but existed for only a few seasons and disbanded in 1924.

There followed a six-year hiatus before the next club to bear the town's name emerged, but this time the story behind their arrival was startlingly different. Gateshead AFC were rather like a thirties version of MK Dons, although the distances involved were far smaller. The club originated in the nearby town of South Shields, itself a location with a bewildering football history, where South Shields Adelaide had been formed in 1899. South Shields Adelaide played at first in the Northern Alliance, moving to the North Eastern League in 1908, by which time the club had dropped the Adelaide from its name.

South Shields became a Football League club in 1919, joining the extended Division Two, but they found life something of a struggle, and suffered relegation to Division Three (North) in 1928. After two seasons in the lower division, the club's financial situation was deteriorating,

so the directors took the unprecedented decision to move to a new location where, they hoped, bigger crowds might boost income and ensure survival.

Having decided against Newcastle, Gateshead was chosen on the grounds that the local council had seemed enthusiastic. A new stadium was built and the club was duly rechristened Gateshead FC, the new name appearing in fixture lists from August 1930. They came very close to gaining promotion in both 1932 and 1950, but remained in Division Three (North) until the regional divisions were replaced by Division Three and Division Four in 1958. Gateshead missed the cut by a solitary point and therefore found themselves in the lower division.

Just two years later the club had to apply for re-election, and surprisingly, given that they had enjoyed 30 moderately successful years in the League, they were voted out in favour of Peterborough United. Thereafter, they played in various local leagues until 1968, when they became founder members of the Northern Premier League, but poor form and mounting financial problems led to the once-proud club being wound up in 1973.

A third, unrelated, Gateshead Town FC played in the Northern Combination league in 1973-74, but then a remarkable repeat of the events of 1929-30 took place.

After the original South Shields FC had been uprooted, a new club had been formed to represent the town in 1936, playing initially in the North Eastern League. In 1968, after spending the previous ten years in a number of short-lived local leagues, they joined the new Northern Premier League, where they played alongside Gateshead. South Shields lasted slightly longer than their neighbours, but they, too, hit the financial buffers in 1974, and once more the club was relocated to Gateshead, becoming Gateshead United. This time, the move was less successful, and United finally went to the wall in 1977.

In the wake of this collapse, two new clubs emerged, a reformed Gateshead FC taking United's place in the Northern Premier League in 1977 and a new South Shields FC starting afresh in the Northern Alliance the following year.

Since then, thankfully, there have been no more relocations, reformations or renamings, and both clubs have continued to the present day.

Glossop North End

With a history stretching back to 1886, Glossop North End are another side whose League career ended many years ago, but who are still plugging away in the lower reaches of the non-League Pyramid.

After spending time in the North Cheshire League, the Football Combination and the Midland League, Glossop North End were elected to Football League Division Two for the 1898-99 season and made an immediate impact. Finishing their debut campaign as runners-up to Manchester City, they were promoted to Division One, at which point they shortened their name to Glossop FC.

It was a move that brought them no luck, and they were relegated again after just one season in the top flight. Thereafter they simply faded away, spending most of their remaining time in the League in the lower reaches of Division Two. The 1908-09 season's FA Cup competition brought a rare moment of excitement when the club reached the quarter-finals, where they lost to Bristol City after a replay.

Finishing bottom of the table in the final season before the First World War, Glossop failed to secure re-election, and their League career was over. In the years since then, they have played their football in the Manchester League, the Lancashire Combination and the Cheshire League, becoming founder members of the North West Counties Football League when the last two merged in 1982. Reverting to their original name in 1992, Glossop North End have enjoyed some success in local cup competitions and reached the final of the FA Vase in 2009, losing to Northern League Division One side Whitley Bay.

Glossop North End prepared for the big day at Arsenal's London Colney training ground, a courtesy extended to the non-League side through their links with the Premiership club, which stretch back almost 100 years to the time Sir Samuel Hill-Wood, later chairman of Arsenal (and grandfather of current Arsenal chairman Peter Hill-Wood), was chairman of Glossop.

Grimsby Town

Grimsby Town's formation, originally as Grimsby Pelham, came about as a result of a meeting of cricketers in 1878, in the Wellington Arms, Freeman Street. The name Pelham, which was the surname of local landowners the Earls of Yarborough, was later dropped. Grimsby Town were elected to Division Two in 1892. They have been at their Blundell Park ground in Cleethorpes since 1899.

The club's most recent successes were in the seventies when, under first Lawrie McMenemy and then George Kerr, they returned to football's second tier, and the nineties, 1998 finding them there again after a play-off win at Wembley. They also won the Football League Trophy that year at the same venue. After five seasons, their relegation coincided with ITV Digital's collapse, the £2 million debts they owed causing a fire sale of players and another relegation.

It is fair to say that it has been mainly downhill from there. Mariners fans will be hoping that their sojourn in the non-League sector will be a short one and they can resume their previous status that had lasted for 99 years. If not, they are another big name to have made the journey to the Conference thanks to the 'two up, two down' system that has operated since 2003.

Kidderminster Harriers

A club with a long history but only a fleeting acquaintance with the Football League, Kidderminster Harriers spent the majority of their first 100 years of existence in the Birmingham & District League, or the West Midlands League as it later became known, and almost all the remainder in the Southern League.

Like so many non-League clubs, things really began to happen for the Harriers after the creation of the Alliance Premier League, although they were not among its founder members, achieving promotion from the Southern League in 1983. Eleven years later, the dream of a Football League place almost became reality, but the celebrations that followed their 1994 Conference championship win were ruined by the news that their Aggborough stadium fell short of League standards and they would not be allowed to make the step up.

Six years later the Harriers were Conference champions again, and this time they were ready for the big day. Their first season in Division Three was moderately successful, the club finishing sixth out of 24, and their future in the League looked more secure when they finished tenth in their second campaign.

Sadly, the momentum couldn't be maintained, and the club soon found itself in financial difficulties. The expense of improvements to Aggborough, combined with the collapse of ITV Digital and disappointing attendances, meant that the Harriers began to struggle. Unable to strengthen their squad, they were soon fighting for survival rather than promotion, and after five seasons they found themselves relegated back to the Conference. Now, after a period of adjustment, Kidderminster are back among the promotion contenders.

Luton Town

Of all the clubs currently playing non-League football Luton Town have the most League experience, having enjoyed the highs and lows of life at the top for over 90 years.

Their first taste of League football came in the final years of the 19th century when Burton Swifts failed to secure re-election to Division Two at the end of the 1896-97 season. The Hatters were elected to take their place and gave a reasonable account of themselves in their first campaign, finishing halfway down the table, but

thereafter they found themselves increasingly unable to compete. They finished the 1899-1900 season with only five wins from their 34 games, one off the bottom of the table.

Luton's problems were not only on the field of play, though. The majority of Football League clubs were still from the north of England, where professionalism had been the norm for several years, and so they found themselves with far higher travel and accommodation bills than most, and their modest gate receipts simply didn't cover their costs. Luton resigned from the League in 1900, and returned to the Southern League they had helped to found six years earlier.

In 1905, the club moved to their present home, Kenilworth Road, and settled down to life in the Southern League until they found themselves members of the Football League once again in 1920, when the Southern League's top division was commandeered to create the new Football League Division Three. Once more the Hatters entered a period of relative stability, finishing more often in the top half of the table than the bottom, but they began to hit their stride in the mid-thirties, and secured promotion to Division Two in 1937. The promotion side featured the legendary Joe Payne, who scored 55 times in 39 games that season, but who will always be remembered for the 10 goals he scored in Luton's 12-0 demolition of Bristol Rovers the previous year.

After the war, and another period of consolidation, Luton enjoyed their most successful spell to date, finishing in second place behind Birmingham City on goal average in 1955 to secure promotion to the top flight for the first time. Four years later, the Hatters appeared in their first major cup final, losing 2-1 to Nottingham Forest in the FA Cup, but the tide was turning, and the sixties proved to be a trying time for Luton fans as the club slipped inexorably down the League and suffered relegation to Division Four just ten years after they had made it to the top.

By 1971, they were back in Division Two

(then the second tier), where they spent all but one of the next 12 seasons before a return to the top flight in 1982 ushered in the club's second golden era. After struggling to establish themselves, Luton recorded their best-ever League position by finishing seventh in 1987, and went on to beat Arsenal 2-1 in the League Cup final in 1988. They reached the final in 1989, but lost to Nottingham Forest.

In 1992, Luton waved goodbye to the top flight once more, and further relegations in 1996 and 2001 took them back to the lowest tier of the League. In typical fashion, the club bounced back, but a combination of financial problems and a managerial merry-go-round meant that the revival was short-lived, and three successive relegations saw this once-proud club begin life outside the League for the first time in almost 90 years at the start of the 2009-10 season.

Maidstone United

Another club whose origins lie in the demise of an earlier incarnation, the current Maidstone United started life as Maidstone Invicta in 1992, just days after the liquidation of the town's ill-fated Football League club.

The original Maidstone United had been around since 1897, playing as an amateur side until 1971 when they joined the semi-professional Southern League. Their stated ambition was to bring League football to the town within ten years, and early indications were that they might just be able to do so. But, having secured promotion to the top flight of the Southern League in only their second season, Maidstone United then had to wait another 16 years to realise their dream.

In the meantime, they became founder members of the Alliance Premier League in 1979, and in 1984, three years before the introduction of automatic promotion and relegation between the Alliance and the Football League, Maidstone became Alliance champions but failed to secure the votes required for entry to Division Four. Five years later they triumphed again, and automatic promotion made the dream reality.

Sadly, the reality fell far short of expectations. United recovered from a shaky start to reach the Division Four play-offs in their debut season, but lost in the semi-final to eventual winners Cambridge United. They started the 1990-91 season with high hopes, but a switch to a more direct style of football under new manager Graham Carr proved unpopular with fans, particularly when results started going against them, and support waned.

Dwindling gates were only part of the problem, though. United had spent huge sums of money in their efforts to attain League status, and a failed attempt to get planning permission for a new stadium on land the club had already bought merely added to the financial gloom. Players were sold in a desperate attempt to keep the club afloat, but by 1992 United had been forced into liquidation and, without any prospect of attracting a buyer, went out of business at the start of the 1992-93 campaign.

Maidstone Invicta were immediately formed from the core of United's youth side and assumed the former club's name two years later. They have since worked their way up from the lower reaches of the football Pyramid to the top flight of the Isthmian League, where the quest to return League football to Maidstone continues.

Mansfield Town

Mansfield's League career is notable more for events off the field of play than on it, with two major footballing scandals hitting the club in the space of just over ten years in the fifties and sixties.

For the first 30 years of their existence, Mansfield played their football in a selection of regional leagues including the Nottinghamshire & District, the Central Alliance, the Nottinghamshire & Derbyshire and the prestigious Midland Counties League, where they enjoyed considerable success. The quality of the Stags' football at this time can be measured by their FA Cup run in the 1928-29 season, during which they defeated Division Three side Barrow at Holker Street and disposed of Division Two's Wolves at Molyneux on the way to a 2-0 defeat by top-flight Arsenal at Highbury.

After several years of trying to secure election to Division Three (North) in the twenties, Mansfield were eventually able to achieve a Football League place by switching their attention to Division Three (South), a move which they correctly deduced would allow them to attract more votes from the directors of clubs in the north and thus afford them a better chance of success.

They took their place in the League at the expense of Newport County for the 1931-32 season although, ironically, they found themselves transferred to Division Three (North) after just one season. Their geographical location and the need to balance the regional divisions meant that Mansfield were switched between the Division Three (North) and Division Three (South) twice more before coming to rest in the northern section in 1948.

In the early fifties, the club was rocked by accusations of financial irregularities, the fallout from which saw several former Mansfield players and officials banned from the game. Once the dust had settled, the club continued its rather mundane existence in the lower reaches of the League until 1963, when promotion to Division Three finally gave long-suffering fans something to cheer about. Unfortunately, the celebrations were rather undermined by the revelation that several Mansfield players were among those under investigation for alleged involvement in match-fixing associated with a betting ring. The result was that a total of ten players, including three from Mansfield, were later imprisoned for their part in the scam.

On the field, things were rather less exciting, and the Stags found themselves back at the bottom in 1972, although a brief resurgence in the latter half of the decade saw them enjoy a single season in the second tier before a rapid return to the doldrums. Promotions and relegations followed, and 1987 saw them winning the Freight Rover Trophy, but the general trend was downwards, and in 2008, after 77 largely uneventful years as a League side, Mansfield slipped quietly into the Conference.

Merthyr Tydfil

A glance at the Football League tables from the twenties will reveal the name 'Merthyr T' – but this has nothing to do with the recent Southern League Premier Division side Merthyr Tydfil, who were formed in 1945 and went bust in 2010. The earlier club were Merthyr Town, who were members of the Football League for nine years from 1921 to 1930.

Merthyr Town were one of a number of Welsh sides that joined the Southern League, where they played from 1909 until the Football League was extended to three divisions by the simple expedient of absorbing the Southern League's top flight in 1920. Their time in the League was essentially a story of slow decline, the eighth place that they achieved in their debut season proving to be their best finish. A Welsh Cup final appearance in 1924 provided some light relief, and some seasons went slightly better than others, but the general trend was towards the bottom of the table where they arrived with a bump, after several near-misses, in 1930. Voted out in favour of the ill-fated Thames AFC, Merthyr Town survived a few seasons back in the Southern League before folding in 1934.

Nelson

Formed in 1881, the history of Nelson FC is punctuated by several periods of inactivity, although each of the club's reincarnations can legitimately claim to descend from the last. Their first taste of league football came in 1889, when they were among the founder members of the Lancashire League. They were champions in 1895-96 and runners-up two years later, but folded during the 1898-99 season and did not compete the season after that. They rejoined the Lancashire League for 1900-01, then moved to the Lancashire Combination for 1901-02, staying there until suspending operations in 1916.

After the First World War, Nelson FC were reactivated, briefly joining the Central League before helping to start the new Football League Division Three (North) in 1921. Their first few years in the League were eventful to say the least – they were promoted to Division Two at the end of their second season, relegated again in their third and almost bounced back at the first attempt, finishing runners-up in 1925.

Things went downhill from there, and by the end of the decade they were struggling to compete. After finishing in the lower reaches of the division in each of their last four seasons, they failed re-election in 1931 and slipped back down to the Lancashire Combination, making way for Chester.

By 1936, the club had gone out of business, but in 1946 they were revived and picked up where they had left off ten years earlier, taking up a place in the Lancashire Combination. There they stayed until 1983, becoming founder members of the North West Counties Football League, where they play their football to this day.

New Brighton

West Cheshire League side New Brighton share their name with an older club that existed between 1921 and 1983, but a name is all they have in common.

The earlier New Brighton club could trace their roots back to 1910 and the formation of South Liverpool FC, who ran into financial difficulties in 1921 and were declared bankrupt. As is so often the way, a new club rose from the ashes of the old, and New Brighton took over from South Liverpool in the Lancashire Combination until making a successful bid to join the newly expanded Football League Division Three (North) in 1923.

New Brighton spent their time as a League club entirely in the same division, finishing bottom of the table at the end of the 1950-51 season and being voted out in favour of Workington. Thereafter, they spent 30 years as a non-League side, eventually grinding to a halt in the face of overwhelming debt in 1983.

The club enjoyed rather more exciting times in the FA Cup, with three fourth-round appearances to their credit, including a particularly impressive run as a non-League side in 1956-57, during which they knocked out three League clubs on their way to a salutary 9-0 defeat at Burnley.

The name was revived in 1993, the new club starting life in the Birkenhead & Wirral League before switching to the South Wirral League in 1995, and progressing to the West Cheshire League the following year.

Newport County

The current club bearing the name Newport County has been in existence for only 20 years, having been founded as Newport FC in the wake of the winding-up of the earlier Newport County FC in 1989. However, because the hiatus was so brief, and because the new team were soon playing their football at Somerton Park, Newport County's home since 1932, the current club is universally regarded as a continuation of the earlier version.

Formed in 1912, and immediately accepted into the Southern League, Newport County were founder members of the Football League Third Division in 1920, and found themselves in the Third Division (South) when the League expanded further the following year. They played as a non-League side in 1931-32 after finishing bottom of the League and being voted out, but were back in 1932-33, elected to take the place made available by the demise of Thames AFC. There they remained until the outbreak of the Second World War, finishing as champions in the last peacetime campaign.

The 1946-47 season, the only one that Newport ever spent in the second tier, was something of a disaster. They finished bottom of the division, having lost 29 of their 42 games and shipped 133 goals in the process, setting a record for the heaviest ever Football League defeat in the process. Their 13-0 loss at Newcastle in October was summed up by the legendary Len Shackleton who famously quipped, 'They were lucky to get nil!'

The club spent the rest of their time as a Football League club in the lower divisions, although they rallied briefly under Len Ashurst in the early eighties. A Welsh Cup win in 1980 gave Newport County a place in the 1980-81 European Cup Winners' Cup, a young John Aldridge among the players who helped them to the quarter-finals of the competition. In 1982-83, they narrowly missed out on promotion to Division Two, but from there on it was downhill all the way.

By the end of the decade, County were in terminal decline, successive relegations in 1987 and 1988 leading to the loss of Football League status after almost 70 years. Worse was to come, and Newport County failed to finish their first season of non-League football, being officially wound up in February 1989.

Within a few months, Newport AFC had risen from the ashes, starting afresh in the Hellenic League. In 1999 the club was renamed Newport County AFC and now play in the Conference, working towards bringing League football back to Newport. At least they are no longer exiled from the town, being based at the Spytty Park sports arena.

Northwich Victoria

Like Gainsborough Trinity, Northwich Victoria are one of the country's oldest clubs, having been founded in 1874 and named, in a patriotic gesture typical of the times, in honour of the reigning monarch. In 1884, the club reached the quarter-finals of the FA Cup, only to find themselves on the wrong end of a 9-1 scoreline against Blackburn Olympic.

Founder members of the Football Combination in 1890, the Vics embarked on their ill-fated Football League career just two years later, when they became one of the clubs selected to make up the new Division Two. They fared reasonably well in their first season, finishing mid-table, but the switch to professional status proved to be a step too far for the Cheshire side and they were soon struggling to make ends meet. It was little surprise, then, that they found themselves propping up the table at the end of their second season, and resigned from the League.

Reverting to amateur status, Northwich Victoria went on to play in a number of local league competitions until joining the Cheshire County League after the First World War. There, they drifted along until 1968, winning the championship just once along the way, before becoming founder members of the Northern Premier League. Eleven years later, they were in at the start yet again, as one of the clubs making up the newly formed Alliance Premier League. When Northwich were relegated to Conference North in 2005, they were the last club to have been in the Conference National continuously since its formation.

Although not usually regarded as one of the FA Cup's traditional giant-killers, the Vics enjoyed a particularly impressive run in the competition in the 1976-77 season, during which they defeated three League clubs – Rochdale, Peterborough United and Watford – on the way to defeat at the hands of Oldham

Athletic in the fourth round. More recently, Northwich reached the third round in 2005-06, giving a good account of themselves in a 3-0 defeat at Sunderland.

Recent financial problems have led to two periods in administration and the sale of Drill Field, the club's home for more than 125 years. After ground sharing with fierce local rivals Witton Albion for a while, Northwich moved to a new stadium in 2006, but all has not gone smoothly since then and the future of the club still hangs in the balance.

Oxford United

Another Conference side with a good deal of League experience, Oxford United achieved a similar level of success to Luton Town, and, like the Hatters, had been in the top flight of English football just 20 years before losing their League status. With both teams recently in the Conference, it is curious to reflect that between 1985 and 1988 Oxford United v Luton Town was a top-flight fixture.

For almost 60 years after their formation in 1893, Headington United remained a small amateur club, but they turned professional in 1949 after their application to join the Southern League was successful. An ambitious club, Headington quickly became one of the best teams in the Southern League, and steadily improved the facilities at the Manor to create one of the best non-League grounds in the country.

In 1962, having changed their name to Oxford United two years earlier in a bid to raise their profile, the club were voted into the League after the collapse of Accrington Stanley created a vacancy. United adapted to life in the League very quickly, and by 1968 they had moved up to Division Two, then the second tier.

In the seventies, however, Oxford dropped back to Division Three and money increasingly became an issue, but, with the help of the controversial tycoon Robert Maxwell, the club survived. In 1984, they took the Division Three title and regained their position in Division Two, but in 1985 they went one better and achieved what had seemed unthinkable just 20 years earlier – promotion to the top flight. Even more remarkable was the fact that they achieved it with a second successive championship, the first club ever to do so, and took the Milk Cup back to the Manor for good measure.

The glory days were, sadly, over very quickly. Oxford United finished 18th in each of their first two seasons at the top level, but lost the fight in the third, and were relegated at the end of the 1987-88 season. A gradual decline in the club's fortunes followed, and by 2001 they had dropped back to the League's bottom drawer. As is so often the case when clubs are struggling, managers came and went, and money once more became an issue, and in 2006 Oxford's 44-year Football League adventure came to an end.

Rushden & Diamonds

Rushden & Diamonds may have existed for less than 20 years, but they have packed a great deal into their brief history. The club came into being in 1992 as a result of the merger of Irthlingborough Diamonds and Rushden Town and was the brainchild of Max Griggs, a local businessman whose involvement resulted from an approach by Diamonds when the cash-strapped club was looking for sponsorship.

Like most mergers, the idea was far from universally popular, but there is no doubt that the new club has been far more successful than either of its predecessors. Within four years, they had moved from the Southern League Division One to the Conference, where they lost no time in making sure that everyone knew they were serious contenders. In 2001, they finished as Conference champions, achieving Football League status just nine years after being launched.

Their first season in the League saw them maintain the momentum and finish in sixth position, securing a place in the play-offs. Having beaten Rochdale 4-3 on aggregate in the semi-final, Rushden & Diamonds found themselves playing fourth-placed Cheltenham Town at the Millennium Stadium in Cardiff, where a crowd of more than 24,000 saw the Gloucestershire side triumph 3-1. The following year, however, they left nothing to chance, finishing as champions to claim their place in Division Two for 2003-04.

Unfortunately, that was as good as it got and Rushden & Diamonds struggled to compete at the higher level. They made an immediate return to the fourth tier (in its first season as League Two), and narrowly avoided a second successive relegation in 2005, but couldn't do so a second time, dropping back to the Conference in 2006.

Southport

Another long-established club, Southport have a continuous history going back to 1881, although their origins lie in a rugby club of the same name that had existed for several years before that. In fact, Southport Football Club began the 1881-82 season as a rugby side, but a series of heavy defeats and the presence of several other rugby clubs in the area prompted a mid-season switch to the round-ball game.

Founder members of the Central League in 1911, Southport hold the distinction of being the first club to bear a sponsor's name when they played the 1918-19 season under the patronage of the Vulcan Motor Company and were renamed Southport Vulcan.

By 1921, when they joined the Football League as one of the founder members of Division Three (North), they were again known simply as Southport. Their League career was unspectacular to say the least, the club remaining in Division Three (North) until its discontinuation in 1958, whereupon they found themselves in the new Division Four. During this period their best finish was fourth, achieved in 1924-25 and 1938-39, although they were more often to be found in the lower half of the division and finished in the penultimate position on four occasions.

Fans had something to shout about in the 1930-31 season, however, when Southport became the first Division Three side to reach the sixth round of the FA Cup, although a 9-1 defeat at the hands of that year's Division Two champions Everton dampened celebrations somewhat.

There were other FA Cup runs of note, but lasting success in the League proved elusive. Southport won promotion to Division Three in 1967 and briefly looked capable of establishing themselves at the higher level, but by 1970 they were back in the basement. Three years later, they took the Division Four title, their only League championship, but suffered immediate relegation, a blow from which they never recovered. Having finished last but one in each of their last three League seasons, Southport failed re-election in 1978, and Wigan Athletic stepped into the breach.

Since then, Southport have played in a number of competitions, and briefly harboured hopes of a return to League football after achieving promotion to the Nationwide Conference in 2006. Sadly, the side struggled badly and suffered immediate relegation back to the Nationwide Conference North but bounced back in 2010.

Stalybridge Celtic

Formed around 1909 – although there is evidence to suggest they may have been active as early as 1906 – Stalybridge Celtic enjoyed one of the League's shortest memberships, having joined in 1921 as part of the new Division Three (North) and resigned after just two seasons. Prior to this, they had played in the Lancashire Combination and the Central League, and even spent a short time in the Southern League in an attempt to raise the club's profile.

Celtic acquitted themselves reasonably well in the League, finishing seventh in their first season, and mid-table in the second, and it is often assumed that their resignation was the result of financial difficulties, but in reality it was down to a feeling within the club that the crowds they were attracting wouldn't allow them to sustain their League status, and a return to the Cheshire League offered a better chance of a long-term future.

They stayed in the Cheshire League for 60 years, during which time they won the championship just once, in 1980. When the Cheshire League and the Lancashire Combination were amalgamated in 1982, Celtic became founder members of the resultant North West Counties League, winning the championship twice and thereby securing promotion to the Northern Premier League. Between then and now, they have led an up-and-down existence, dividing their time almost equally between the Northern Premier League and the Conference, and have been members of Conference North since its creation in 2004.

Workington

The original Workington Football Club was formed in 1884 and joined the new Cumberland Association League six years later. In the years that followed, the club played in a succession of local and regional league competitions, but they were unable to weather mounting financial problems and folded in 1910.

Reformed in 1921 as Workington AFC, the new club immediately joined the North Eastern League and settled down to a largely uneventful existence as a non-League side. The highlight of the pre-war years came in the 1933-34 FA Cup, when Workington enjoyed a lengthy run that ended in a 2-1 defeat in a fourth-round tie against Preston North End, then in Division Two but about to win promotion to the top flight.

Workington were elected to Football League Division Three (North) in 1951, replacing Merseysiders New Brighton. Initially, the Reds found life in the League difficult, but the arrival of one Bill Shankly as manager in 1954 gave them a much-needed boost, and during the mid-fifties they consistently inhabited the top half of the table. The improvement was short-lived, however, and after a poor showing in 1957-58 Workington were effectively relegated to the new Division Four.

There they stayed, apart from a brief spell in the third tier in the mid-sixties, the climax of which came in 1966 when they finished in fifth place and narrowly missed out on promotion to Division Two. As if exhausted by the endeavour, they finished bottom the following season, and so returned to Division Four.

Against this backdrop of under-achievement in the League, however, Workington fans were comforted by far greater success in the League Cup, their club twice reaching the quarter-finals during the decade. In 1963-64 it was West Ham who blocked Workington's progress into the semi-finals, and the following year it was Chelsea, held to a 2-2 draw at Borough Park, but 2-0 winners in the replay at Stamford Bridge. Workington must have fancied their chances against the Blues, having already seen off Norwich City of Division Two and top-flight Blackburn Rovers on the way to the quarter-finals. For almost 20 years, Workington also held the record for the biggest victory in the competition, their 9-1 demolition of Barrow in 1964 remaining unsurpassed until 1983.

Hampered by a lack of funds throughout their time in the League, Workington were struggling badly by the mid-seventies and had to apply for re-election in each of their last four seasons. In 1977, it was all over, and Workington were voted out. After surviving several subsequent lean spells, the Reds are currently plugging away in Conference North.

Wrexham

When Wrexham became one of the founder members of Football League Division Three

(North) in 1921, they brought with them almost 50 years of history. From their beginnings in 1872 as a team put together to allow local cricketers to maintain fitness during the winter months, they had quickly become one of the pre-eminent clubs in Wales, helping to form the Football Association of Wales in 1876, taking part in, and winning, the inaugural Welsh Cup in 1877-78, and campaigning to standardise the number of players in a team to the 11 so familiar today.

Before signing up to the Football Combination in 1890, they had played a mix of friendly games against both English and Welsh clubs and competitive games in both the Welsh Cup and FA Cup, enjoying considerable success in the former. Apart from a two-season spell in the League of Wales, Wrexham remained in the Football Combination until 1905 when they switched to the Birmingham & District League, their first match in the new competition being against Kidderminster Harriers.

Their League career started modestly, with only one top-10 finish in their first seven seasons, but three times in the late twenties and early thirties Wrexham were promotion contenders, their best effort coming in 1932-33 when they scored 106 goals in their 42 games and finished as runners-up to Hull City. They also made an impression in the FA Cup, reaching the fourth round in 1928 before losing to Division One side Birmingham City, and losing to Bradford City at the same stage of the competition two years later.

In 1957, Wrexham again reached the FA Cup fourth round, where they were rewarded with a glamour tie against Manchester United. The Busby Babes ran out 5-0 winners, but it was a day Wrexham fans wouldn't forget in a hurry.

Wrexham remained in Division Three (North) until the League was reorganised in 1958, when they were just well enough placed to start the following campaign in the new national Division Three. However, this was the start of a dismal period in the club's history, and after a few seasons yo-yoing between Division Three and Division Four, Wrexham finished the 1965-66 season propping up the entire Football League.

Things improved as the sixties came to an end, and in 1971 Wrexham regained their place in Division Three, holding off determined challenges from Swansea and Port Vale to secure promotion as runners-up to Chesterfield. Although their League form thereafter was inconsistent, the club enjoyed a spectacular FA Cup run in 1973-74 that came to an end in the quarter-finals where they lost to Division One side Burnley.

In 1976, they even made it as far as the quarter-finals of the European Cup Winners' Cup, but in all probability it is the 1977-78 season that will be remembered as the club's best. They managed another FA Cup quarter-final appearance, losing narrowly to eventual finalists Arsenal, reached the same stage of the League Cup and won both the Welsh Cup and the Division Three title to earn a place in the second tier for the first time in their history.

Sadly, it was a brief stay, and by 1983 back-to-back relegations had returned them to the League basement. For the final 25 years of their League career Wrexham divided their time fairly quietly between tier three and tier four, with the sensational dismissal of then League champions Arsenal from the FA Cup in 1992 the only real highlight of another lacklustre period in the club's history. In 2008, after a period of instability both on and off the field, Wrexham slipped into the Conference and so ended 87 years of League football at the Racecourse.

York City

In sharp contrast to Wrexham, Midlands League side York City had been in existence only seven years when they were elected to replace Ashington in Football League Division Three (North) in 1929. They made an immediate impression, finishing sixth in their debut season, but this early promise went unfulfilled, and this would be their best showing until finishing fourth at the end of the 1952-53 campaign. Occasional excitement was offered by the FA Cup, their most notable pre-war performances coming during the 1937-38 contest, during which they disposed of Division One sides West Bromwich Albion and Middlesbrough before bowing out in a replayed quarter-final against Huddersfield Town, then also a top-flight side.

Despite finishing in the bottom three in 1953-54, the Minstermen finished fourth again the following season, but surpassed themselves by reaching the FA Cup semi-finals, where they held eventual winners Newcastle United to a 1-1 draw at Hillsborough before losing 2-0 in the replay at Roker Park.

After the reorganisation that created Division Three and Division Four in 1958, York City found themselves in the new bottom tier, but their life in the League from here on would be in distinct contrast to anything that had gone before. They secured promotion to Division Three at the first attempt, but suffered an immediate reverse and spent the next five seasons back in the bottom drawer. Promotion in 1965 was again followed by an immediate return to the lower level, and for the next three seasons running City performed so poorly that they were forced to apply for re-election. In fact, the re-election ballot, which the club somehow survived each time, seemed to be about the only thing that went York's way during the closing years of the sixties.

During the seventies, however, things improved dramatically, and York even spent two seasons in the old Division Two (second tier) in 1974-76. It is strange now to think that Manchester United, Aston Villa, Sunderland, Bolton, Portsmouth and Hull City were among those that York City would have played in their first season in Division Two, while a relegated Chelsea and newly promoted Blackburn Rovers featured on the fixture list for the campaign that followed.

Successive relegations consigned York to the lower reaches of the League yet again in 1977, but seven years later they took Division Four by storm, winning the championship by a margin of 16 points, and winning 31 of their 46 games on the way to becoming the first League club to top 100 points in a season. More FA Cup giant-killing followed, with a 1-0 win over Arsenal in the fourth round of the 1984-85 competition setting up a fifth-round tie with Liverpool, the pre-eminent side of the eighties. Things went better than expected, with York holding the then League champions to a 1-1 draw in the first game, but Liverpool made no mistake in the replay, demolishing City 7-0.

As with so many of the former League sides now playing in the Conference, York's final years in the League were essentially a story of gradual decline, and although there were further promotions and relegations along the way, City finally lost their League status in 2004 after several mediocre seasons in the basement division. But 2010 saw them revive under Martin Foyle's managership and they reached the play-off final.

GIANT-KILLERS

Non-League clubs have claimed some significant scalps over the years. Here are just a few examples of David slaying Goliath.

Yeovil 2 Sunderland 1 (29 January 1949)

If ever there was a David and Goliath encounter, then Yeovil's FA Cup fourth-round tie against Sunderland in the 1948-49 season was it. Yeovil, then a Southern League side, were almost 100 places below Sunderland, whose recent habit of paying huge transfer fees to secure the likes of Len Shackleton and Welsh international Trevor Ford had earned them the nickname of the 'Bank of England club'. Sunderland would finish that season eighth in Division One, and when the fourth-round draw was made, no one expected anything other than a comfortable win.

Yeovil, led by player-manager Alec Stock, were in good form and bullish mood, having cruised into the third round after 4-0 wins at home to Romford and away at Weymouth in the previous rounds, then having beaten Division Two side Bury 3-1 in front of more than 13,000 at the Huish to earn a crack at Sunderland. But shortly before the game Yeovil's hopes of progressing to the fifth round were severely dented by the news that first-choice 'keeper Stanley Hall was unavailable because of injury.

Nevertheless, on the day, over 17,000 hopeful fans squeezed through the turnstiles at the Huish in anticipation of a classic FA Cup scrap. The home side started briskly, creating several early chances, and in the seventh minute they had a breakthrough when a header from Ray Wright dropped invitingly in Alec Stock's path and he drove the ball past Johnny Mapson in the Sunderland goal.

In the second half, Sunderland became much more of a handful, but Yeovil held on to their lead until the 62nd minute, when Dyke made an error and failed to catch a long ball into the box from Sunderland full-back Barney

Ramsden. Jackie Robinson pounced on the loose ball, tapping it over the line for one of the easiest goals of his career.

With the match level at 1-1 after 90 minutes, extra time was played, this being normal practice in the FA Cup in the immediate post-war period. As the first period came to an end, an uncharacteristic mistake by Len Shackleton put Yeovil striker Eric Bryant through on goal, and he slotted the ball home to give the non-League side the advantage. Sunderland were unable to equalise a second time, and Yeovil were assured of a place in FA Cup legend.

In the fifth round they found themselves up against Manchester United, but with Old Trafford still out of commission the tie was played at Maine Road. More than 80,000 turned up to see if Yeovil could cause another major upset, but United made no mistake, running out 8-0 winners.

Derby County 1 Boston United 6 (10 December 1955)

When Midland League side Boston United travelled to the Baseball Ground to take on Derby County in the FA Cup second round in December 1955, no one would have given them much chance of coming away with a victory, let alone pulling off one of the most incredible giant-killing feats in the history of the competition.

Derby had been a top-flight side just three years earlier, and even though they were now in the unfamiliar surroundings of Division Three (North) things were now going well for them and a quick return to Division Two looked likely.

Boston were on good form, rapidly building a reputation as a quality side in a competitive league that featured the reserve sides of several League clubs. They were a club with FA Cup pedigree, too, and had reached the first round proper in each of the preceding three seasons.

The match started very much as might have been expected, with the home side putting early pressure on their guests, but after 26 minutes the deadlock was broken when the Pilgrims took an unexpected lead through former Derby player Ray Wilkins. Ten minutes later, Geoff Hazledene, another of Boston's ex-Rams, doubled the visitors' advantage. Soon afterwards, County pulled one back when former England international Jesse Pye slotted the ball home from the penalty spot, but it was a short-lived revival, and by half-time Johnny Birbeck had put Boston two ahead again.

Reduced to ten men after an injury, Derby simply couldn't get back into a game that they had, in all honesty, lost before half-time. United had their tails up, and Hazledene completed his hat-trick before Wilkins netted a second to bring the final score to 6-1, still a record victory for a non-League side playing away against League opposition in the FA Cup. Boston went on to face Tottenham Hotspur in the third round and lost 4-0, but nothing could take the shine off the Lincolnshire side's incredible achievement four weeks earlier.

There's even a fascinating footnote to this story. In the 1973-74 season Derby County and Boston United were once again drawn to play each other in the FA Cup, this time in the third round. As before, the first tie was to be played at the Baseball Ground, and United produced a spirited performance to hold the League side to a 0-0 draw and take the tie back to York Street.

In the replay, any hopes of a repeat of the Pilgrims' famous victory were soon dispelled, but there's a curious symmetry in the fact that, on this occasion, Derby ran out 6-1 winners.

Worcester City 2 Liverpool 1 (15 January 1959)

Liverpool may not have been enjoying one of the most successful periods in their history when they faced Worcester City in the third round of the 1958-59 FA Cup competition, but they were still a force to be reckoned with, and this often-overlooked giant-killing act deserves far wider recognition.

Liverpool were a Division Two side at the time, having dropped out of the top flight at the end of the 1953-54 season. They would have to wait until 1962 before they made the return journey, but during eight seasons in the second tier they finished outside the top four only once, and their FA Cup record included one quarter-final and three fifth-round appearances. Worcester City, by contrast, were a workmanlike Southern League team, whose 5-2 victory over Division Four side Millwall in the previous round had come as something of a shock.

The tie suffered a postponement due to a frozen pitch, but even though the rearranged game took place on a bitterly cold and misty Thursday evening a crowd of 15,000 squeezed into St George's Lane to watch the Dragons take on the mighty Reds. It's doubtful that any of them seriously entertained the idea of a Worcester victory.

Liverpool were unhappy with the state of the pitch, which was still partly frozen, but were in for an even bigger shock just nine minutes into the game, when City centre-forward Harry Knowles whipped in a cross and a mix-up between Liverpool defender John Molyneux and Scottish international keeper Tommy Younger left City striker Tommy Skuse with a tap-in to put the home side one up.

The conditions were undoubtedly playing a part, and the remainder of the first half saw few clear goal-scoring opportunities for either side, but the Reds started the second half having shifted up a gear, and City had a fight on their hands. Liverpool's England international Alan A'Court was in fine form but City 'keeper Johnny Kirkwood had the game of his life and the Worcester defence stood firm in the face of sustained pressure from the increasingly frustrated visitors.

Liverpool's defence came to City's aid again in the 81st minute, gifting the home side an unexpected second goal. The ball bounced between Younger and Liverpool centre-half Dick White, whose bungled attempt to clear resulted in a delicate lob over the hapless 'keeper into the back of the net. Liverpool were then awarded a controversial penalty. With almost ten minutes left to play, Geoff Twentyman converted the spot kick to set Worcester nerves jangling.

In the end, it was too late to save Liverpool, and City were able to celebrate one of the all-time great FA Cup shocks. In the next round, the Dragons went to Bramall Lane to take on Division Two side Sheffield United under far better playing conditions and lost 2-0, but acquitted themselves well.

Nuneaton Borough 2 Swansea Town 0 (7 January 1967)

Nuneaton Borough were on song during the 1966-67 season, finishing as Southern League Premier Division runners-up and enjoying a lengthy run in the FA Cup. Boro' battled their way from the first qualifying round to the third round proper, playing a total of nine games before losing by the odd goal at Rotherham on the last day of January 1967.

Their FA Cup adventure began at Atherstone Town, where Boro' triumphed 6-1, and then switched to Manor Park, where Loughborough felt the full force of the Boro' attack, suffering an 8-2 reverse. Burton Albion proved a tougher nut to crack in the next round, but one goal was enough to see them through to the final qualifying round, where they took a replay to see off Macclesfield Town and reach the first round proper for the first time in 12 years.

Boro' booked a place in the second round draw with a 2-0 away victory over Amateur Cup holders Wealdstone, and were rewarded with a home tie against Division Three strugglers Swansea Town. The Swans had needed a replay to get past non-League Folkestone in the first round, although their emphatic 7-2 victory in the second game must have boosted their confidence a little.

On the day, though, Swansea proved to be no match for the Southern League side and lost 2-0, leaving Boro' to take on Division Two's Rotherham United in the third round. Boro' held the League side to a 1-1 draw, a disappointing result given the balance of play, especially in the second half, but the trip to Millmoor three days later marked the end of Nuneaton's FA Cup run. Despite again looking the more dangerous side and creating the better chances, Boro' lost to the only goal of the game.

Hereford United 2 Newcastle United 1 (5 February 1972)

Hereford United clearly hadn't read the script when they went up to St James' Park to do battle with Newcastle in the third round of the FA Cup in January 1972. The Southern League side, playing their football four divisions below the Magpies, had already played five FA Cup ties before travelling up to the North East. The match was postponed twice because of torrential rain, so by the time the two sides squared up to each other on 24 January, the remainder of the year's third-round ties had been decided.

Newcastle had spent only six seasons outside the top flight since the war, and although they tended to under-achieve in the League, they had three post-war FA Cup wins and six quarter-final appearances to their credit. Their star-studded side included half a dozen international players and future England striker Malcolm MacDonald.

Within 17 seconds of the kick-off, the Newcastle faithful were shaking their heads in disbelief and Hereford were, incredibly, in front. Awarded a free kick almost immediately after the kick-off, Hereford lobbed the ball into the Newcastle box. Brian Owen ghosted in behind the Newcastle defence and tucked the ball into the back of the net. The Magpies were quickly back on terms with a goal from MacDonald, and they took the lead minutes later when John Tudor added a second, but Hereford player-manager Colin Addison evened things up with a 25-yard shot to force a replay at Edgar Street.

Like the first game, the replay was delayed because of poor weather, and had been postponed three times before finally going ahead on 5 February, when it was played alongside the year's fourth-round ties. The exact number of people who witnessed the match will never be known – Edgar Street had an official capacity of just over 14,000, but the official figure of 16,100 is probably about right. *Match of the Day* cameras were on hand to record events for posterity, and an unknown 26-year-old called John Motson had been sent along to provide the commentary.

The pitch was heavy after all the recent rain, and the playing surface quickly deteriorated. The visitors made the early running, clearly intending to kill the game by scoring as soon as possible, but Hereford 'keeper Fred Potter was in defiant mood and repulsed several early Newcastle attacks. MacDonald made a nuisance of himself, missing a sitter after taking the ball round Potter, and then having a goal disallowed after John Tudor fouled the Hereford 'keeper. In a bizarre 30 seconds, the resultant free kick was taken and hit Tudor before rebounding towards the Hereford goal, where it hit the bar and came out to Newcastle's Terry Hibbitt. Hibbitt despatched a stinging shot that also hit the bar and came back into play, and only then did Hereford finally manage to clear their lines.

The longer the game went on, the worse the pitch became and the conditions inevitably began to take their toll. As the game entered its last 10 minutes, it seemed likely that the first goal to be scored would settle the tie. That first goal went to Newcastle in the 82nd minute, and Hereford looked doomed. Substitute striker Ricky George was sent on as Hereford gave it everything they had. In the 85th minute the ball bobbled on the uneven pitch and sat up perfectly for Ronnie Radford, who unleashed a 30-yard thunderbolt that buried itself in the top corner of the Newcastle net.

Radford's dramatic equaliser sent the match into extra time, where Ricky George's fresh legs proved decisive. At the end of the first half of extra time Radford fed the ball to Dudley Tyler who found George who turned and slotted the ball into the Newcastle goal. Hereford had completed one of the greatest FA Cup upsets of all time.

Just four days later, Hereford played their fourth-round match against West Ham United, again at Edgar Street. The local heroes held the nervous Londoners to a 0-0 draw, but their FA Cup run finally came to an end at Upton Park on 14 February when they lost 3-1.

Northwich Victoria 3 Watford 2 (8 January 1977)

The 1976-77 season was particularly memorable for Northwich Victoria, who were not only involved in a thrilling battle for the Northern Premier League championship that went right to the wire but also enjoyed their best run in the FA Cup for almost a century, reaching the fourth round for the first time since 1884.

Their first-round opponents were Division Four strugglers Rochdale, who proved to be a stern test. Having held the League side to a 1-1 draw at Spotland, the Vics must have been relieved to get a second chance at home, but the replay ended all square at 0-0, and the two sides reconvened a week later at Maine Road. This time, the Vics prevailed, winning 2-1 to set up a home game against Peterborough United, then enjoying a relatively successful spell in Division Three, in the second round.

With Peterborough 1-0 up early in the game, things didn't seem to be going too well for the Cheshire side when fate intervened and thick fog descended on the Victoria Stadium, causing the game to be abandoned midway through the first half. Three days later, it was a very different story, with the Vics running out 4-0 winners to book a place in the third round.

Their next opponents would be Watford, who were adjusting well to life in Division Four after suffering relegation 18 months previously. Although the Hornets would finish the 1976-77 season in seventh position, there were already signs of the dramatic improvement in form that would see them secure successive promotions in 1978 and 1979, and eventually carry them on to the top flight.

It turned out to be a classic example of FA Cup giant-killing, with a crowd of just over 9,000 at the Drill Field witnessing a gripping contest whose outcome was in the balance right up to the final whistle. Watford took a 2-1 lead in the first half, only to suffer a second-half onslaught from the Vics that culminated in a Frank Corrigan goal 10 minutes from time to give the non-Leaguers an historic victory. Corrigan enjoyed his 15 minutes of fame, and Northwich Victoria looked forward to the fourth round draw.

In the event, they got a home tie against Oldham Athletic. This was switched to Maine Road, where 29,000 saw the Vics' FA Cup run end in a 3-1 defeat.

Birmingham City 1 Altrincham 2 (14 January 1986)

Altrincham's famous victory over Birmingham City in the third round of the 1985-86 FA Cup remains the last time a non-League side turned over top-flight opposition away from home. On the way to St Andrews, Alty had already overcome League opposition, beating Division Three side Blackpool 2-1 at Bloomfield Road, but Birmingham were odds-on favourites to win this one, even if they were struggling in the League.

The first half was fairly quiet, neither side making many chances, but things became much more interesting after the break, with three goals in 15 minutes deciding the tie. Birmingham's Robert Hopkins was both hero and villain, putting the home side ahead with the game's first goal after 62 minutes, and providing Altrincham with their winning goal 13 minutes from time when he went in for a tackle and the ball ricocheted off his boot and flew into the Birmingham net past a helpless David Seaman. In between, a mistake in the Birmingham defence had let Ronnie Ellis in for Altrincham's equaliser.

Altrincham's opponents in the next round were York City, then in Division Three (third tier) and on a good run of form that had seen them pushing for a promotion spot. The Minstermen beat Altrincham 2-0, going on to lose to eventual Cup winners Liverpool.

Sutton United 2 Coventry City 1 (7 January 1989)

Twenty years on, Sutton United's unexpected win over Coventry City in the third round of the FA Cup is still the last time that a Conference side knocked out top-flight opposition. True, the men from Gander Green Lane were on a roll, having begun to make a name for themselves in the Conference after gaining promotion from the Isthmian League a couple of seasons earlier. What's more, the previous season's FA Cup run, during which they had disposed of League opposition in the form of Aldershot and Peterborough and made a nuisance of themselves against Middlesbrough before losing narrowly in a replay at Ayresome Park, had surely served notice that they weren't to be taken lightly. But no one could have expected what was to come on that blustery afternoon in January 1989.

Coventry were then sitting in sixth position in the League. Although they had been involved in a good few relegation dogfights, Coventry seemed to be a permanent fixture in the top flight after more than 20 consecutive seasons there, and they had pulled off an unexpected FA Cup victory of their own just two years earlier, beating hot favourites Tottenham Hotspur to lift the trophy in 1987. Seven of that FA Cup-winning side were among those who lined up against Sutton, but it was clear from the start that United were not about to roll over.

A goal from captain Tony Rains sent the home side in ahead at half time, but the Sky Blues drew level shortly after the break, and Sutton nerves were jangling. Matthew Hanlon settled them to some extent by putting the home side ahead again seven minutes later, and could have settled the tie had he not blasted the ball over the bar from 12 yards out a few minutes after that.

As the time ticked away, Coventry's efforts to retrieve the situation became ever more frantic. Cyrille Regis forced a spectacular save out of Sutton's keeper Trevor Roffey. Keith Houchen, scorer of Coventry's winning goal in the final against Tottenham, hit the bar, and Steve Sedgley's follow-up rebounded off the angle of post and bar. Towards the end of the game, a header from Brian Kilcline was scrambled off the line, but Sutton United held firm to pull off one of the biggest FA Cup shocks of all time.

Their luck ran out spectacularly in the fourth round when they travelled to Carrow Road and lost 8-0 to a Norwich City side who were then among the top five in the country. But Sutton fans will always be able to look back on the day that their boys made FA Cup history and sent the Sky Blues home with red faces.

Havant & Waterlooville 4 Swansea City 2 (16 January 2008)

Hampshire side Havant & Waterlooville hit the headlines in January 2008 with a shock third-round win over Swansea City, who were at that point riding high at the top of League One (third tier). Having battled their way through from the second qualifying round, the Hawks had already seen off Conference National side

York City in the first round proper, and stepped up a gear to defeat League Two's Notts County at Meadow Lane in the second round, where Tony Taggart stunned the Magpies by scoring the only goal of the game with just three minutes left on the clock.

Swansea, sitting 83 places above the Hawks, may have been enjoying the high life in the League, but their Cup form had been rather shaky. The Swans had reached the third round without facing League opposition, their ties in the two earlier rounds both being against Isthmian League sides, but they had been unconvincing in their 2-1 win against Billericay Town in the first round, and had needed a replay to overcome Horsham and secure their place in the third round draw, so the prospect of yet another non-League encounter must have set the alarm bells ringing in South Wales.

The draw had favoured City, and home advantage looked to have proved decisive as the minutes ticked away with the Welsh side leading 1-0. But just when they thought they had it in the bag, Rocky Baptiste popped up to score a late equaliser to take the tie back to Hampshire.

The replay took place 11 days later, by which time the fourth round draw had been made, and the two sides knew that the winner would be rewarded with a dream trip to Liverpool. It was a classic blood and guts FA Cup encounter that got off to an unexpected start when the home side were awarded a corner in the fourth minute. The ball was sent into the Swansea goalmouth, where an unfortunate Garry Monk managed to head the ball into his own net under pressure from Hawks striker Richard Pacquette.

Swansea twice came close to equalising in the minutes that followed, and began to put the non-Leaguers under pressure, but the Hawks held firm and snatched an unexpected second goal after 25 minutes when midfielder Jamie Collins drilled the ball home after Swansea failed to clear their lines from a corner. Thirteen minutes later Rocky Baptiste put the home side 3-0 up, getting on the end of a wayward shot from Pacquette, although the visitors replied almost immediately, Guillem Bauza's 20-yard shot taking the slightest of deflections on its way into the Havant & Waterlooville net.

Swansea spurned two more golden opportunities to get back into the game before half time, Leon Britton missing a penalty and Dennis Lawrence having to watch his downward header bounce high over the bar. At the beginning of the second half, Richard Pacquette missed the chance to put the Hawks 4-1 up when he hit his close-range shot directly at Swans keeper Dorus De Vries.

Two minutes later Swansea pulled another one back through Jason Scotland and the tide seemed to be turning in favour of the visitors. But the Hawks exploited Swansea's defensive frailty yet again in the 65th minute, when Tom Jordan, son of former Scottish international Joe, popped up at the far post to head the last goal of the game and secure that match of a lifetime at Anfield.

After the game, Jamie Collins revealed the inspiration behind the win: 'Our motivation was that Swansea kept calling us a pub side. We wanted to come out and prove that we don't just come and kick teams. We come out to try and play football, we try to play the right way, and I think in large spells of the game, we outplayed them.' And ten days later, the Hawks even managed to give the Reds a scare, twice taking the lead in a game that eventually ended in a 5-2 win for the Premiership side.

NEAR MISSES

For every successful giant-killer, there are perhaps half a dozen other non-League sides who give the big boys a serious scare before bowing to the inevitable. Here, we pay tribute to some of those who came close to causing a major upset, those who briefly grabbed the headlines and gave some of the biggest clubs in the land food for thought.

Manchester United 1 Walthamstow Avenue 1 (31 January 1953)

Manchester United have rarely fallen foul of the giant-killers over the years, but there have been several occasions on which they've come close. More than half a century before Exeter's shock draw at Old Trafford in 2005, the amateurs of Walthamstow Avenue came away from their fourth-round FA Cup tie at the 'Theatre of Dreams' with a 1-1 draw, an incredible achievement given that United were the reigning Football League champions.

Before the kick-off, no one was in any doubt that United would score a hatful, but with 10 minutes to go they were leading by the only goal of the game when Jimmy Lewis popped up and grabbed an equaliser. When the replay was held at Highbury five days later, Lewis went one better, netting both Walthamstow's goals, but Matt Busby's men made no mistake at the second time of asking, running out 5-2 winners.

Eleven months later, the plucky amateur side was at it again, travelling to East Anglia to take that year's Division Three (South) champions Ipswich Town to a replay in the second round. Like United, Ipswich lived to fight another day, but it's interesting to note that they clearly learned nothing from the experience since they were held to a draw by Bishop Auckland in a third-round tie the following season before losing the replay 3-0!

Walthamstow Avenue ceased to exist more than 20 years ago, absorbed in 1988 by Leytonstone/Ilford, with the resultant merger becoming known as Redbridge Forest. Forest themselves lasted just four years before being involved in another merger and becoming part of Dagenham & Redbridge.

Arsenal 2 Bedford Town 2 (7 January 1956)

Between the late fifties and the late sixties, Southern League side Bedford Town earned themselves something of a reputation as giant-killers. Perhaps their finest hour came in a tie they would ultimately lose, when they held the mighty Arsenal to a 2-2 draw at Highbury in the third round of the FA Cup in January 1956.

More than 55,000 people watched as the Gunners' attempts to win the tie were frustrated by a stubborn Bedford defence, but if they were concerned during that first encounter, they must have been seriously worried during the second, as the Eagles came within an ace of pulling off one of the biggest shocks of all time. The non-League side not only took an unexpected lead but they held on to it until just 4 minutes from time, eventually losing 2-1 in extra time having had two potential goals disallowed for offside.

The following November, Bedford dumped Division Three (South) strugglers Norwich City out of the Cup in round one and, in the years that followed, they claimed several more League scalps including Newcastle United, Exeter City, Brighton & Hove Albion and Oxford United.

Newcastle United 1 Hendon 1 (5 January 1974)

Newcastle United made it to the FA Cup final in 1974, but their journey to Wembley was far from smooth. In fact, they almost fell at the first hurdle, as Isthmian League champions Hendon threatened to emulate Hereford's achievement at the same stage of the competition two years before.

Like Hereford, Hendon had to travel to St James' Park for the tie, but whereas Hereford had got off to a flying start, Hendon found themselves under pressure from the word go. The Magpies started well, clearly mindful of the need to avoid further embarrassment. Malcolm MacDonald almost opened the scoring before

Pat Howard put the home side one up, but Hendon dug deep and managed to keep the score at 1-0 until the break.

In the second half, the balance of play gradually shifted, with Hendon's confidence growing minute by minute. Newcastle were unable to extend their lead, and the longer the game went on, the more likely it seemed that an upset might be on the cards. When Hendon captain Rod Haider grabbed an equaliser, Geordie nerves began to jangle.

At Watford's Vicarage Road stadium four days later Newcastle booked their place in the fourth round with a 4-0 win, but the non-Leaguers made their exit with heads held high.

Wrexham 1 Blyth Spartans 1 (18 February 1978)

Blyth Spartans have caused a few FA Cup upsets over the years, but their greatest achievement came in 1978 when they became one of the few non-League sides to make it into the fifth round. Their opponents were Wrexham, a club in good form who would finish the season as Division Three champions, but Blyth had already seen off a Stoke City side that were then enjoying a good run in Division Two and must have thought they were in with a shout.

Sadly, it wasn't to be, and Blyth's FA Cup run was effectively killed off by a controversial decision right at the end of the game. With a minute left on the clock, Blyth were leading 1-0 when Wrexham were awarded a corner. The ball was lofted into the area and caught by the Blyth 'keeper, who prepared to launch it upfield. The referee, however, decided that the corner had to be retaken because the flag had not been in place first time round.

Wrexham equalised from the retake and forced a replay, which took place nine days later in front of 42,000 fans at St James' Park. This time, the Dragons took a two-goal lead and, although the non-Leaguers made a fight of it and pulled one back, the plum sixth-round tie against Arsenal was theirs.

Barnsley 1 Enfield 1 (24 January 1981)

Isthmian League champions Enfield made headlines back in 1981 with an FA Cup run that extended into the fourth round and a trip to Oakwell to face Division Three high-fliers Barnsley. The Yorkshiremen were on their way to a runners-up slot and promotion to Division Two, and went into the tie unbeaten in 16 games. Enfield had already disposed of League opposition – former giant-killers Hereford United in the second round, and Division Four strugglers Port Vale in the third round – so a classic FA Cup tie was in prospect.

More than 24,000 fans packed Oakwell, and they weren't disappointed. Enfield battled away and had two goals disallowed before Trevor Aylott gave the home side the lead on the stroke of half-time. As the second half wore on, the non-Leaguers redoubled their efforts and Peter Burton snatched a headed goal to equalise and take the tie back to London.

The replay took place at White Hart Lane, but there was no fairy-tale ending for the Isthmian League hopefuls. Enfield threw everything they had at a stubborn Barnsley defence from the outset, but were denied by the woodwork and some inspired 'keeping. A goal from Aylott meant the Yorkshiremen went in ahead at half-time, and despite coming close in the second half, Enfield were unable to reply. Ronnie Glavin added a second and Aylott a third to put the tie beyond doubt.

Manchester United 0 Exeter City 0 (8 January 2005)

Alex Inglethorpe had been in the Exeter job for less than a month when his team outplayed Doncaster Rovers in the second round (thanks to a 45-yard strike from Dean Moxey) to set up a dream tie at Old Trafford.

The other Alex – Sir Alex Ferguson – figured his reserves and youth players should have enough in them to beat the non-League side and duly sent out a team with David Bellion leading the line and Phil Neville captaining the side. But City's players put on the performance of their lives, with rookie keeper Paul Jones playing a blinder, while Moxey could have won the game at the death but blasted wide.

The replay at Exeter's St James' Park saw the likes of Ronaldo and Rooney take to the field, but even then Exeter put up a battling display before eventually going down 2-0.

Burton Albion 0 Manchester United 0 (8 January 2006)

You'd have thought Fergie would have learned from Manchester United's humbling at the hands of Exeter the year before. Although his side was stronger than the year before – Silvestre, Saha and Solskjaer were in the line-up – United struggled on a heavy pitch and Burton had the best of the first half.

The non-League side matched United in the second half as well and were unlucky not to get a penalty when future World Cup winner Gerard Pique handled in the box, but the Brewers were more than happy with a goalless draw.

Manager Nigel Clough was already looking forward to the replay at Old Trafford. 'I don't know how much this will mean to the club in financial terms but if you had seen the look on my players' faces at the end, you would realise it will mean an awful lot more for them just to get the chance to play at Old Trafford,' he said.

Ferguson preferred to focus on the romantic element of the result rather than his own disappointment. 'We didn't want a replay and I didn't expect one. If we had taken our chances we wouldn't have had to play one but the money will give Burton a lifeline, just as it did for Exeter last year,' said the United boss. 'They worked their socks off and there is nothing wrong with the result as far as football is concerned.'

Although Burton lost the replay 5-0, the cash from both games enabled Clough to build the side that ran away with the Conference the following season.

N THE SHADOW OF GIANTS

Non-League clubs struggling to make a go of things in the shadow of bigger neighbours

In the north, football clubs have often been the latecomers, competing for support with the long-established Rugby League clubs. Horwich RMI decided in 1995 that if you couldn't beat them you could join them. They relocated to Hilton Park, home of Rugby League club Leigh Centurions. Once agreement had been reached to share the 10,000-capacity stadium, Horwich officially changed their name to Leigh RMI to reflect their new surroundings. Hilton Park is nicknamed the Coliseum for rugby fixtures in view of the 'Centurions' nickname of the Rugby League team.

Five years after this move, Leigh RMI reached the Conference, the highest level of non-League football. With Leigh traditionally being a Rugby League town, the football club averaged attendances of less than 200. Relegated to the Northern Premier League, the club rebranded itself Leigh Genesis in 2009 as it relocated to a new 12,700-capacity purpose-built stadium at Leigh Sports Village, a sporting development project sponsored by Wigan Council for the town of Leigh, at which they would continue to ground share with Centurion. This arrangement proved unworkable, however, and they played many home games in 2009-10 elsewhere.

Havant & Waterlooville have already made friends with their big-city neighbours Portsmouth to the extent that Pompey stage their reserve matches at West Leigh Park to save wear on the Fratton Park pitch. In 2009 they also made season tickets available to Portsmouth FC 'Pompey Blue' members for £40 to encourage them to visit not only when their reserves were playing but also when the first team play away – only for Havant & Waterlooville fans to complain that they were losing out. Some decided to get their season tickets that way and enjoy a three-figure saving!

Eastleigh enjoy a close relationship with

nearby Southampton. Matthew Le Tissier turned out for the Spitfires, then in the Wessex League, in 2002 after his retirement, while former Saint Jason Dodd managed the semi-pro team for a short period. Other Saints to have turned out in white include Francis Benali, Nicky Banger and David Hughes.

Le Tissier admitted: 'I've really enjoyed my time with Eastleigh. It's much more relaxed than the professional game and I've taken a light-hearted approach to it. If I'd taken it too seriously I would have ended up being sent off by now with some of the refereeing!'

Oxford United and Oxford City have enjoyed contrasting fortunes in the non-League game. United began life as Headington United, reaching the League in 1962 and hitting the top flight in 1986. They also won the League Cup that year and enjoyed 44 years as a League club, but were relegated from the lowest League division in 2006. Four years later they found their way back via the play-offs.

City, by contrast, have never risen higher than the Southern League Premier Division, which they reached in 2008, but were the county's premier club when formed in 1882. In the eighties Bobby Moore was appointed manager with his former West Ham United team-mate Harry Redknapp as assistant – a little-known first step to the Tottenham dug-out. City are arguably no longer in the shadow of giants even if their modest Court Place Farm ground lacks the creature comforts of the Kassam Stadium.

Liverpool have made seven friendly appearances in six seasons at the Racecourse ground. Wrexham's now-traditional July meeting with the Reds – whose reserves played their home games at Wrexham's ground until moving to Tranmere in 2009 – has provided a much-needed source of funds for the club,

particularly during their 18-month period of administration.

Dragons boss Brian Carey highlighted the special relationship enjoyed between the two clubs: 'Liverpool are the one club who have really helped us out, particularly when we were in administration. Smaller clubs are often very much at the mercy of the bigger clubs and we are just thrilled to bits that they are helping us out and we can't thank them enough for coming again. We have a relationship with Liverpool which we are really proud of.'

The connection between Wrexham and Liverpool chief executive Rick Parry – both of his sons are involved in the Dragons' youth set-up – has often been credited with helping to forge the friendship.

THE ENGLAND C INTERNATIONAL TEAM

The England C National Football Team represents England at non-League level. Formed in 1979, and previously known as the England National Game XI and the England Semi-Pro national team, it features players who play for clubs outside the Football League. Many players who have been capped have gone on to play at a higher level.

Home matches are played at various League and non-League grounds around the country. Friendly matches are played with equivalent teams from other nations, and compete in the Four Nations Tournament each season, along with Scotland, Wales and the full Gibraltar teams. They won the tournament for the seventh time in May 2008, winning all three of their matches without conceding a goal. The team have been managed by Paul Fairclough since January 2003 and at the time of writing are also the current holders of the European Challenge Trophy.

Managers

Paul Fairclough (2003-)
Steve Avory (2002-2003)
John Owens (1997-2002)
Keith Wright (1980-1985)
Howard Wilkinson (1979-1980)

Notable former players

Junior Agogo
Marcus Bignot
Andy Bishop
George Boyd
Mark Carter
Andy Clarke
Danny Collins
Paul Furlong
Jerry Gill
Steve Guppy
Karl Hawley
Barry Hayles
Andy Hessenthaler
Terry Hibbitt
David Howell
Lee Hughes
Steve Jones
Scott Kerr
Michael Kightly
Craig Mackail-Smith
Aaron McLean
Steve Morison
Trevor Peake
Gary Roberts
Alan Smith
Mark Stimson

EXILES
Border disputes and crossover clubs

England v Wales

The history of Welsh football was, for many years, shaped as much by the country's landscape as it was by the people who played and followed it. The difficulty of travelling from one part of the country to another, especially in a north-south direction, led to the formation of numerous local league competitions, and these were the mainstay of the game in the Principality for almost a century.

From the earliest days, though, many of the top Welsh sides looked to English clubs to provide them with stiffer competition, and it wasn't long before some abandoned the localised Welsh game altogether. Wrexham spent their early years playing in local cup competitions and taking on both English and Welsh sides in friendly matches, but in 1890 they joined the Combination, an early league competition primarily composed of clubs from Wales and the North West of England.

It should be noted that the Combination, which ran from 1890 until 1911, has no connection with the current Football Combination, which started life in 1915 as the London Combination. It was, however, an important early competition that provided an escape route for several ambitious Welsh sides during its lifetime.

Apart from a couple of seasons spent in the Welsh League between 1894 and 1896, Wrexham have always played their football in English leagues, returning to the Combination until 1905, moving to the Birmingham & District League from then until 1921, and then appearing in various divisions of the Football League itself until dropping down to the Conference in 2008.

In the years leading up to the First World War, a number of Welsh clubs followed Wrexham's lead and signed up to English league competitions, most of them joining the Southern League. The most familiar amongst them were Cardiff City, Newport County and Swansea Town, but there were several others, including Barry Town, Ebbw Vale, Merthyr Town and Mid Rhondda.

When the Southern League's First Division was effectively taken over and renamed by the Football League in 1920, Merthyr Town, Newport County and Swansea Town were amongst those who suddenly became Football League Division Three clubs, while Cardiff's pre-eminence amongst the Welsh sides was recognised when they were awarded a place in Division Two. Further expansion the following year saw Aberdare Athletic and Wrexham join their compatriots in the Football League.

There have been no further Welsh additions to the Football League, but several other notable Welsh clubs have spent at least some of their existence in the English game.

Bangor City

Bangor City played in local leagues for several years before joining the Combination in 1898. After the Combination disbanded in 1911, Bangor went back home to the North Wales Alliance, but the rather chaotic state of football in North Wales at the end of the twenties prompted their return to England. In the thirties, forties and fifties they played in the Lancashire Combination, the Cheshire League and Northern Premier League, becoming founder members of the Alliance Premier League in 1979.

Rhyl

Like Bangor City, Rhyl played in local leagues before joining the Combination in 1898, and returning to Wales in 1911. After spells in the North Wales Coast League and the North Wales Alliance, Rhyl became founder members of the Welsh National League in 1921, but they, too, found themselves looking to the east once again as the thirties began. Moving first to the Birmingham and District League, and later, when the distances involved began to make life difficult, to the Cheshire League, Rhyl remained in English football for the next 56 years, spending several seasons in the North West Counties League and the Northern Premier League before returning to Wales in 1992.

Barry Town

Barry Town also spent a long period playing in English football, joining the Southern League shortly after their formation as Barry FC in 1912 and staying there for the next 70 years. In 1982, they resigned from the Southern League and joined the Welsh League, which they dominated for the remainder of the decade, winning the championship on five consecutive occasions from 1983 to 1987, and again in 1989. The lack of competition led them to return to the Southern League for the 1989-90 season, although they headed back to Wales in 1993.

Caernafon Town

Caernarfon Town played with distinction in the Welsh League (North) between their formation in 1937 and 1980, when they sought, and were granted, permission from the Football Association of Wales to apply for membership of the Lancashire Combination. Two years later they became members of the new North West Counties League, gaining promotion to the Northern Premier League in 1985. Ten years later they, too, returned home to join the League of Wales.

Merthyr Tydfil, Colwyn Bay and Newtown

Merthyr Tydfil spent a single season in the Welsh League in 1945-46, winning the championship and making an immediate move to the Southern League, where they stayed until enjoying a six-year spell as a Conference side from 1989. They were relegated back to the Southern League in 1995 but resigned in 2010 for financial reasons, reforming as Merthyr Town.

Colwyn Bay, meanwhile, spent a short period in the Birmingham & District League during the thirties, but otherwise played all their football in Welsh leagues from their formation in 1901 until they joined the North West Counties League in 1984. In 1991 they were promoted to the Northern Premier League, where they remain to this day.

Of all the Welsh clubs to have played in the English league system, Newtown stayed the least time across the border, spending just four seasons in the Northern Premier League from 1988-89 after a series of championship wins in the Mid-Wales League between 1975-76 and 1987-88.

The League of Wales

For many years, the idea of Welsh clubs plying their trade in the English league system was simply accepted, but it became a very big issue in the early nineties, when the League of Wales was formed.

The formation of the new league was prompted by a number of developments in the international game. Alun Evans, Secretary of the Football Association of Wales, was convinced that the Welsh international football team was under threat from FIFA. His reasoning centred on the belief that the presence of Wales, Scotland, Northern Ireland and England as separate countries that each had a permanent seat on the International Football Association Board was resented by many FIFA members, and that Wales was particularly vulnerable since it didn't have a national league of its own.

Evans' argument was given weight by the fact that the idea of the four home nations' national sides being replaced by a combined UK side had also been raised by some FIFA members. In addition, the introduction of a new Welsh national league was in line with UEFA's growing insistence that clubs should not play in a 'foreign' league.

The formation of the League of Wales prompted one of the most acrimonious disputes in the world of football in recent years. The FAW clearly needed to make the new league as strong as possible, but the three pre-eminent Welsh sides – Cardiff City, Swansea City and Wrexham – were members of the Football League, and there was no prospect of persuading them to join up. However, there was a chance of getting those Welsh sides playing non-League football across the border to switch.

But eight clubs – Bangor City, Barry Town, Caernarfon Town, Colwyn Bay, Merthyr Tydfil, Newport County, Newtown and Rhyl – soon known as the 'Irate Eight', initially wanted to remain in the English game. Three of them – Bangor, Newtown and Rhyl – elected to return to Wales prior to the new league starting, while the remainder were forced by new FAW regulations to play their home games in England. Barry Town spent a season in exile at Worcester City, before deciding that they, too, would return to their homeland, leaving four clubs to fight on. In 1995, the remaining four won a court ruling that allowed them to remain within the English Pyramid and play their home games in Wales. Surprisingly, despite this victory, Caernarfon Town had a change of heart and joined the League of Wales for the 1995-96 campaign.

UEFA still regards the presence of the six Welsh clubs in the English system as an anomaly. However, it's an anomaly that seems to be tolerated in view of the fact that none of them are allowed to enter the Welsh Cup, and therefore no longer benefit from an easy route into Europe. Since 1995, those English clubs situated close to the Welsh border who had traditionally been allowed to enter the Welsh Cup have also been barred from the competition, following a UEFA ruling that the League of Wales should provide the route into European football.

One club has recently moved in the opposite direction, playing their football in the Welsh Pyramid but having a home ground situated in England. The New Saints of Oswestry Town & Llansantffraid Football Club (TNS) moved to a new purpose-built stadium in Oswestry in 2007, leaving behind their home ground of 14 years, Treflan, in Llansantffraid, the village where the club had started life almost 50 years earlier.

Llansantffraid FC played in the lower reaches of Welsh football for almost 30 years without making much impression, but the late eighties saw a dramatic upturn in their fortunes, and three promotions in four years brought them to the then new League of Wales. There, they confounded predictions and made themselves at home, adding a Welsh Cup victory in 1996 to their list of achievements.

In 1997, Oswestry-based company Total Network Solutions offered the Welsh club a sponsorship deal, a condition of which was that the club changed its name to that of the company. Over the next few years, TNS went from strength to strength, winning the Welsh Premier League title several times and playing in Europe, and in 2004 they entered into a merger with nearby Oswestry Town, an English club that played its football in the Welsh system. The merged club was still known as TNS until 2006, when Total Network Solutions was taken over by British Telecom, but by the time they moved to Oswestry's Park Hall ground in 2007 they had become known as The New Saints of Oswestry Town & Llansantffraid Football Club, retaining the TNS initials whilst reflecting the club's heritage.

The new order in Wales has had some interesting knock-on effects. AFC Wimbledon found themselves on the wrong end of an 18-point deduction (reduced to three on appeal) in 2007 after they signed and played Jermaine Darlington without obtaining international clearance. Darlington, the first man to play for both Wimbledon and AFC Wimbledon, had retired from football after a spell with Cardiff City but was persuaded to return to the non-League game. He had never played outside the English FA-governed system, but AFC Wimbledon officials did not realise that Cardiff's location across the border demanded clearance for the player.

Even the now-defunct Chester City, representing an English town, and playing their football in the English Pyramid, had to be careful when their Deva Stadium was built. The complex straddled the England-Wales border, and to ensure that there would be no question about their being able to continue in the English league, the club's offices were built on the English side.

England v Scotland

Berwick Rangers, founded in 1884, are technically in England but play in the Scottish League. The town of Berwick-upon-Tweed is near to the Scottish border and is closer to Edinburgh than to

Newcastle-upon-Tyne. The old town is on the Scottish side of the traditional border, the River Tweed, and Berwick was formerly part of Scotland. The time (and expense) involved in travelling to away matches against English opposition would be greater than it is to travel to matches in Scotland. The club also formerly played in the East of Scotland League, which contains other nearby Borders teams, prior to joining the Scottish League in 1955.

They were the only English team to do so until Gretna, the town on the borders of England and Scotland famed for its wedding industry. Formed in 1946, Gretna played in the English football Pyramid from 1947 until being co-opted into the Scottish League in 2002. Their rise was meteoric, funded by Sunderland-born millionaire Brooks Mileson, and they achieved top-flight football after three consecutive promotions. Unfortunately the club struggled in the Scottish Premier League and were placed in administration in March 2008 after Mileson withdrew his support due to illness. At the end of the season, all of the club's staff were made redundant and Gretna, unable to undertake to fulfil their forthcoming fixtures, were compulsorily relegated to Scottish League Division Three.

This demotion prompted the immediate withdrawal of the only remaining offer to buy the club, and Gretna resigned their place in the Scottish Football League on 3 June. The supporters' trust formed a new club, Gretna 2008, which was accepted into the East of Scotland Football League in July 2008.

The prospect of Rangers and Celtic one day playing in the English Premiership has long been a topic of debate. It would certainly add spice to the English game having the two Scottish giants in regular competition south of the border, but would greatly devalue the Scottish Premier League.

WORKS TEAMS

Many clubs started life as teams of workmates: footballers who worked and played together

Airbus UK

When promoted to the League of Wales for the first time in 2004, Airbus UK FC followed in the footsteps of TNS in becoming Britain's second team to bear the name of their sponsor. Based in Broughton, North Wales, they are the works team of the Airbus aerospace factory, where the wings of the European Airbus airliner are produced, and are consequently nicknamed the Wingmakers or the Planemakers.

The club shared Conwy United FC's ground before their own, the Airfield, had its pitch brought up to League of Wales standards. The Airfield is adjacent to an operational runway, and so has unusual retracting floodlights. Formed in 1946 as Vickers-Armstrong, the club has borne the names of several factory owners including de Havilland, Hawker Siddeley, British Aerospace and BAE Systems.

Braintree Town

The club was formed in 1898 as Manor Works FC, the works team of the Crittall Window Company. They joined the North Essex League almost immediately, changing their name to Crittall Athletic in 1921 and becoming founder members of the Eastern Counties League in 1935. After winning the championship in 1936-37, they joined the Essex County League, where they finished runners-up in their debut season, but for 1938-39 they were back in the ECL. The club severed its links with Crittall in 1981, becoming Braintree Town FC.

Cammell Laird

Cammell Laird started life as the works team for the famous Merseyside shipyard of that name. The yard is sadly now gone but Lairds carried on to celebrate their centenary in 2007. They currently play in the UniBond League Division One South.

Cammell Laird have a reputation for a welcoming atmosphere at Kirklands, but face fierce competition for crowds from such neighbouring clubs as Tranmere Rovers, Liverpool and Everton. Cammell Laird usually have the lowest average gates in their division. There have been suggestions that they should change their name to Birkenhead Town in order to create an identity with the town, but die-hards feel it would be sad to lose the link to the history of the club.

Edinburgh City

There has been more than one Edinburgh City FC. The current club that plays at Meadowbank Athletics Stadium was originally Postal United – so named because most of the players worked for the Royal Mail – and adopted the historic name in 1986. It is said that they traced the one director of the original club still alive and 'paid' a bottle of whisky for the rights to the name!

Ferranti Thistle

Scottish football club Ferranti Thistle was formed in 1943 as the works side of the Ferranti engineering firm, playing in the East of Scotland League. On their election to the Scottish Football League in 1973, the club moved to the Meadowbank Stadium in Edinburgh and renamed themselves Meadowbank Thistle, but moved again at the start of the 1995-96 season, this time to the New Town of Livingston.

In the 1986-87 season, Meadowbank Thistle won the Scottish League Division Two championship and were promoted to Division One. They finished runners-up the following season, but were denied promotion to the

Scottish Premier Division due to a reduction in the size of the division.

Thereafter, their fortunes declined steadily and in 1992 they suffered relegation to Division Two. When the Scottish Football League was reorganised in 1994 to create four divisions of ten clubs each to replace the earlier configuration of two divisions of 12 clubs and one of 14, Meadowbank Thistle remained in Division Two (the third tier), but in 1995 they were relegated again. In the wake of the relegation, and in the face of considerable opposition from fans, the club were relocated to the town of Livingston, under which name they started the 1995-96 season in Division Three.

The club bounced back and, after finishing champions of Division One in 2000-01, gained promotion to the Scottish Premier League after just six seasons in existence. Livingston's first SPL campaign, 2001-02, brought more success as they finished third and qualified for the UEFA Cup. They gained their first national trophy in 2004, the Scottish League Cup, a 2-0 win secured over Hibernian at Hampden Park, but financial administration and relegation followed two years later.

Ford United

The works team of the car giant's Dagenham, Essex, plant was the stepping stone for at least one professional footballer in Fulham and Gillingham 'keeper Jim Stannard. When he came back to manage the club in the early 2000s, they had changed their identity to Redbridge despite objections from Dagenham & Redbridge. They are currently in the Ryman League Division One North.

Leigh RMI

Leigh Railway Mechanics Institute Football club, usually known as Leigh RMI, are based in Leigh, Greater Manchester. The club was founded in 1896 and was known as Horwich RMI FC until 1995, when they relocated from Horwich to Hilton Park, home of Rugby League club Leigh Centurions. Leigh's finest hour was an FA Cup draw with Fulham in 1998, when the London club was being managed by Kevin Keegan. The club rebranded themselves Leigh Genesis in 2009.

Metropolitan Police FC

The club was formed in 1919, 90 years after the creation of the law enforcement body from which it took its name. The Blues, as they were inevitably dubbed, joined the Spartan League in 1928, and they remained in that competition until 1960. They currently play in the Ryman League Division One.

In 1984, when in the Isthmian League, the Met reached the first round proper of the FA Cup and were drawn at home to Dartford, a tie that was subsequently featured on BBC Television's *Match of the Day* programme. Their home ground at Imber Court, East Molesey in Surrey, is about one and a half miles from the historic Hampton Court Palace and was

acquired by the force for use as a sports ground in 1919.

The rules of eligibility, which can be changed at the club's AGM, and do get altered from time to time, state that 75 per cent of the playing staff must be employees of the Metropolitan Police (not necessarily police officers). This is a condition of the club's use of the Imber Court facilities. The football club don't deny that they would like more freedom to sign non-police players, but it just isn't allowed.

The other 25 per cent are required to be 'persons of good character'. Having a relative in the police is no longer essential, although it still helps. However, if the football management attempted to sign a player with more than the most petty of criminal records, the committee wouldn't allow it. Furthermore, any police officer sent off while playing for Met Police runs the risk of disciplinary proceedings at work.

Sunderland Nissan

Works team Sunderland Nissan, who competed in the Northern League until 2009, were the unfortunate victims of the credit crunch when the Japanese car makers pulled the plug on funding, leaving manager Wilf Constantine and his players jobless.

He said: 'I was looking for two or three more players, and I felt that I would have had a good squad to challenge for the league next season. And then suddenly came the bombshell that the club was resigning from the league. I just wasn't expecting it, and I don't think many other people were as well. I had no idea, no indication, no hint. But I can understand why the company did it, because people are losing their jobs at Nissan.'

To make matters worse, the players were unable to find other teams until the club paid the £1,000 fine for resigning after the league's deadline.

Vauxhall Motors FC

Vauxhall Motors FC was founded in 1963 in Ellesmere Port, Cheshire, in the wake of the opening of a new car plant. By 1970 the club had achieved several promotions and played on a company-owned ground at Hooton Park, but for the past 20 years they have played at Rivacre Park, opened in 1987 by then England manager Bobby Robson. The Motormen have enjoyed considerable FA Cup success in the past few years, even defeating Queens Park Rangers in a penalty shoot-out in a first-round replay at Loftus Road in 2002.

FAMOUS FOOTBALLERS WHO STARTED IN NON-LEAGUE

Jermaine Beckford

Current Everton striker Beckford is typical of many non-League players in having been rejected by the professional game at an early age only to come back stronger. He began at Chelsea, where he was part of the youth set-up until released in 2003. He later played for Isthmian Premier League side Wealdstone, where he scored 35 goals in 40 games, and over thirty clubs showed an interest in the prolific striker. He had a trial with Championship side Crystal Palace and in 2006 appeared in a reserve fixture against Arsenal. But it was Leeds who came in for Beckford and he joined them for £45,000, making up an ex-non-League strikeforce with ex-Barnet man Trésor Kandol.

DJ Campbell

Mercurial striker Dudley (DJ) Campbell was a beneficiary of Yeading's 2004-05 FA Cup run, their draw against Newcastle putting him in the shop window. He secured a transfer to local League neighbours Brentford, and then went on to a brief top-flight stay with Birmingham before moving on to Leicester for £1.6 million and (on loan) Blackpool. Campbell has played for the England National Game XI, now known as England C.

Stan Collymore

After starting his career as an apprentice footballer with Walsall, and Wolverhampton Wanderers, Collymore was released to sign for then Conference team Stafford Rangers in 1990-91. His knack for scoring, notching eight goals, many spectacular, in his first season, won him a professional contract with Crystal Palace at the age of 19. Southend United, Nottingham Forest and Liverpool followed, then Villa, Leicester and Bradford, but he never fulfilled the potential that had been apparent early on. He is currently a media pundit.

Alan Devonshire

Midfielder Devonshire made his name playing for West Ham United (1976-1990) and England (eight caps between 1980 and 1983). After finishing his career at Watford he went into non-League management with Maidenhead United and, from 2003, Hampton & Richmond. In his first season he guided them to fifth place in the Ryman Division One South, which, due to reorganisation of the leagues, was enough to see the club promoted to the Ryman Premier Division. He has since taken them to the Conference South, guiding his team to third place in the league and into the play-offs for the Conference National.

Kerry Dixon

Starting life with Chesham and Dunstable Town, Dixon transferred to Reading for £20,000 in 1980. Three years later Chelsea bought him for £150,000. He appeared for England in the 1986 World Cup (eight caps, four goals). With 193 goals in total to his name, Dixon is Chelsea's second highest scorer of all

time, behind only Bobby Tambling. He is also seventh in the club's all-time appearances list. Having player-managed Doncaster in 1997, Dixon has coached southern non-League sides Borehamwood, Letchworth and Hitchin Town.

Wade Elliott

A former non-League player with New Forest non-leaguers Bashley, he was spotted by ex-Bournemouth player Jimmy Case who organised a trial match for him at Bournemouth. He then trained with Bournemouth over the Christmas holidays and signed for them in February 2000 for a fee of £5,000. He gained the reputation of an honest professional with the Cherries before heading north for fame if not, by the standards of football's over-inflated wages, fortune at Burnley. He scored the play-off final goal that ensured his club top-flight football in 2009. He has twice been Burnley Player of the Year.

Les Ferdinand

After playing for Southall in the FA Vase final at Wembley in 1986, Les Ferdinand joined Hayes at the age of 19. In most of the next season he made 39 appearances, scoring 19 goals and being sent off once. He was transferred to QPR in March 1987 for the then unheard-of fee for a non-League club of £30,000. But when QPR sold him to Newcastle United for £6 million in 1995, the £600,000 Hayes received funded the club's first few seasons in the Conference. Little wonder he has a suite named after him at the Church Road ground!

Steve Finnan

Limerick-born defender Steve Finnan began his career at non-League Welling United, making 41 appearances for the Wings over a two-year period. In 1995 he left southeast London for the Midlands, joining Birmingham City, but made only 15 appearances for the Blues before spending some time on loan at Notts County. He made a permanent move to Meadow Lane in 1996, quickly establishing himself and becoming a target for bigger clubs. In November 1998, he moved to Fulham for £600,000 and while there came to the notice of Ireland manager Mick McCarthy, who recognised his efforts with an international call-up.

Between 2003 and 2008 Finnan enjoyed considerable success with Liverpool. He made over 200 appearances for the Reds, but was less in demand after the arrival of Rafa Benitez, and left for Spanish club Espanyol in 2008. He made a return to the Premiership with Portsmouth for 2009-10.

Steve Guppy

Guppy was working on building sites when he was spotted by Southampton playing for his local team, Colden Common, in 1989. He failed to break into the first team so joined then non-League Wycombe Wanderers in September 1989. Moves to Newcastle, Port Vale, Leicester and Celtic raised his profile, and his Beckham-esque crossing ability helped him win a full England cap, playing against Belgium in 1999. After drifting down the leagues he joined Stevenage Borough with whom he won the FA Trophy in 2007. Guppy remains the only footballer to have played for England Under-21, England semi-pro, England B and the full England teams.

Barry Hayles

Carpenter-turned-striker Hayles was first noticed as a Stevenage player, helping them to the Conference title in 1996. His performances in their FA Cup run earned him a move to Bristol Rovers in 1997. After just one season, Hayles moved to Fulham for a fee of £2 million in 1998, helping the club through two promotions to get to the Premier League. Since then he has become a nomad, numbering Sheffield United, Millwall, Plymouth, Leicester and Cheltenham among his clubs. He has also played ten times for Jamaica, his parental country of birth.

Steve Heighway

Born in Dublin, winger Steve's early education took place in Sheffield and Stockport. He was overlooked by professional clubs and played in the non-League game while completing a degree in economics at the University of Warwick. In 1970, Heighway was studying for his final exams and playing for Skelmersdale United when he was spotted by Liverpool's scouting system. Heighway's academic achievements won him the nickname 'Big Bamber', team-mate and fellow academic Brian Hall being 'Little Bamber', both after *University Challenge* TV host Bamber Gascoigne. He was part of Bill Shankly's successful Liverpool team of the seventies.

Lee Hughes

Hughes started in non-League football with Kidderminster Harriers and played for them in the Football Conference, as well as having a part-time job as a roofer. He scored 35 goals in the 1996-97 season when they were beaten to promotion to the Football League by Macclesfield Town. Called up to the England C national football team, he was then sold to West Bromwich Albion for £200,000, a record fee paid for a non-League player. He described it as a dream come true, being a lifelong supporter of the club. Returning to WBA after a spell at Coventry City, he was involved in a fatal car crash and in 2004 began a prison sentence. He played in the Staffordshire County Senior League for Featherstone FC, the prison football team. Released in 2007, in 2009 he was playing with Notts County.

Vinnie Jones

The future Wimbledon hard man was in many ways the archetypal non-League footballer, mixing Saturdays on the park with hod-carrying duties on the building site in the week. He started his football career in 1984 at Alliance Premier League side Wealdstone, then played one season with second-level Swedish club IFK Holmsund in 1986 and helped them win the league before signing for Wimbledon, then on the cusp of the top flight. He did not return to non-League in his latter playing days, preferring the bright lights of Hollywood.

Trésor Kandol

Zaire-born, Spanish-based Trésor Osmar Kandol is a Congolese international who between 2007-10 played for Leeds United, having been signed from Barnet. Before Barnet, he played at Chesham United, Darlington, Dagenham & Redbridge, Thurrock, Bournemouth, Cambridge United and Luton Town. He usually celebrates his goals with a somersault, like his cousin Lomano Trésor LuaLua. While at Barnet in 2006, Kandol was sent to prison for 13 weeks for a series of driving offences.

Paddy Kenny

Keeper Kenny started his football career with amateur side Ovenden West Riding before he joined UniBond First Division Bradford Park Avenue in 1997. He was described by then Avenue boss Trevor Storton as a 'young Peter Schmeichel'.

He was ever present during the 1997-98 season, making 55 appearances in total, and had trials with Birmingham, Bradford and Bury. But it was the Lancashire club who would sign Kenny for £10,000 in August 1998. He followed boss Neil Warnock to Sheffield United in 2002 and won international recognition for Eire. In 2009, however, he was banned for 10 months after failing a drugs test due to a banned substance in a cough medicine he bought over the counter. He moved to QPR in 2010.

Michael Kightly

When non-League winger Kightly signed for Wolves in early 2007 for a bargain £20,000 it was rumoured Manchester United were also keen to sign him, an indication of his promise. A trainee with Southend United, he spent a spell on loan with Farnborough before signing for

Grays in July 2005.

He missed a sizeable chunk of the 2007-08 season through an ankle injury, but was rewarded with a new four-year contract in the summer. And he made 41 appearances in all competitions as Wolves clinched the Championship title in 2008-09, scoring eight goals before suffering a broken metatarsal in a behind-closed-doors friendly in March. Michael had also become a regular member of the England Under-21 squad.

Dave Kitson

In his late teens Kitson gave up on football with his local club Hitchin Town, and concentrated on his day job at supermarket chain Sainsbury's as a frozen food stacker. However, shortly after this he was signed by Cambridge United after being spotted playing against their reserve side in a friendly against Arlesey Town.

He was sold to Reading in December 2003 for £150,000. A move to Stoke for a club record £5.5 million flopped and he returned to Reading on loan, but started 2009-10 back at the Potteries and in better form.

Eddie McGoldrick

McGoldrick started out at non-League side Kettering Town, but following a transfer to Nuneaton Borough he established himself as a utility player in the early eighties before moving into the Football League with Northampton Town, where he collected a Fourth Division title medal in 1987. McGoldrick then had successful spells at Crystal Palace, Arsenal and Manchester City, was capped at international level for the Republic of Ireland and was a member of Ireland's 1994 World Cup squad. After leaving professional football in 1999, he had short spells as manager of Corby Town in 2000 and Bashley in 2003 before becoming player-manager at Corby Town.

Alan Pardew

The man who managed Southampton in 2009-10 enjoyed a long playing career in non-League at Whyteleafe, Corinthian Casuals, Dulwich Hamlet and Yeovil Town before entering the League with Crystal Palace, Charlton and Barnet. Pardew was also in the England semi-professional squad while working as a glazier and a cab driver, and at one stage he gave up football for six months while working in the Middle East.

Paul Parry

Picked up by Hereford after being rejected by Bristol City, winger/striker Parry was the club's leading scorer and was sold to Cardiff in 2003. After 200 appearances including an FA Cup final, he joined Preston North End for £300,000. He conquered a fear of flying to gain 12 full caps for Wales (scoring once) but retired from international football in 2008. He made his Wales debut in 2004 as a substitute in the 4-0 win over Scotland. At the time, he had made only five appearances since joining Cardiff and had been playing Conference football six weeks earlier.

Stuart Pearce

The future Nottingham Forest and England full-back failed a trial at Queens Park Rangers, then rejected Hull City in favour of training and working as an electrician and plumber. For almost five years, he played in the non-League game with his local side, Wealdstone, then among the biggest names of non-League football in the Alliance Premier League. In 1983 then top-flight club Coventry offered £30,000 (a huge sum at the time for a semi-professional player) for Pearce, and he was on his way to glory. He is now an England coach.

Kevin Phillips

After being rejected as a striker for Southampton, Kevin Phillips resumed his career at non-League Baldock Town as a right-back. He moved from Baldock to Watford, thence to Sunderland, with whom he was the Premier

League top scorer in the 1999-2000 season with 30 goals (he then went on to win the Golden Boot for the whole of Europe in that season). He has also had spells at Southampton (again), Aston Villa, West Bromwich Albion and currently Birmingham City.

Cyrille Regis

Regis was the first of the three Black Pearls (with Jason Roberts and Les Ferdinand) to go from Hayes to League football and international caps. Born in French Guiana, he joined Hayes from Molesey of the Athenian League in the summer of 1976 at the age of 19, and played with a maturity that belied his age, scoring 24 goals in 61 appearances. At the end of his first season, he was signed by Johnny Giles for West Bromwich Albion, on the recommendation of chief scout Ronnie Allen, for an initial £5,000. England caps followed and moves to Coventry City, Aston Villa, Wolverhampton Wanderers and Wycombe Wanderers at the end of his career.

Jason Roberts

A nephew of Cyrille Regis, Jason made his debut for Hayes in November 1995. He scored two goals against Slough Town in the Conference in March 1997, running the ball from the halfway line past his opponent, and was instrumental in the 5-1 demolition of Stevenage Borough at Broadhall Way in August 1997. A week later, he signed for Wolverhampton Wanderers for a non-League record fee of £250,000, plus a percentage of any sell-on. During his time at Hayes Jason made 50 appearances and scored 16 goals. A Grenada international, he currently plays for Blackburn Rovers.

Chris Smalling

Chris Smalling's move to Fulham from Isthmian League Premier Division side Maidstone United in 2008 proved that the game's elite still has an eye on the non-League game. While with Maidstone, Smalling was also scouted by Middlesbrough but, having spent time at academies of clubs in the Football League, was happy to play for his local club – good experience that helped him to get used to the physical side of the game. Fulham manager Roy Hodgson numbers Maidstone as one of his former clubs and snapped Smalling up. The 19-year-old made his Premiership debut in May 2009 and by September was playing in Europe. Sir Alex Ferguson then signed him in an extraordinary £8 million transfer in January 2010, making his a meteoric climb – from Maidstone to Manchester United in less than two years.

Shaun Teale

Central defender Shaun Teale started his playing career with Weymouth before moving along the coast to AFC Bournemouth for a £50,000 fee in 1989. He hit the top flight with Aston Villa, later moving to Tranmere Rovers and to Motherwell in Scotland before re-entering the non-League game as player-manager of Burscough in the UniBond Premier Division. While he was there, the side won the 2003 FA Trophy. He has since managed Northwich Victoria and Chorley, but is now a restaurateur.

Paul Terry

Though he made a limited impact in the Football League during spells with Yeovil and Leyton Orient, Paul Terry, elder brother of Chelsea and England captain John, is a non-League stalwart who has a wealth of experience with Grays and Rushden & Diamonds.

His career started in 1999 with Dagenham & Redbridge, for whom he made 130 appearances before moving to Yeovil in 2003. He made over 150 League and cup appearances for Yeovil in his four years there, helping the club to the League Two championship in 2004-05. A cruciate knee ligament injury ruled him out for much of the 2006-07 season, at the end of which he was out of contract and moved to Leyton Orient, where he spent two seasons.

After making a handful of appearances for Grays at the start of the 2009-10 campaign, Terry spent the season with fellow Conference side Rushden & Diamonds.

Andy Townsend

Current media pundit Andy Townsend began his career with Athenian League club Welling. After making 105 appearances he signed for Weymouth for £13,500 in 1984. His value had grown to £35,000 when he was transferred to Southampton less than a year later, following this with a million-plus move to Chelsea. He then captained Aston Villa to the League cup twice and Eire in the 1994 World Cup campaign before moving to Middlesbrough in 1997, West Bromwich Albion in 1999 and ending up on television, radio and in the newspapers.

Chris Waddle

Future England winger and current media pundit Waddle began his footballing career with Pelaw Juniors, moving on to Whitehouse SC, Mount Pleasant SC, HMH Printing, Pelaw SC, Leam Lane SC and Clarke Chapman before joining Tow Law Town in the 1978 close-season. After unsuccessful trials with Sunderland and Coventry City and a spell working in a sausage and meat pie factory he was eventually taken on by Newcastle United in July 1980 for a fee of £1,000. Following his departure from the pro game in 1999, Waddle enjoyed two seasons with Worksop Town, making 60 appearances and scoring three goals. His most notable appearance was in a 12-0 Northern Premier League record win against Frickley Athletic. He also had a brief spell with Glapwell and made one appearance for Stocksbridge Park Steels in the Northern Premier League First Division. He still turns out in the Wragg League Sheffield for HSBC Over-35s and for Devonshire Arms FC in the Sheffield Imperial League.

Ian Wright

Striker Wright came to professional football relatively late. Despite trials at Southend and Brighton during his teens, he was unable to win a professional contract and looked set to pursue a job as a full-time plasterer as he played for amateur and non-League teams. He was left disillusioned about his chances of a career as a professional footballer.

Wright also served 14 days in Chelmsford Prison for driving without tax and insurance. Crystal Palace signed him in August 1985, three months short of his 22nd birthday, and his goals helped the club to the top flight via the play-offs in 1989. He went on to Arsenal and England and is now a TV pundit. He retained an interest in non-League, taking his place on the board of directors of Isthmian League Ashford Town in 2007 following his purchase of a stake in the club.

Not forgetting the man in black…

Mark Halsey

Top referee Halsey, a native of Hertfordshire, is a former goalkeeper who spent 12 years playing non-League football before he started refereeing in 1989. In December 1984 he played one game for Barnet before joining St Albans City and in the early nineties would train with Barnet in Potters Bar to keep himself prepared for the rigours of officiating top-flight games. In 1999 he was promoted to Premier League status, and FIFA the following year. In 2009 it was revealed he was fighting cancer, but he returned to refereeing after treatment.

FAMOUS FOOTBALLERS WHO FINISHED IN NON-LEAGUE

Gordon Davies

A latecomer to the professional game, Davies both started and finished his career in non-League football. He played for Merthyr Tydfil alongside his day job as a PE teacher until March 1978, when he was signed by Fulham at the age of 23. He spent six seasons with the Cottagers, scoring 114 goals in 247 appearances, before moving briefly on to Chelsea and then, in October 1985, to Manchester City. Davies swiftly returned to Fulham, where he spent another five seasons and became the club's record goal-scorer, amassing 159 League goals in a total of 394 games. After he left Fulham for the second time, he spent a short time back in his native Wales with Wrexham before finishing his playing days with Northwich Victoria, retiring at the age of 37 in 1993.

Jimmy Greaves

Ex-Spurs and England hotshot Greaves is the most famous footballer to have finished his career in non-League. Having retired at the age of 31, he made a comeback at the age of 38, playing for Barnet FC in the then Southern League. Playing from midfield, he netted 25 goals and was their player of the season, despite a well-known alcohol problem which he finally beat in 1978.

Bontcho Guentchev

Bulgarian international Guentchev, who played in the World Cup in 1994 and Euro 1996, spent the majority of his career playing in England for Ipswich Town but also had spells at FC Etar Veliko Tarnovo, Sporting Lisbon, CSKA Sofia and Luton Town before finishing his career in non-League with Hendon and Carshalton Athletic, helping the latter back to the Ryman Premier Division after relegation the previous season. He retired to run a café/bar in West London called 'Strikers', but came out of retirement in 2006 to play for Hendon, scoring his first goal since his return to the club in March 2007 against Hayes in the Middlesex Senior Cup. He also persuaded his oldest son Lubomir to join Hendon from Bulgarian side Naftex-Burgas.

Matt Jansen

Mercurial striker Jansen was on the verge of an England international cap, having been called up to the squad in 2002 while with Blackburn, but suffered a head injury in a motorbike accident later that year and quit professional football four years later. After trying out with Wrexham in the Conference he started the 2009-10 season with Leigh Genesis, managed by former team-mate Garry Flitcroft, in Northern Premier League Division One North.

Ian Moores

Striker Moores started his career at Stoke in 1974, moving to Tottenham Hotspur in 1976, but he made only 29 appearances for Spurs in two years before the arrival of Ossie Ardiles and Ricky Villa made him surplus to requirements. In September 1978 he signed for Leyton Orient, and for the next four years he was a first-team regular, but when Orient suffered relegation in 1982, Moores moved to Bolton for the 1982-83 season.

Between 1983 and 1988 he played with considerable success for Apoel in Cyprus. Returning to England, he signed for Tamworth, with whom he won the FA Vase in 1989, scoring a goal in the replay of the final. He retired from playing the following year, working in personal finance and coaching at youth level until his death from lung cancer in 1998 at the age of 43.

Clive Walker

A tricky winger who played for Chelsea, Sunderland, Fulham, QPR and Brighton, Walker's spell at Conference club Woking under manager Geoff Chapple helped them to win the FA Trophy in 1994; when he left in 1997 he had played 203 games for them, scoring 91 goals.

He is still the oldest player to play for his last club, Cheltenham Town, having been in his 42nd year when he retired.

He is now a pundit, and credits his non-League career with the change. 'Woking's FA Cup successes meant that we were on the television a lot and Sky showed a lot of our games. As I was the old pro from Chelsea, they often used me for interviews, but I enjoyed it.'

Christopher Wreh

Talented but undisciplined Liberian Wreh scored the goal in 1998 that took Arsenal to the FA Cup final, picking up a winner's medal against Newcastle. Loan spells and a disastrous move to Saudi Arabia later, he ended up in the Ryman Premier League with Bishop's Stortford, managed by former Gunner Martin Hayes. Failing to show for a game got him the sack, and his next step was even further down, to Buckingham Town. He then retired from the game in 2005 to concentrate on a musical project, Soul Rebel.

CHARACTERS

Half a dozen individuals who have brought colour and sometimes controversy to the non-League game

Geoff Chapple

Chapple is probably the most successful English non-League football manager. His achievements include winning the FA Trophy five times in seven years with Woking (1994, 1995 and 1997) and Kingstonian (1999 and 2000).

He was a semi-pro player in the Southern and Isthmian Leagues before plunging into his managerial career with Windsor & Eton. He first joined Woking in the 1984-85 season and went on to lead them on their famous FA Cup run in 1991, which saw them beat West Bromwich Albion 4-2 at The Hawthorns. As well as the five FA Trophy wins came six promotions within and from the Isthmian League structure, several FA Cup giant-killings and a clutch of minor cups.

Surprisingly he never took charge of a League team, his managerial career never extending beyond the Conference. According to a review of his biography, 'This was a manager who never supervised training, would avoid speaking to players unless he had to, showed little interest in tactics and often signed key players who had been found and approached by his assistant. There's no doubt that Chapple had firm views on how the game should be played – he was devoted to an eye-pleasing, passing game – and had the patter and people skills of a high-calibre salesman, his career outside football.'

He later had a second spell with Woking, although this time he was not so successful and parted company with the club in October 2002. He returned to the club as commercial manager in the autumn of 2008. His story was told in a book by Clive Poulton, *Geoff Chapple – The Story Behind the Legend.*

Chris Kelly

Chris Kelly was the star player of Leatherhead's cup-fighting seventies side, described by the *Daily Mail* as 'Leatherhead's answer to Stan Bowles and Rodney Marsh' and earning the nickname 'The Leatherhead Lip' for his readiness to talk up the team on national television.

With the tabloids building up the heavyweight rivalry between Muhammad Ali and Joe Frazier, the Mail compared striker Kelly – an upholsterer by trade – with Louisville's finest. Having scored the winner at the Goldstone ground and denigrated future opponents Leicester on *Match of the Day*, *Nationwide* and even *Tomorrow's World*, he scored at Filbert Street to put the amateurs 2-0 up. But Leicester, with their array of stars, recovered in the second half of the epic cup-tie, eventually winning 3-2.

Kelly, who had a spell with Millwall but didn't enjoy the professional game, returned to Leatherhead as commercial manager and remained an outspoken character. In 2006 Leatherhead's FA Cup dream took them to League Two Torquay where they led before slipping to a 2-1 defeat.

Tony Kempster

Kempster was the man who arguably brought more than anyone else to non-League football over the last decade. His passion came from his father who played for Ruislip Town in the Hellenic League, and Tony himself played non-League football and was a referee.

He had always been interested in computers and in the nineties combined his two passions to create the ultimate non-League football website. 'Tony's English Football Site', as it was unassumingly named, opened for business in 1997-98 and contained the statistics that bring the game alive – 'Fixtures, Results, Tables, Maps & Mileages for all leagues to Step 7 of the Pyramid and selected leagues below that'. An estimated 200,000 people checked his site every Saturday, and almost 300,000 checked it on the last day of the season.

After retiring from his job at Nestlé, Tony became fascinated by the annual restructuring of the leagues and began a dialogue with leagues up and down the country as well as the Football Association. His views on the structure of the game were often sought by the authorities before they made decisions.

In 2008 the Football Supporters' Federation honoured him with their annual award for Services to Supporters. But he was already ailing and died on 14 June 2009. The site, www.tonykempster.co.uk, has been maintained in a frozen state since the end of the 2008-09 season – and, while a successor has been mooted, is still well worth consulting.

Ian Ridley

Journalist and author Ridley, whose biographies include co-written efforts with Tony Adams, Steve Claridge and Paul Merson, took control of Weymouth FC in 2003-04 and appointed former Millwall, Leicester and Birmingham striker Claridge as manager.

Within a season gates had more than doubled from around 500 to 1,200 and the club's fortunes turned around from relegation fodder to promotion candidates in the Conference South. But a boardroom takeover caused Ridley to leave in September 2004.

After five troubled years Ridley made a surprise return to the chair on 18 March 2009 following discord between past and present members of the board, which was fuelled by more than ten successive defeats in the Conference. Bobby Gould, the former manager of Wales, was unable to turn the situation around and the club were relegated, having gained only a single point since February.

Ridley had his work cut out and was behind a rescue package in late 2009 that kept the club from administration. But a battle with prostate cancer led him to step down once this had been achieved.

Graham Westley

Westley was born in Hounslow, London, in 1968. After becoming an apprentice with Queens Park Rangers he made two League appearances for Gillingham before joining Barnet, then in the Football Conference. He later played for a number of non-League clubs, including Wycombe Wanderers, Kingstonian, Wealdstone, Farnborough Town, Harlow Town, Enfield, Aylesbury United, Harrow Borough, Tooting & Mitcham United, Molesey and Walton & Hersham.

In 1999 he bought a controlling interest in Farnborough Town and appointed himself as manager, but left the club in controversial circumstances to take over at Stevenage Borough in January 2003. During his three-and-a-half-year stint at Broadhall Way, he turned them from relegation candidates to play-off finalists.

He left the club when his contract expired in June 2006, but after short spells with Rushden & Diamonds (December 2006-February 2007) and Kettering Town (April-May 2007) he returned to Stevenage in May 2008. At the end of the 2008-09 season, Westley took Boro' to the Conference National play-off semi-finals and helped them secure the FA Trophy against York City at Wembley Stadium. In 2010 he achieved his long-held dream to be a League manager when he took Stevenage up as Conference champions.

Always an inveterate self-publicist, Westley has been a columnist in the *Non-League Paper* and is happy to state his often controversial case.

Tony Williams

Williams represented England Under-18 against Scotland before playing for Corinthian Casuals, Dulwich Hamlet and Kingstonian. After launching the *Rothmans Football Yearbook* in 1970 as founder and co-compiler he was asked to join Rothmans (although a non-smoker!) in the company's public relations department. He was soon able to persuade them that Rothmans should become the first ever sponsor of the Isthmian League.

After the cigarette company pulled out of their sports sponsorship Tony produced the first *Non-League Directory* in 1978, launching *Non-League Football* magazine with *The Mail on Sunday* and then *Team Talk*.

After his ten years with Hungerford Town, he served Yeovil Town as a director for seven years. Tony Williams Publications now publishes a variety of non-League titles, while the man himself received the GLS Lifetime Award for promoting non-League football.

14 THE NON-LEAGUE PAPER, Sunday,

Nationwide — NATIONWIDE CONFERENCE

Four off as seasonal spirit slips

Halifax Town 1
Cartwright (7), Sandwith (8), Colley (7), Dudgeon, Yates, Midgley (7), Bushell (7), Owen (7), Sagare (7), Farrell (7), Mallon (7). Subs:Hockenhull (7), Lee (8), Killeen, Hudson (7), Allan.

Scarborough 0
Walker (6), Hotte (6), Cryan (7), Redmile, Lyth (6), Marcelle (7), Gill, Kelly (7), Kerr (6), Sestanovich (8), Quayle (6). Subs:Capper, Williams (6), Whitman (6), Senior (6), G. Downey.
Referee: R Desmond (Swindon)

STAR MAN: Kevin Sandwith (Halifax) **ENTERTAINMENT:** ★★★☆☆

By **MARTYN HINDLEY**

REFEREE Robert Shoebridge took centre stage for a festive clash which was bereft of any seasonal niceties – taking the shine off a Halifax victory that puts them back in contention for a play-off place.

The Ripley official flashed four red and five yellow cards in a Yorkshire derby that boiled over before half-time.

The flashpoint came 13 minutes before the interval when a thumping challenge from Boro's Wayne Gill on Halifax midfielder Ryan Mallon sparked off several altercations and forced the officials into action.

Gill appeared to have been dismissed for the initial challenge while the home pair of Adam Yates and James Dudgeon earned an early bath for retaliation.

Mr Shoebridge's four-card trick was completed when Boro centre-half Matt Redmile followed them into the book and the bath for his role in an unsightly scuffle that made it nine-a-side.

The brawl was a disgraceful end to a half which up to then had been exciting enough.

It took 24 minutes for the first meaningful effort but when it came, Mark Quayle's snap shot was foiled by Kevin Sandwith's last-ditch interception.

Then came the rash of cards – more hate-mail than Christmas greetings.

Andy Farrell's late challenge on Mark Hotte earned him a caution before the powderkeg blew in spectacular fashion two minutes later.

Among the carnage, Jimmy Kelly had two attempts at catching out Mark Cartwright – a right-footed piledriver ending on the terracing and then a carbon copy minutes later.

Cartwright had one further piece of action, but could barely claim to have been over-employed by Ashley Sestanovich's 20-yarder.

The sides were well matched throughout – as their league placings of 13th and 15th would indicate.

The deciding strike came for the hosts with just 18 minutes remaining – a harsh judgement on Scarborough in a game which had largely been reduced to a farce by the multiple dismissals.

Craig Midgley was unfortunate to see his shot from eight yards cannon back off the upright and Jake Sagere's rebound effort bobbled around a packed penalty area off the legs of Ashley Lyth.

Just when it seemed that that the Seadogs had cleared the danger, Christian Lee smashed home through the crowd to snatch all three points.

The goal stung Scarborough into a series of attacks and the immediate arrival of Tristram Whitman for Scott Kerr signalled manager Ruiseell Slade's attacking intentions.

They came closest to levelling though a Chris Senior bicycle kick which drifted well wide, and although Kelly made several attempts at the most spectacular goal of the season, Cartwright was only seriously tested by Colin Cryan's late drive which was well parried.

MATCH STATS

HALIFAX v SCARBORO

HALIFAX		SCARBORO
5	SHOTS ON TARGET	8
2	SHOTS OFF TARGET	8
3	CORNERS	3
2	OFFSIDE	2
16	FOULS CONCEDED	17
2	YELLOW CARDS	3
2	RED CARDS	2

Stats & player ratings supplied by PA

NICKNAMES

Just about every football club, from the Premiership to the local Sunday League, has a nickname. At the simplest level it may be a shortened version of the club's name or a reference to the colours the team plays in, but sometimes it will be a reference to something in the club's history, or perhaps a local industry. Whatever its origin, a club's nickname is an integral part of its identity, handed down from one generation of fans to the next.

There are hundreds of clubs across the country with interesting nicknames and fascinating stories to tell about their origins, but there simply isn't room to tell them here, so the following round-up has been limited to those clubs recently playing in the Conference.

Barrow may be known to the current generation of fans as the Bluebirds, but for a while in the late sixties there was a move to adopt the rather more curious nickname of the Ziggers. It never caught on, although the name was used for the Barrow AFC National Supporters' Club Newsletter for a time. A 1997 edition of the *Holker Street Newsletter* goes some way to explaining what it was all about:

John Woods, who was editor at the time, changed the name of the then imaginatively titled *Newsletter* to *The National Zigger* as a link with the most successful period in the club's history. The Zigger was...a stuffed kitbag that was paraded around Holker Street before games started, to the chant from the Holker Street end of 'Zigger, zagger, zigger, zagger, oi, oi, oi!' The Zigger was featured on the front cover of the magazine *Football League Review* in September 1968 along with the club's mascot, Jimmy Caldwell.

There was a campaign to have the Ziggers adopted as the club nickname, but it never took off and was finally replaced by the Bluebirds. Jimmy is quoted as saying, 'The older fans don't seem to go for our Zigger, but we keep trying.'

Like Barrow, Conference National sides Altrincham (the Robins), Crawley Town (the Red Devils), Kettering Town (the Poppies) and Salisbury City (the Whites) all have nicknames derived from the team colours, while several others are known simply by abbreviations of the club name. Cambridge United (United, the U's), Ebbsfleet United (the Fleet), Forest Green Rovers (the Green), Hayes & Yeading United (United), Kidderminster Harriers (the Harriers), Rushden & Diamonds (the Diamonds) and Stevenage Borough (Boro') are among the latter group.

The now-defunct Chester City, often referred to simply as the Blues, are another club whose nickname comes from the club colours, but older fans will also know them as the Seals, a name derived from the Sealand Road ground that the club called home for almost a century. In 1974 the club adopted a new badge that depicted two seals, the design being chosen from entries submitted to a competition organised by a local newspaper, but the badge was replaced by the current version ten years later, and with the move to the Deva Stadium in 1992, the old nickname began to be heard less often. A new club, Chester FC, nicknamed the Blues, has sprung from the ashes

Telford United v Southport
Tuesday 3rd September 1996 K.O. 7.45pm

and started 2010-11 in the Evo-Stik Division One North.

Fans of League returnees Oxford United can choose club colours or an abbreviation, with their side being known either as United or the Yellows, but they have a third option, the Boys From Up The Hill – a hangover from the days when the club was known as Headington United.

Eastbourne Borough are another side that boasts a nickname from their days playing under another name. Formed in 1964 as Langney FC, the club became Langney Sports in 1968, and played under that name until 2001, when the name Eastbourne Borough was chosen to raise awareness of the club's location, but fans still refer to their team as the Sports. Histon fall into the same category, although the origins of their nickname, the Stutes, go back rather further in time. Between 1904 and their move to the Eastern Counties League in 1965, the club were known as Histon Institute, but almost half a century after they shortened their name the old nickname lives on.

Like Altrincham, Welsh club Wrexham's choice of colours is reflected in their nickname of the Robins, but the side are also known as the Red Dragons, combining the club colours with a dash of national pride.

Geographical location plays a part in some of the other Conference National sides' nicknames, with Gateshead being known as the Tynesiders, and York City as the Minstermen, while Tamworth, like Chester, take theirs from the name of their home ground, the Lamb Ground, being known to fans as the Lambs.

Local history has given Luton Town its nickname of the Hatters, Luton having been associated with hat-making since the 17th century, while Grays is an area rich in aggregate production, and so Grays Athletic are also known as the Gravelmen or sometimes the G-Men.

Last but not least, AFC Wimbledon have a far more recent local connection to thank for one of their nicknames, the children's favourites the Wombles having lived on Wimbledon Common, of course. Traditionally known as the Dons, Wimbledon also became known as the Crazy Gang in the late eighties, a name originally applied to some of their more exuberant players but gradually adopted by the fans as a name for the club as a whole.

Conference North also has its share of clubs whose nicknames are based on club colours, including Alfreton Town, Ilkeston Town, Redditch United and Workington (all known as the Reds) and Southport (the Yellows), while an interesting variation on the theme is offered by Harrogate Town, whose yellow and black strip has earned them the nickname the Sulphurites. Rather less interestingly, they are also known as Town, and stand alongside Blyth Spartans (the Spartans), Solihull Moors (the Moors), Stalybridge Celtic (Celtic) and Stafford Rangers (Rangers) in this respect.

Ilkeston Town's fans also use an abbreviation as an alternative nickname for their team, but in this case it's actually an abbreviation that locals use when talking about the town itself, which is widely referred to as Ilson.

Local geology provides Southport with their alternative nickname, the Sandgrounders. Southport is built on a bed of sand, and the term has been used to refer to the town's inhabitants for many years, so it was a natural choice as a nickname for the club. Local industry led to Hinckley United being dubbed the Knitters. The club was formed in 1997 from a merger of Hinckley Athletic and Hinckley Town, and a competition was held to find a nickname. The winning entry was chosen to reflect the fact that wool and hosiery have been staples of commerce in the local area for over 300 years.

Another club whose nickname stems from local industry is Corby Town, dubbed the Steelmen. Opposition fans have a rather less flattering term for Corby's followers, calling them 'plastic Jocks', a reference to the influx of Scottish steelworkers that coincided with the club's formation in 1948, and to this day Corby number many Scots among their fans.

For many years, Fleetwood Town were known as the Fishermen, Fleetwood being a noted deep-sea fishing port, but in recent years they've been another of the clubs known by a shortened version of their official name, the Fleet. Their fans refer to themselves in more humorous terms, as 'Macs' (after the rock band Fleetwood Mac) or the 'Cod Army' as well as the more traditional 'Woodies'.

Gainsborough Trinity are a long-established club who started life in 1873 as a church side called Trinity Recreationalists, but they had changed to their current name by the time they joined the Midland League in 1889. They're still known as the Recreationalists, and sometimes even as the Holy Blues, reminding fans of their origins all those years ago, but they're also often referred to rather more simply as Trinity.

The now defunct Farsley Celtic weren't usually referred to as Celtic, but the Celts, their alternative nickname of the Villagers reflecting the time when Farsley was a village community a few miles outside Leeds. These days, the urban sprawl has all but engulfed Farsley, which became part of the Metropolitan Borough of Leeds more than 30 years ago.

Droylsden is another town that has been absorbed by a nearby city, this time Manchester. The former mill town lies just four miles from the city centre, and its football club has the unusual nickname of the Bloods, which it shares with Saffron Walden Town. The origin of the name is unclear – it may be connected with the adoption of a red and white strip in the early twenties, but the more usual explanation is that it derives from the name of the club's home ground, the Butchers Arms.

Another club with an obscure nickname is Northwich Victoria, known to many as the Vics, but also, more puzzlingly, the Trickies. There's no such mystery about Vauxhall Motors' nickname, the former works team being known simply as the Motormen.

Finally, there are four Conference North clubs whose nicknames are types of animal. Eastwood Town are known as the Badgers, having played for many years in black and white stripes, although their current kit consists of a white shirt with black trim and black shorts. Gloucester City and Hyde

United are both known as the Tigers, in City's case because of their deep yellow and black striped shirts, but in United's case it was simply a name the fans bestowed on the club in recognition of their battling spirit as they struggled to compete in the early days of the Northern Premier League.

Last of the four is AFC Telford, known as the Bucks. The current club rose from the ashes of Telford United, who played their home games at Bucks Head until 2000, when the ground was redeveloped and renamed New Bucks Head.

Continuing the wildlife theme, Conference South has Lewes, known as the Rooks. The name comes from the club badge, the design of which includes a tower representing Lewes Castle, but which also looks like a rook from a traditional pattern chess set. As an aside, Lewes play at one of the most unusually named football grounds in the country, the Dripping Pan, so called because it stands on land formerly used by monks from the local priory, who used to evaporate water from the local river there to produce salt.

Two sides in the league are known as the Dragons – Basingstoke Town, from the design of the club badge, and Worcester City, because they play at St George's Lane. Worcester City have more nicknames than any other club in the Conference, being known not only as the Dragons, but also as City, the Blues, the Loyals, the Royals, and the Faithfuls, the last three stemming from the city of Worcester's steadfast support for the Crown during the English Civil War.

Hampton & Richmond Borough are known as the Beavers, which may be derived from the name of their home ground, the Beveree Stadium, or the adjacent Beaver Close, although a more fanciful suggestion is that the proximity of the River Thames and an ancient stream that runs down to it might have made the vicinity an ideal habitat for beavers before they became extinct in the UK during the 16th century.

Conference South boasts an unusually high number of clubs whose nicknames are those of birds. Lewes, as we've seen, are known as the Rooks, while Havant & Waterlooville are known as the Hawks, a clever development of the initial letters of the club's name. Both Dorchester Town and Maidenhead play in black and white, and have thus earned the nickname the Magpies, and there are no prizes for guessing why Weston-super-Mare are known as the Seagulls.

Last on the ornithological list is Staines Town, known as the Swans because of the town's connection with the annual census of the swan population on the Thames ('swan upping') that stretches back hundreds of years. Staines are also known as the Wheatsheafers, after their home ground, Wheatsheaf Park, and occasionally as the Linos, a reflection of the town's former main industry, making linoleum. But club nicknames can spring from the most unlikely sources, and Staines fans have recently taken to calling the club 'The Massive', after comedian Ali G's famous 'Staines Massive'. With a player named Ali Chaaban in the side, Staines supporters soon took to chanting 'Who needs Ali G when we've got Ali C?'

Relatively few Conference South sides have nicknames abbreviated from the club's official name, only Bath City (City), St Albans City (the Saints, or City), Welling (the Wings) and, as noted above, Worcester City falling into this category, although Thurrock, who were known as Purfleet FC until 2003, are still known as the Fleet.

The range of colours is rather greater in Conference South, too, with Bishop's Stortford (the Blues), Chelmsford City (the Clarets) and Dover Athletic (the Whites) alongside two rather less obvious examples in Weymouth and Woking. Weymouth's famous FA Cup run in the 1949-50 season certainly brought the Terras to the nation's attention, but it's doubtful that many people realised that the name was derived from the club's earliest strip, which featured terracotta-coloured shirts. Woking, meanwhile, are known as the Cards, the name being a reference to the 'Cardinal red' in their red and white shirts.

The remaining clubs in the league all have nicknames associated in some way with their locality. In Newport County's case, they have two to choose from, one referring to their home town, and the other to the fact that they were unable to play there at one stage. Newport has long been a centre of steel production, giving the club their original nickname, the Ironsides, but when Newport County were reformed after liquidation in 1989 and forced to play their 'home' games in the Gloucestershire town of Moreton-in-Marsh, they were quickly dubbed the Exiles, a name that has stuck.

Braintree Town are known as the Iron, a reference to their beginnings as Manor Works FC, the works team of the Crittall Window Company, famous for their iron window frames. Crittall were once the leading window manufacturers in the country, and their windows were fitted to the ill-fated Titanic. Despite a series of name changes before the club adopted its current title in 1968, the nickname has endured to this day.

Finally we come to Eastleigh, known as the Spitfires. The famous World War 2 fighter first flew from Eastleigh Airport in March 1936. The airport has since expanded to become Southampton International Airport, but the locals have a sense of history and when the club held a competition to find a suitable nickname for the club, the Spitfires was looked on as an ideal suggestion.

NON-LEAGUE MISCELLANY

Loan me a Ground!

Many Premiership and Championship reserve sides now host their games at lower/non-League grounds to avoid wear and tear on their home playing surface. Here is a selection of current arrangements:

Club	Ground	Host
Arsenal	Underhill	Barnet FC
Aston Villa	Marston's Stadium	Hinckley United FC (in winter months)
Birmingham City	Damson Park	Solihull Moors
Burnley	Crown Ground	Accrington Stanley
Blackburn Rovers	Sports Village	Leigh Genesis
Bolton Wanderers	County Ground, Leyland	Lancashire FA
Everton	Stobart Stadium Halton	Widnes
Manchester United	Moss Lane	Altrincham FC
Newcastle United	Kingston Park	Newcastle Falcons
Portsmouth	West Leigh Park	Havant & Waterlooville FC
Reading	Cherrywood Road	Farnborough FC
Sunderland	Welfare Park	Eppleton Colliery Welfare
West Ham United	Woodside Park	Bishop's Stortford FC
Wolves	New Bucks Head	Telford United FC

Model (Semi-)Professionals

When Nike employ world-class footballers to star in their TV adverts they look at non-League doubles whose time comes cheaper. Ashley Sestanovich, for instance, stood in for Thierry Henry during filming for a Nike advert in Rome. The boyhood Arsenal fan told the BBC at the time: 'I met Thierry Henry when I was filming an advert for a Nike commercial in Rome and I played the part of his body double. I met all the players – the likes of Ronaldo, Ronaldinho and Luis Enrique were all there. Sylvain Wiltord, Patrick Vieira and Thierry Henry were there from Arsenal and it was great to see them face-to-face – but I would like to meet them on the pitch at some point.' Sestanovich, who played for Scarborough, Farnborough Town and Grays among others, also acted as Thierry Henry's body double for a series of TV adverts for Renault cars.

Mat Mitchel-King divided his time between the Blue Square Premier League with Histon and international catwalks as a male model before signing for Crewe in 2009. His portfolio includes working as a body double for Rio Ferdinand for Nike. He explained his role as Ferdinand's double, saying: 'For the Nike advert I do all the stuff from a distance and they film Rio for the close stuff. I have met Rio once, just small talk really. When you see him you don't know what to expect, but at the end of the day he is a human being, just a very talented one. On the film set, it is actually the players that look to you for guidance and advice. We are more like colleagues, so we have to keep a level of professionalism and not ask for autographs.'

Fair-Play Footballers

Corinthian Casuals was formed when two leading amateur sides came together in 1939, both having histories stretching far back into the 19th century. The Corinthians (formed 1882) carried a famous name signifying their position as honest, upstanding purveyors of early Association Football. They can claim to have inspired the formation of a top Brazilian side, a Swedish cup competition and the colour of Real Madrid's shirts. They merged with Casuals, formed in 1883.

Many more people have heard of Corinthian Casuals than know where they play (Tolworth, Surrey). Their president is Jimmy Hill OBE and their stated aim is 'to promote fair play and sportsmanship, to play competitive football at the highest level possible whilst remaining strictly amateur and retaining the ideals of the Corinthian and the Casuals Football Clubs.'

Posh non-League Foundations

Peterborough have a keen eye on the non-League game courtesy of director of football Barry Fry. Their team of 2008-09 that achieved promotion to the Championship contained the cream of non-League talent gathered over the past Craig Mackail-Smith, George Boyd, Aaron Mclean and Shaun Batt.

In January 2009 they created a coup by signing Hampton & Richmond striker Ben Wright who chose them in preference to Premier League Fulham. Hampton & Richmond manager, Alan Devonshire, described Wright as the best talent he has witnessed in the 11 years he has been involved in non-League football, and the sought-after striker, who has scored 13 goals for the Blue Square South outfit since signing from Fleet Town at the beginning of the season, was glad his future had been settled: 'I am delighted to be here and it is definitely a club that is going places. The manager Darren Ferguson and director of football Barry Fry have indicated how ambitious the club is and I can't wait to get started. I am a bit different to what you might expect from a striker. I like to make things happen, I feel I am quite good technically and my finishing has improved a lot. My manager at Hampton & Richmond, Alan Devonshire, has helped me a lot.'

Other non-League captures include Rene Howe (Kettering) and Scott Rendell (Cambridge United).

By Royal Appointment

Barry Davies MBE, the former BBC football commentator, is Windsor & Eton's president. The patron is His Royal Highness Prince Philip, their badge contains a cartoon of the castle and they are known as the Royalists.

Davies was possibly the last television football commentator to keep his loyalties to himself during his career; he revealed on a radio interview with Simon Mayo in 2007, after he had retired from football commentary, that he supports Windsor & Eton. (Rival John Motson is a Barnet fan.)

'Barry has got very, very involved since he came on board 18 months ago and is always down here,' said club secretary Stephen Rowland. 'The chairman encouraged him to stay involved in football and I think he's

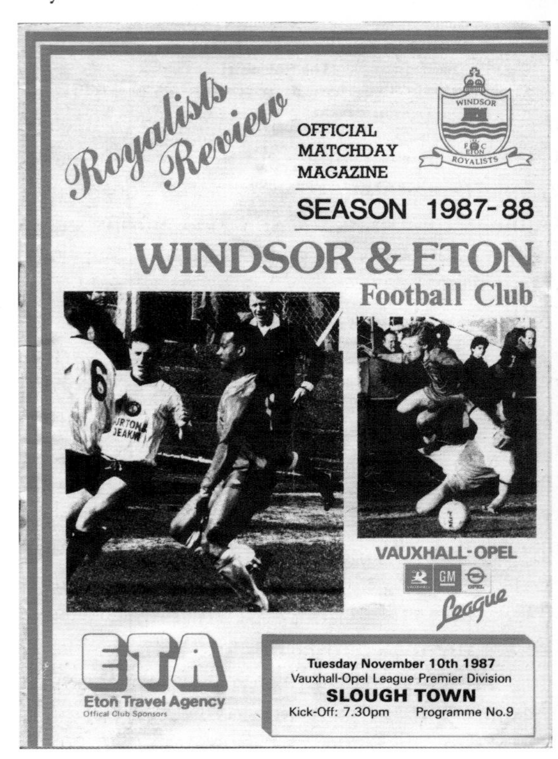

enjoying it. Prince Philip has also been down a few times for things like end-of-season dinners, which is pretty special. We are one of only two clubs in the country to have Royal patronage and it's nice to have that on our headed paper.'

She's in Charge!

On 18 February 2009 Donna Powell became the first female to manage a professional male football club in Britain when she rose from the rank of turnstile operator to manage Fisher Athletic in their Conference South game against Eastleigh. However, she wasn't actually a manager in the true sense of the term, as Dave Mehmet was never actually relieved of the position – it was a reward for having raised £250 for the ailing club. Powell was unable to prevent a 2-1 defeat, this result one of 16 consecutive League reverses between 19 November and 9 March which saw the club relegated in late March 2009. They were wound up weeks later.

Non-League on Big Screen

Yeading FC's Warren ground was the setting for the successful 2002 film *Bend It Like Beckham*, the vehicle for a young Keira Knightley to stake a claim to fame. Sharp-eyed fans noted the film contained a scene where the fictitious girls' football team travelled in a Yeading FC van. *The Mean Machine*, starring Yeading player Nevin Saroya alongside Vinnie Jones and released in 2001, had been filmed at the Warren as were a number of TV commercials. When Yeading merged with Hayes in 2007, Hayes' Church Road became the new club's ground. However, the Warren is still used for youth and reserve team purposes. It is intended that it be redeveloped when the property market picks up, at which point Church Road will be sold and the Warren will commence hosting first-team football once more.

Terras Hit for Nine

When Weymouth lost their Blue Square Premier game against Rushden & Diamonds 9-0 on 22 February 2009 the *Non-League Paper* described it as 'not a football match (but) a snuff movie'. Weymouth were forced to field a youth team after their players put in a 14-day notice to the club, having not been paid since the turn of year. The club had reportedly stopped paying for the players' insurance, so the youth team had to turn out instead. Boys against men.

The Weymouth boys held out for 8 minutes before Rushden scored, and the visitors were 4-0 up by half-time. Goalkeeper Pro Domo made a string of fine saves, but his defence was hopelessly ill-equipped to deal with Rushden's full-time professionals. The crowd did their best to get behind the team, and the Rushden players reportedly offered their own encouragement to the Weymouth players to keep going.

The final tally of 9-0 equalled the record win for the Conference, held jointly by Hereford United against Dagenham & Redbridge in 2004, Sutton against Gateshead and Runcorn against Enfield, both in 1990.

Lager, lager, lager!

In the 2007-08 season, Havant & Waterlooville played and beat Bognor Regis Town, Fleet Town, and Leighton in the FA Cup preliminary rounds before vanquishing York City and League sides Notts County and Swansea City in the competition proper. Their reward was a trip to Anfield to play Liverpool – truly the stuff of dreams.

The Conference South team led twice before losing 5-2, but their performance, acclaimed by the Kop, belied the words of Swansea manager Roberto Martinez who described them as 'nothing but a pub team'.

The South Coast minnows were sponsored by Carlsberg, who also sponsor Liverpool – and with FA rules stating that the same sponsorship logo cannot appear on both teams' shirts, the Hawks' shirts were modified to display the word 'probably' in the familiar Carlsberg font. Subsequent to the game, a banner stating

'H&W – Probably the greatest Pub Team in the world' found its way around the world via newspapers and the internet – great advertising for the lager firm.

Year-Round Sportsmen

With cricket and football seasons overlapping these days, there aren't many 'year-round' sportsmen left. But Burgess Hill goalkeeper Joe Adams had a really good reason for missing a match in September 2009 – he was scoring 79 for his team Glynde & Beddingham in the National Village Cricket Championship Final. He was fortunate that his manager Gary Croydon was a cricketer too, 'so he's very understanding'.

Another cricketer to get involved in the non-League game is Adi Aymes, formerly the wicketkeeper of Hampshire CCC, who is employed by Havant & Waterlooville as a fitness coach. One of his successors, Iain Brunnschweiler, played for Southern League AFC Totton, while back in the seventies Surrey cricketer Graham Roope was an occasional goalkeeper for then Southern League Wimbledon FC.

In an unrelated move, first-class cricket umpire Ian Gould became chairman of Southern League Division One Midlands club Burnham in the summer of 2009. Gould, 52, was born in the nearby village of Taplow and was keen to put something back into local sport.

Cricket was also the cause of a strange departure for a non-League player. Dean Chandler was released by Yeovil in 2000, according to the Western Gazette, because he played in a cricket match arranged as part of team-mate Tony Pennock's testimonial, while injured.

Non-League Goes Pop

Non-League pop stars are few and far between, but they do exist. Danyl Johnson was a successful contestant in the 2009 *X Factor*, having been plucked from the obscurity of the London Falcons Sunday team. Fellow contestant, Olly Murs, competed at a higher level as a forward for Witham Town in the Ryman Division One North, having already starred on Noel Edmonds' *Deal Or No Deal*.

Then sometime Totton/Brockenhurst goalkeeper Iain Brunnschweiler played guitar alongside Coldplay drummer Will Champion in a little-known Southampton band called 'Fat Hamster'. Brunnschweiler recalled: 'We were quite young, about 12 or 13 years old, and used to go to the youth activities group at church. We got together with another lad, David Milln, to form a three-piece band. I played the guitar and tried to sing, but I was absolute rubbish!' Nevertheless he put his talents to good use in 2007 when AFC Totton recorded their FA Vase final song.

Minter's Magnificent Seven

On 22 November 1922 Isthmian League Dulwich Hamlet took on St Albans City in a replayed FA Cup fourth qualifying round match that was to make history. Hamlet had won the FA Amateur Cup just two years earlier, while St Albans were the reigning Athenian League champions. Each side possessed a legendary England amateur international centre-forward. Dulwich's Edgar Kail bagged over 400 goals for Dulwich and was the last player to appear for both the amateur and full England teams. Wilfred Minter scored a remarkable 356 goals in 362 matches for St Albans, refusing all offers to turn professional in favour of working in the family business.

It was Hamlet's Davis who struck first after 15 minutes before Minter replied with a quick-fire hat-trick to put City 3-1 in front after half an hour. Thirty minutes later Davis had hit two more and Kail had helped himself to a double to put the side 5-3 up. But Minter was just warming up and in the next 10 minutes hit his second hat-trick of the match.

At 6-5 to City, it looked like they had done enough but Nicol popped up to equalise for Hamlet with just five minutes remaining. Kail scored a spectacular goal to give Hamlet the lead in extra time before the inevitable Minter equaliser with five minutes left. Both teams would have settled for a replay but, with the last action of the game, Davis headed his fourth goal to win it 8-7 for Dulwich.

Wilfred Minter had scored seven goals away from home but was still on the losing side – a unique feat in the long history of the FA Cup.

Put the Chairman On!

Non-League chairmen have a habit of trying to get on the field of play. The first was Doncaster's John Ryan, who accumulated his fortune altering people's appearances. The former owner of the plastic surgery giant Transform led the club to the Football League and had his reward when, in April 2003, he took the field against Hereford United in Donny's final Conference game of the season. It was the fulfilment of a childhood dream. He came on as a substitute in the 89th minute and, in doing so, entered the *Guinness Book of Records* as the oldest player of all time. He was allocated the number 28.

In 2009 Bookham chairman Simon Butler, 46, posed boss Glyn Manderville a problem by turning out for the Combined Counties club's reserve team, flying in weekly from his ski holiday business in the Alps. He admitted his best years as a player were behind him, but suggested the manager had his number should his talents be needed in the first team!

Accrington All-Change

When Accrington Stanley were promoted to the Football League as Conference champions in 2006 the team relegated to give them their place was Oxford United. Ironically when a financial crisis forced the old Accrington Stanley to resign from the League in 1962, the club that replaced them the following season was Oxford! At least the promotion shook off the stigma of the eighties TV advertisement for milk that featured a budding football player saying, 'Accrington Stanley – who are they?'

The Old and the New

Stevenage Borough's FA Trophy final with Kidderminster in 2007 was the first-ever competitive match to be held at the 'new' Wembley after its multi-million-pound renovation. The game, which attracted a record attendance for the competition of 53,262, ended in a 3-2 victory for Stevenage. Their Steve Guppy and Kidderminster's Jeff Kenna became the first players to have played at both the new Wembley and the old Wembley.

Bishops Bless United

The Munich air crash that decimated Manchester United in 1958 has been well documented elsewhere, but few appreciate the role that non-League football played in the aftermath.

Jimmy Murphy, United's acting manager with Matt Busby still hospitalised, approached amateur giants Bishop Auckland to bolster his squad with Derek Lewin, Warren Bradley and Bob Hardisty. The trio, all England amateur internationals, were brought into Old Trafford to strengthen the reserve side, giving the kids in the team a helping hand. Playing in front of fanatical 10,000-plus crowds took the players by surprise when they made their debut against Burnley at Old Trafford.

United persuaded winger Bradley to sign a semi-professional contract after promising to find him a teaching job in the city. After helping United miraculously finish First Division runners-up to Wolverhampton Wanderers he was called up by the full national team, becoming the only Englishman to win full and amateur caps in the same season. Lewin and Hardisty left Old Trafford at the end of the season, but Bradley went on to make 63 first-team appearances, scoring 20 goals, before returning to non-League in 1963 with Macclesfield after a brief stint at Bury.

The bond between Manchester United and Bishop Auckland still continues. When the Bishops moved into their Tindale Crescent ground for the 2010-11 season the floodlights at the new stadium were donated to the club by United and once graced Old Trafford.

Up for the (FA) Cup

The 2008-09 season saw eight non-League clubs competing in the third round – there would have been nine had Droylsden not been disqualified for fielding an ineligible player in the replay against Chesterfield. It is a number that sets an all-time record for the competition and, say non-Leaguers, looks to be the future.

'On any given day, any team in our league is capable of beating those in the league above,' said Kidderminster Harriers manager Mark Yates. 'Whether they can do it on a consistent basis is another matter. Because of the amount of foreigners at the top end of the game, better English players have filtered down to our level. There's only about three or four clubs in the Conference Premier that aren't professional now. So if the fitness levels are improving and the quality is improving, there's no surprise that the gap is closing.'

For the record, the teams were Barrow, Histon, Blyth Spartans, Forest Green Rovers, Kidderminster Harriers, Kettering, Eastwood Town and Torquay.

Grounds for Delay

Fleetwood Town's Highbury Stadium surely holds the record for the longest gap between the first and second games played at any sporting venue. Fleetwood Town has been based at Highbury for almost 70 years, having previously played at two other locations in the town. The first game at Highbury was in September 1939, but the second didn't take place until August 1946! The Second World War broke out days after the first match and all football was immediately suspended for the next seven years.

What's In A Name?

A record in name changes was set by a club that had four names in the space of six years. Originally Emley, they changed their name to Wakefield & Emley, before slightly changing it a season later to Wakefield-Emley, and then becoming simply Wakefield. Running them close were Runcorn, who started life as Runcorn FC at their own ground, then becoming Runcorn FC Halton when they ground-shared at Widnes Rugby Club, and then in 2006 reforming as Runcorn Linnets and ground sharing at Witton Albion.

Manager Merry-Go-Round

Grays Athletic hold the record for the most managers in a three-year period. The merry-go-round began when Mark Stimson left the club to join Stevenage Borough at the end of the 2005-06 season and Frank Gray was appointed as new manager. However, after just 14 games, his last being a disappointing 0-1 home defeat to Bromley, he was sacked (over the phone as chairman Mick Woodward was on holiday at the time).

Woodward appointed himself as manager for a short while and player/coach Jamie Stuart took charge of an Essex Senior Cup match with Woodward assisting but then appointed ex-Everton player Andy King as manager. King handed in his resignation in January 2007 and was replaced by Justin Edinburgh, his assistant at the time, who became the fourth manager during the season. Grays eventually finished 19th in the league, just avoiding relegation. In total Grays fielded over 50 players in all competitions.

In February 2008 Edinburgh departed by mutual consent, leaving the club fourth in the Conference National. Chairman Woodward took the helm for a second time until the end of the 2007-08 season, promoting goalkeeping coach Gary Phillips to assistant manager and also appointing Neil Smith and Tim O'Shea as coaches to help with training and tactics.

Gary Phillips was boss at the start of 2009-10, but his job was advertised by the club with him still in situ as the club looked to cull their

three-man coaching team. Phillips and his assistants Alan Lewer and John Yems were among those to have applied for the job, which went to ex-West Ham man Julian Dicks.

Oldies But Goldies

Sheffield FC, which officially came into being on 24 October 1857, isn't just the oldest football club in the world. It has links with the mighty Real Madrid, the two being the only clubs in the world to have been awarded the FIFA Order of Merit. The awards were made at a special ceremony in Paris in 2004, when Sheffield FC's chairman, Richard Tims, stood proudly shoulder to shoulder with the legendary Alfredo Di Stefano and Emilio Butragueno. Real received the award for being the most successful club in Europe during the preceding 100 years. Sheffield FC received their citation in recognition of their historical importance to the world's most popular sport, and for their contribution to its development into the game we love today. This has included taking football kit to Africa.

For most of this time, Sheffield FC led a quiet, unspectacular existence, the only real highlights coming in the Amateur Cup competition that Sheffield themselves suggested to the FA in the early 1890s. Professional teams were dominating the FA Cup competition, so the FA introduced the FA Amateur Cup in 1893, and 11 years later Sheffield FC beat Ealing 3-1 at Bradford's Valley Parade to win the coveted trophy. More than 80 years would pass before they had another shot at the Amateur Cup, by which time it had been replaced by the FA Vase. In the 1977 final, Sheffield FC held Billericay to a 1-1 draw at Wembley, but lost the replay at the City Ground, Nottingham, 2-1. They celebrated their 150th anniversary at the end of the 2006-07 season with a place in the UniBond League First Division.

NON-LEAGUE MEDIA

BBC Non-League Football Show

Broadcast weekly on Monday nights throughout the season, the BBC *Non-League Football Show* is a Radio London programme. Host Caroline Barker joined BBC Radio London in 2004 and since then has represented the station at many major sporting events. She was born in Chelmsford, and spent many of her childhood Saturdays in the stands at Chelmsford City's New Writtle Street ground.

The show began broadcasting in 2007 and at the time of writing was in its third season. Most of non-League's biggest names have been guests, while the audience for the show has been expanded by the internet; and its weekly Podcast is listened to across the world.

Setanta

The collapse of Irish television company Setanta in June 2009 after losing the rights to 23 Premiership games and suffering a subsequent haemorrhaging of 700,000 subscribers brought to an end two seasons of unprecedented non-League television coverage.

Restricted in their ability to show Premiership football, Setanta added the Conference to their portfolio, showing selected games live on Thursday nights. This gave the Conference a shop window, though rescheduling games on the one night in the week when there were no clashes with other games left loyal supporters unimpressed. Viewing figures regularly passed 100,000, which rivalled the Scottish Premier, the Football League and even the Championship.

Setanta earned praise for its innovative and high-quality coverage of more than 50 live Blue Square matches a season, but many industry insiders believed it did not make economic sense. In the first year of the deal it showed more than 70 matches, but problems with scheduling games at short notice led to cutbacks.

Setanta sought and were granted unlimited access to managers, changing rooms and other areas from which the likes of Sky had been excluded, and so genuinely expanded the scope of TV coverage with mid-match interviews and the like. Their demise, however, led to worries for Conference clubs whose budget for 2009-10 included the money from the TV rights due to the fact that Setanta did not go under until the close season. Clubs typically banked £70,000 per season from a £12 million, five-year deal, representing around 15-25 per cent of annual budget. The news came as a blow to clubs, most of whom had budgeted for the TV money. Fortunately a Premier League payout announced in September 2009 helped soften the blow.

Hopes were high as the 2009-10 season began that the Conference could follow the Setanta deal, with a similar arrangement with ESPN, the sports broadcasting company that picked up the 46 live Premier League matches previously held by Setanta and launched a stand-alone UK channel to screen them. But after examining the rights held by its collapsed predecessor the Disney-owned broadcaster declined.

It is believed that including rights and production costs, the league would have cost ESPN upwards of £2 million a year to cover. In August 2010 a subscription-based channel, Premier Sports TV, announced that it would show 30 matches per season from the Blue Square Premier over the coming three years. This would be funded by a monthly viewing fee of £6.99.

The Non-League Paper

The Non-League Paper has had an eventful history since it was launched in 2000, but editor David Emery has remained reassuringly in place and it still appears today as the only national weekly publication of its kind.

The paper went into administration in 2002 due to reported 'financial irregularities', and again in June 2006, but in August the title was offered a last-minute reprieve when a buyer, BHT Media, emerged with a rescue package. It was relaunched by BHT and became a pull-out section in *The Football Paper*, but previous owners Greenways Media reacquired it just seven months later and continue to publish it to this day.

Speaking at the time, David Emery said: 'It is almost seven years to the day since I launched the Non-League Paper, so from my point of view, football's coming home.'

At the start of the 2007-08 season *Non-League Today* was launched as a rival to *The Non-League Paper* by its former news editor, David Watters. The *NLP* beefed up its coverage, took on non-League player Stuart Hammonds and Stevenage manager Graham Westley as columnists and claimed that, despite the competition, sales figures on the first day of the season were, at 39,512, better than any first-day sale in the past three years. The challenge of *Non-League Today* was seen off, the newcomer closing in January 2009.

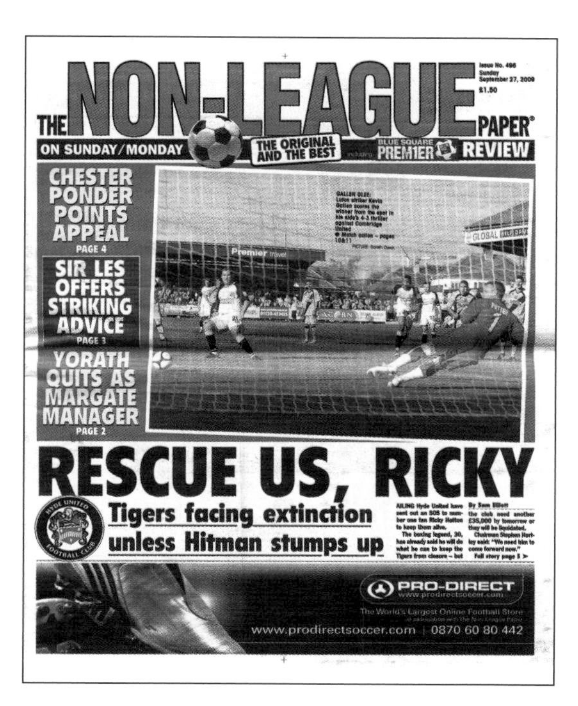

THE NON-LEAGUE PAPER®

Issue No. 496
Sunday
September 27, 2009
£1.50

ON SUNDAY/MONDAY

THE ORIGINAL AND THE BEST

BLUE SQUARE PREM1ER REVIEW

CHESTER PONDER POINTS APPEAL
PAGE 4

SIR LES OFFERS STRIKING ADVICE
PAGE 3

YORATH QUITS AS MARGATE MANAGER
PAGE 2

GALLEN GLEE: Luton striker Kevin Gallen scores the winner from the spot in his side's 4-3 thriller against Cambridge United
Match action – pages 10&11

RESCUE US, RICKY

Tigers facing extinction unless Hitman stumps up

By Sam Elliott

AILING Hyde United have sent out an SOS to number one fan Ricky Hatton to keep them alive.

The boxing legend, 30, has already said he will do what he can to keep the Tigers from closure – but the club need another £35,000 by tomorrow or they will be liquidated.

Chairman Stephen Hartley said: "We need him to come forward now."

Full story page 5 >

PRO-DIRECT
www.prodirectsoccer.com
The World's Largest Online Football Store
www.prodirectsoccer.com | 0870 60 80 442

WEBSITES

Not an exhaustive guide – things change too rapidly in cyberspace for that – but a point of reference to start you web-trawling. Happy hunting!

www.nonleaguedaily.com
A guide covering the Conference to the local leagues.

www.nonleaguenews.co.uk
A handy news feed detailing articles about any specified club.

http://nln24.com
'Real football for real fans', with plenty of features and blogs.

http://nonleaguezone.com
A fans' forum for each division of the non-League game.

http://www.midlandsnonleaguefootball.co.uk
Fascinating and often thought-provoking regional site.

http://fchd.info
The Football Club History Database, covering the clubs of England and Wales from the biggest names down to village clubs and long-forgotten names from the past.

www.tonykempster.co.uk
Now frozen, Tony Kempster's site is still a treasure trove of information.

http://nonleaguefootballlive.com
Does what it says on the tin – a national live-score service for those who can't be there. Some lively forums attached.

www.thenonleaguefootballpaper.com
Associated with the Sunday-published paper.

www.non-league.org
Very good for the tipster, with analysis of current form etc.

www.bbc.co.uk/london/radio/nonleague/nl_the_non_league_show
Associated with the radio show, and offers a weekly Podcast.

http://www.thepyramid.info
Details of composition and structure of non-League football in England, from the Conference to county leagues, plus links to official League sites.

www.nonleaguescotland.co.uk
Essential for fans interested in goings-on north of the border.

www.pyramidpassion.co.uk
A celebration of non-League football grounds and culture, now frozen.

www.confguide.com
Home to the liveliest fan forums.

www.footballconference.co.uk
Official Conference site.

http://evostikleague.pitchero.com
Official Northern Premier League site.

www.isthmian.co.uk
Official Isthmian League site.

www.southern-football-league.co.uk
Official Southern League site.

http://www.mikeavery.co.uk/Results.htm
English football statistics. Fixtures, results and tables in Kempster style.

http://www.nonleaguematters.co.uk
The proposed successor to the Kempster site.

www.gameoftwohalves.net
A football history information site about non-League soccer in the North of England.

www.nonleaguedaily.com
Good, often updated guide to the non-League game.

STATISTICS

Football Conference (Alliance Premier League)

Founding members 1979	Level of football 2009-10
AP Leamington	Southern League Premier Division (as Leamington FC) *
Altrincham	Conference National
Bangor City	Welsh Premier League
Barnet	League Two
Barrow	Conference National
Bath City	Conference South
Boston United	Northern Premier League Premier Division
Gravesend & Northfleet	Conference National (as Ebbsfleet United)
Kettering Town	Conference National
Maidstone United	Isthmian League Premier Division
Northwich Victoria	Conference North
Nuneaton Borough	Southern League Premier Division
Redditch United	Conference North
Scarborough	Wound up in June 2007 §
Stafford Rangers	Conference North
Stevenage Borough	Conference National
Telford United	Wound up in May 2004 †
Wealdstone	Isthmian League Premier Division
Weymouth	Conference South
Worcester City	Conference South
Yeovil Town	League One

* AP Leamington was a works team that ceased operations in 1988 after Automotive Products decided to sell the Windmill Ground, on which they played, for housing development. Homeless, the club remained dormant for 12 years before being revived as Leamington FC in 2000.

§ Scarborough Athletic, formed by the Scarborough FC Supporters' Trust in the wake of the demise of Scarborough FC, currently play in the Northern Counties East Premier Division. Scarborough FC continued initially as a youth side, with an adult team known as Scarborough Town added in 2008. Scarborough Town currently play in the Wearside league.

† AFC Telford United, formed by the Telford United Supporters' Trust in the wake of the demise of Telford United, currently play in the Conference North.

CONFERENCE NATIONAL CHAMPIONS AND PLAY-OFF WINNERS

1979-80	**Altrincham**	
1980-81	**Altrincham**	
1981-82	**Runcorn**	
1982-83	**Enfield**	
1983-84	**Maidstone United**	
1984-85	**Wealdstone**	
1985-86	**Enfield**	
1986-87	**Scarborough (first year of automatic promotion)**	
1987-88	**Lincoln City**	
1988-89	**Maidstone United**	
1989-90	**Darlington**	
1990-91	**Barnet**	
1991-92	**Colchester United**	
1992-93	**Wycombe Wanderers**	
1993-94	**Kidderminster Harriers (not promoted *)**	
1994-95	**Macclesfield Town (not promoted §)**	
1995-96	**Stevenage Borough (not promoted †)**	
1996-97	**Macclesfield Town**	
1997-98	**Halifax Town**	
1998-99	**Cheltenham Town**	
1999-2000	**Kidderminster Harriers**	
2000-01	**Rushden & Diamonds**	
2001-02	**Boston United**	
2002-03	**Yeovil Town**	
	Play-off winners	Doncaster Rovers
2003-04	**Chester City**	
	Play-off winners	Shrewsbury Town
2004-05	**Barnet**	
	Play-off winners	Carlisle United
2005-06	**Accrington Stanley**	
	Play-off winners	Hereford United
2006-07	**Dagenham & Redbridge**	
	Play-off winners	Morecambe
2007-08	**Aldershot Town**	
	Play-off winners	Exeter City
2008-09	**Burton Albion**	
	Play-off winners	Torquay United
2009-10	**Stevenage Borough**	
	Play-off winners	Oxford United

* Kidderminster Harriers were not promoted due to their ground not being of the required standard.

§ Macclesfield Town were not promoted due to their ground not being of the required standard,

although Football League games had been staged at Moss Rose between 1990 and 1992, when Chester played their home games at Macclesfield pending the completion of the Deva Stadium.
† Stevenage Borough were not promoted due to their ground not being of the required standard.

Conference North Champions and Play-off Winners

2004-05	**Southport**	
	Play-off winners	Altrincham
2005-06	**Northwich Victoria**	
	Play-off winners	Stafford Rangers
2006-07	**Droylsden**	
	Play-off winners	Farsley Celtic
2007-08	**Kettering Town**	
	Play-off winners	Barrow
2008-09	**Tamworth**	
	Play-off winners	Gateshead
2009-10	**Southport**	
	Play-off winners	Fleetwood

Conference South Champions and Play-off Winners

2004-05	**Grays Athletic**	
	Play-off winners	Eastbourne Borough (not promoted *)
2005-06	**Weymouth**	
	Play-off winners	St Albans City
2006-07	**Histon**	
	Play-off winners	Salisbury City
2007-08	**Lewes**	
	Play-off winners	Eastbourne Borough
2008-09	**AFC Wimbledon**	
	Play-off winners	Hayes & Yeading United
2009-10	**Newport County**	
	Play-off winners	Bath City

* In 2004-05, the Conference North and Conference South champions won automatic promotion to the Conference National, while the play-off winners in each division played each other to determine who would secure a third promotion place – Altrincham beat Eastbourne Borough 2-1 in the play-off final held at Stoke City's Britannia Stadium. Altrincham were promoted to the Conference National, while Eastbourne Borough remained in the Conference South.

CONFERENCE LEAGUE CUP

Season	Winner	Runner-up
1979-80	Northwich Victoria	Altrincham
1980-81	Altrincham	Kettering Town
1981-82	Weymouth	Enfield

1982-83	Runcorn	Scarborough
1983-84	Scarborough	Barnet
1984-85	Runcorn	Maidstone United
1985-86	Stafford Rangers	Barnet
1986-87	Kettering Town	Hendon
1987-88	Horwich RMI	Weymouth
1988-89	Yeovil Town	Kidderminster Harriers
1989-90	Yeading	Stamford
1990-91	Sutton United	Barrow
1991-92	Wycombe Wanderers	Runcorn
1992-93	Northwich Victoria	Wycombe Wanderers
1993-94	Macclesfield Town	Yeovil Town
1994-95	Bromsgrove Rovers	Kettering Town
1995-96	Bromsgrove Rovers	Macclesfield Town
1996-97	Kidderminster Harriers	Macclesfield Town
1997-98	Morecambe	Woking
1998-99	Doncaster Rovers	Farnborough Town
1999-2000	Doncaster Rovers	Kingstonian
2000-01	Chester City	Kingstonian
2001-02	not held	
2002-03	not held	
2003-04	not held	
2004-05	Woking	Stalybridge Celtic
2005-06	not held	
2006-07	not held	
2007-08	Aldershot Town	Rushden & Diamonds
2008-09	AFC Telford United	Forest Green Rovers
2009-10	not held	

The Conference League Cup was discontinued in 2001, but reintroduced as the Football Conference Challenge Cup for the 2004-05 season. With the completion of a sponsorship deal early in the season, it became known as the Carthium Cup, but the collapse of the Carthium Group shortly afterwards resulted in a second renaming, to the National Conference Cup, pending another sponsorship deal. Gladwish Land Sales stepped into the breach two months later, and it was renamed the GLS Cup, its fourth name in only three months.

The reorganisation of the Conference led to the abandonment of the competition after its inaugural season, but it was relaunched again in 2007 with new sponsors Setanta.

Northern Premier League Champions

1968-69	Macclesfield Town
1969-70	Macclesfield Town
1970-71	Wigan Athletic
1971-72	Stafford Rangers
1972-73	Boston United

1973-74	Boston United
1974-75	Wigan Athletic
1975-76	Runcorn
1976-77	Boston United
1977-78	Boston United
1978-79	Mossley
1979-80	Mossley
1980-81	Runcorn
1981-82	Bangor City
1982-83	Gateshead
1983-84	Barrow
1984-85	Stafford Rangers
1985-86	Gateshead
1986-87	Macclesfield Town

(With the introduction of Division One in 1987, the Northern Premier League was renamed the Northern Premier League Premier Division.)

Northern Premier League
Premier Division Champions

1987-88	Chorley
1988-89	Barrow
1989-90	Colne Dynamoes
1990-91	Witton Albion
1991-92	Stalybridge Celtic
1992-93	Southport
1993-94	Marine
1994-95	Marine
1995-96	Bamber Bridge
1996-97	Leek Town
1997-98	Barrow
1998-99	Altrincham
1999-2000	Leigh RMI
2000-01	Stalybridge Celtic
2001-02	Burton Albion
2002-03	Accrington Stanley
2003-04	Hucknall Town
2004-05	Hyde United
2005-06	Blyth Spartans
2006-07	Burscough
2007-08	Fleetwood Town
2008-09	Eastwood Town
2009-10	Guiseley

Northern Premier League
Division One Champions

1987-88	Fleetwood Town
1988-89	Colne Dynamoes
1989-90	Leek Town
1990-91	Whitley Bay
1991-92	Colwyn Bay
1992-93	Bridlington Town
1993-94	Guiseley
1994-95	Blyth Spartans
1995-96	Lancaster City
1996-97	Radcliffe Borough
1997-98	Whitby Town
1998-99	Droylsden
1999-2000	Accrington Stanley
2000-01	Bradford Park Avenue
2001-02	Harrogate Town
2002-03	Alfreton Town
2003-04	Hyde United
2004-05	North Ferriby United
2005-06	Mossley
2006-07	Buxton

(In 2007, the Northern Premier League Division One was split to create two regional competitions: Division One North and Division One South.)

Northern Premier League
Division One North Champions

2007-08	Bradford Park Avenue
2008-09	Durham City
2009-10	FC Halifax Town

Northern Premier League
Division One South Champions

2007-08	Retford United *
2008-09	Retford United
2009-10	Mickleover Spoirts

* Retford United were not promoted due to their Cannon Park ground not being of the required standard. Runners-up Cammell Laird were promoted in their place.

Southern League

	Division One	**Division Two**
1894-95	Millwall Athletic	New Brompton
1895-96	Millwall Athletic	Wolverton L&NWR
1896-97	Southampton St Mary's	Dartford
1897-98	Southampton Royal Artillery	Portsmouth

(For the 1898-99 season, Division Two was divided into two sections, London and South-West, with a play-off contested between the winners of each section.)

	Division One	**Division Two (London)**	**Division Two (SW)**
1898-99	Southampton	Thames Ironworks	Cowes
	Division Two play-off – Thames Ironworks won 3-1		

(For the 1899-1900 season, the league reverted to the old format.)

	Division One	**Division Two**
1899-1900	Tottenham Hotspur	Watford
1900-01	Southampton	Brentford
1901-02	Portsmouth	Fulham
1902-03	Southampton	Fulham
1903-04	Southampton	Watford
1904-05	Bristol Rovers	Fulham Reserves
1905-06	Fulham	Crystal Palace
1906-07	Fulham	Southend United
1907-08	Queens Park Rangers	Southend United
1908-09	Northampton Town	Croydon Common

(For the 1909-10 season, Division Two was split into an 'A' section and a 'B' section, with the winners of each section contesting a play-off for the Division Two championship.)

	Division One	**Division Two (A)**	**Division Two (B)**
1909-10	Brighton & Hove Albion	Stoke	Hastings & St Leonards
	Division Two play-off – Stoke won 6-0		

(For the 1910-11 season, the league again reverted to the previous format.)

	Division One	**Division Two**
1910-11	Swindon Town	Reading
1911-12	Queens Park Rangers	Merthyr Town
1912-13	Plymouth Argyle	Cardiff City
1913-14	Swindon Town	Croydon Common
1914-15	Watford	Stoke
1919-20	Portsmouth	Mid Rhondda

(At the end of the 1919-20 season, the majority of the teams in the First Division moved into the new

Third Division of the Football League. The Southern League was therefore split into two national sections for England and Wales, with the winners of each section contesting a play-off for the Southern League championship.)

	English Section	Welsh Section
1920-21	Brighton & Hove Albion Res.	Barry
	Championship Play-off – Brighton & Hove Albion Res. won 2-1	
1921-22	Plymouth Argyle Res.	Ebbw Vale
	Championship Play-off – Plymouth won 3-0	
1922-23	Bristol City Res.	Ebbw Vale
	Championship Play-off – Ebbw Vale won 2-1	

(For the 1923-24 season, the league was split into two regional sections, with the winners of each section contesting a play-off for the Southern League championship.)

	Eastern Section	Western Section
1923-24	Peterborough & Fletton United	Yeovil & Petters United
	Championship Play-off – Yeovil & Petters United won 3-1	
1924-25	Southampton Res.	Swansea Town Res.
	Championship Play-off – Southampton Res. won 2-1	
1925-26	Millwall Reserves	Plymouth Argyle Res.
	Championship Play-off – Plymouth Argyle Res. won 1-0	
1926-27	Brighton & Hove Albion Res.	Torquay United
	Championship Play-off – Brighton & Hove Albion Res. won 4-0	
1927-28	Kettering Town	Bristol City Res.
	Championship Play-off – Kettering Town won 5-0	
1928-29	Kettering Town	Plymouth Argyle Res.
	Championship Play-off – Plymouth Argyle Res. won 4-2	
1929-30	Aldershot	Bath City
	Championship Play-off – Aldershot won 3-2	
1930-31	Dartford	Exeter City Res.
	Championship Play-off – Dartford won 7-2	
1931-32	Dartford	Yeovil & Petters United
	Championship Play-off – Dartford won 2-1	
1932-33	Norwich City Res.	Bath City
	Championship Play-off – Norwich City Res. won 2-1	

(For the 1933-34 season an extra section, the Central Section, was introduced to provide additional fixtures. The Central included teams from the other two sections and did not contribute to the overall championship.)

	Eastern Section	Western Section	Central Section
1933-34	Norwich City Res.	Plymouth Argyle Res.	Plymouth Argyle Res.
	Championship Play-off – Plymouth Argyle Res. won 3-0		

1934-35	Norwich City Res.	Yeovil & Petters United	Folkestone
	Championship Play-off – Norwich City Res. won 7-2		
1935-36	Margate	Plymouth Argyle Res.	Margate
	Championship Play-off – Margate won 3-1		

(For the 1936-37 season, the Eastern and Western sections were merged into a single division. Additional fixtures were obtained through the Midweek Section, which did not contribute to the overall championship.)

	Southern League	**Midweek Section**
1936-37	Ipswich Town	Margate
1937-38	Guildford City	Millwall Res.
1938-39	Colchester United	Tunbridge Wells Rangers

(For the 1945-46 season, the Midweek Section was not played due to power restrictions after the Second World War.)

	Southern League
1945-46	Chelmsford City
1946-47	Gillingham
1947-48	Merthyr Tydfil
1948-49	Gillingham
1949-50	Merthyr Tydfil
1950-51	Merthyr Tydfil
1951-52	Merthyr Tydfil
1952-53	Headington United
1953-54	Merthyr Tydfil
1954-55	Yeovil Town
1955-56	Guildford City
1956-57	Kettering Town
1957-58	Gravesend & Northfleet

(For the 1958-59 season the Southern League was again divided into two sections: North-Western and South-Eastern. The winners of each section contested a play-off for the Southern League championship.)

	North-Western Section	**South-Eastern Section**
1958-59	Hereford United	Bedford Town
	Championship Play-off – Bedford Town won 3-0	

The following season saw the two sections merged to form a Premier Division, and a new Division One introduced.

	Premier Division	**Division One**
1959-60	Bath City	Clacton Town
1960-61	Oxford United	Kettering Town
1961-62	Oxford United	Wisbech Town
1962-63	Cambridge City	Margate

1963-64	Yeovil Town	Folkestone Town
1964-65	Weymouth	Hereford United
1965-66	Weymouth	Barnet
1966-67	Romford	Dover
1967-68	Chelmsford City	Worcester City
1968-69	Cambridge United	Brentwood Town
1969-70	Cambridge United	Bedford Town
1970-71	Yeovil Town	Guildford City

(For the 1971-72 season, Division One was regionalised.)

Season	Premier Division	Division One North	Division One South
1971-72	Chelmsford City	Kettering Town	Waterlooville
1972-73	Kettering Town	Grantham	Maidstone United
1973-74	Dartford	Stourbridge	Wealdstone
1974-75	Wimbledon	Bedford Town	Gravesend & Northfleet
1975-76	Wimbledon	Redditch United	Minehead
1976-77	Wimbledon	Worcester City	Barnet
1977-78	Bath City	Witney Town	Margate
1978-79	Worcester City	Grantham	Dover

(For the 1979-80 season, 13 Southern League Premier Division clubs joined the newly formed Alliance Premier League. The Southern League Premier Division and Division One were subsequently merged to form two regional divisions.)

	Midland Division	Southern Division
1979-80	Bridgend Town	Dorchester Town
1980-81	Alvechurch	Dartford
1981-82	Nuneaton Borough	Wealdstone

(For the 1982-83 season, the Premier Division was reintroduced above the regional divisions.)

	Premier Division	Midland Division	Southern Division
1982-83	Leamington	Cheltenham Town	Fisher Athletic
1983-84	Dartford	Willenhall Town	Road-Sea Southampton
1984-85	Cheltenham Town	Dudley Town	Basingstoke Town
1985-86	Welling United	Bromsgrove Rovers	Cambridge City
1986-87	Fisher Athletic	VS Rugby	Dorchester Town
1987-88	Aylesbury United	Merthyr Tydfil	Dover Athletic
1988-89	Merthyr Tydfil	Gloucester City	Chelmsford City
1989-90	Dover Athletic	Halesowen Town	Bashley
1990-91	Farnborough Town	Stourbridge	Buckingham Town
1991-92	Bromsgrove Rovers	Solihull Borough	Hastings Town
1992-93	Dover Athletic	Nuneaton Borough	Sittingbourne
1993-94	Farnborough Town	Rushden & Diamonds	Gravesend & Northfleet
1994-95	Hednesford Town	Newport County	Salisbury City

1995-96	Rushden & Diamonds	Nuneaton Borough	Sittingbourne
1996-97	Gresley Rovers	Tamworth	Forest Green Rovers
1997-98	Forest Green Rovers	Grantham Town	Weymouth
1998-99	Nuneaton Borough	Clevedon Town	Havant & Waterlooville
1999-2000	Boston United	Stafford Rangers	Fisher Athletic

(For the 2000-01 season, the regional divisions were renamed the Western and Eastern divisions.)

	Premier Division	Western Division	Eastern Division
2000-01	Margate	Hinckley United	Newport IOW
2001-02	Kettering Town	Halesowen Town	Hastings Town
2002-03	Tamworth	Merthyr Tydfil	Dorchester Town
2003-04	Crawley Town	Redditch United	King's Lynn
2004-05	Histon	Mangotsfield United	Fisher Athletic
2005-06	Salisbury City	Clevedon Town	Boreham Wood

(For the 2006-07 season, the two regional divisions were renamed Division One Midlands and Division One South & West.)

	Premier Division	Division One Midlands	Division One South & West
2006-07	Bath City	Brackley Town	Bashley
2007-08	King's Lynn	Evesham United	Farnborough
2008-09	Corby Town	Leamington	Truro City
2009-10	Farnborough	Bury Town	Windsor & Eton

Isthmian League Champions

1905-06	London Caledonians
1906-07	Ilford
1907-08	London Caledonians
1908-09	Bromley
1909-10	Bromley
1910-11	Clapton
1911-12	London Caledonians
1912-13	London Caledonians
1913-14	London Caledonians
1914-19	Postponed due to the First World War
1919	Leytonstone
1919-20	Dulwich Hamlet
1920-21	Ilford
1921-22	Ilford
1922-23	Clapton
1923-24	St Albans City
1924-25	London Caledonians
1925-26	Dulwich Hamlet
1926-27	St Albans City
1927-28	St Albans City

1928-29	Nunhead
1929-30	Nunhead
1930-31	Wimbledon
1931-32	Wimbledon
1932-33	Dulwich Hamlet
1933-34	Kingstonian
1934-35	Wimbledon
1935-36	Wimbledon
1936-37	Kingstonian
1937-38	Leytonstone
1938-39	Leytonstone
1939-45	Postponed due to the Second World War
1945-46	Walthamstow Avenue
1946-47	Leytonstone
1947-48	Leytonstone
1948-49	Dulwich Hamlet
1949-50	Leytonstone
1950-51	Leytonstone
1951-52	Leytonstone
1952-53	Walthamstow Avenue
1953-54	Bromley
1954-55	Walthamstow Avenue
1955-56	Wycombe Wanderers
1956-57	Wycombe Wanderers
1957-58	Tooting & Mitcham United
1958-59	Wimbledon
1959-60	Tooting & Mitcham United
1960-61	Bromley
1961-62	Wimbledon
1962-63	Wimbledon
1963-64	Wimbledon
1964-65	Hendon
1965-66	Leytonstone
1966-67	Sutton United
1967-68	Enfield
1968-69	Enfield
1969-70	Enfield
1970-71	Wycombe Wanderers
1971-72	Wycombe Wanderers
1972-73	Hendon

(With the introduction of Division One in 1973, the Isthmian League was renamed the Isthmian League Premier Division.)

Isthmian League Premier Division Champions

1973-74	Wycombe Wanderers
1974-75	Wycombe Wanderers
1975-76	Enfield
1976-77	Enfield
1977-78	Enfield
1978-79	Barking
1979-80	Enfield
1980-81	Slough Town
1981-82	Leytonstone & Ilford
1982-83	Wycombe Wanderers
1983-84	Harrow Borough
1984-85	Sutton United
1985-86	Sutton United
1986-87	Wycombe Wanderers
1987-88	Yeovil Town
1988-89	Leytonstone/Ilford
1989-90	Sutton United
1990-91	Redbridge Forest
1991-92	Woking
1992-93	Chesham United
1993-94	Stevenage Borough
1994-95	Enfield
1995-96	Hayes
1996-97	Yeovil Town
1997-98	Kingstonian
1998-99	Sutton United
1999-2000	Dagenham & Redbridge
2000-01	Farnborough Town
2001-02	Gravesend & Northfleet
2002-03	Aldershot Town
2003-04	Canvey Island
2004-05	Yeading
2005-06	Braintree Town
2006-07	Hampton & Richmond Borough
2007-08	Chelmsford City
2008-09	Dover Athletic
2009-10	Dartford

Isthmian League Division One Champions

1973-74	Dagenham
1974-75	Staines Town
1975-76	Tilbury

1976-77	Boreham Wood
1977-78	Dulwich Hamlet
1978-79	Harrow Borough
1979-80	Leytonstone/Ilford
1980-81	Bishop's Stortford
1981-82	Wokingham Town
1982-83	Worthing
1983-84	Windsor & Eton
1984-85	Farnborough Town
1985-86	St Albans City
1986-87	Leytonstone/Ilford
1987-88	Marlow
1988-89	Staines Town
1989-90	Wivenhoe Town
1990-91	Chesham United
1991-92	Stevenage Borough
1992-93	Hitchin Town
1993-94	Bishop's Stortford
1994-95	Boreham Wood
1995-96	Oxford City
1996-97	Chesham United
1997-98	Aldershot Town
1998-99	Canvey Island
1999-2000	Croydon
2000-01	Boreham Wood
2001-02	Ford United

(For the 2002-03 season, Division One was reorganised into North and South regions.)

	Division One North	**Division One South**
2002-03	Northwood	Carshalton Athletic
2003-04	Yeading	Lewes

(For the 2004-05 season, Division One North and South were reorganised into new Divisions One and Two.)

	Division One	**Division Two**
2004-05	AFC Wimbledon	Ilford
2005-06	Ramsgate	Ware

(For the 2006-07 season, Divisions One and Two were reorganised again into Division One North and South regions.)

	Division One North	**Division One South**
2006-07	AFC Hornchurch	Maidstone United
2007-08	Dartford	Dover Athletic

2008-09	Aveley	Kingstonian
2009-10	Lowestoft Town	Croydon Athletic

Isthmian League Division Two Champions

1977-78	Epsom & Ewell
1978-79	Farnborough Town
1979-80	Billericay Town
1980-81	Feltham
1981-82	Worthing
1982-83	Clapton
1983-84	Basildon United

(For the 1984-85 season, Division Two was reorganised into North and South regions.)

	Division Two North	Division Two South
1984-85	Leyton Wingate	Grays Athletic
1985-86	Stevenage Borough	Southwick
1986-87	Chesham United	Woking
1987-88	Wivenhoe Town	Chalfont St Peter
1988-89	Harlow Town	Dorking
1989-90	Heybridge Swifts	Yeading
1990-91	Stevenage Borough	Abingdon Town

(For the 1991-92 season, Division Two North and South were merged and Division Three was added.)

	Division Two	Division Three
1991-92	Purfleet	Edgware Town
1992-93	Worthing	Aldershot Town
1993-94	Newbury Town	Bracknell Town
1994-95	Thame United	Collier Row
1995-96	Canvey Island	Horsham
1996-97	Collier Row & Romford	Wealdstone
1997-98	Canvey Island	Hemel Hempstead Town
1998-99	Bedford Town	Ford United
1999-2000	Hemel Hempstead Town	East Thurrock United
2000-01	Tooting & Mitcham United	Arlesey Town
2001-02	Lewes	Croydon Athletic

(For the 2002-03 season, with the reorganisation of Division One into North and South regions, Division Three was renamed Division Two.)

	Division Two
2002-03	Cheshunt
2003-04	Leighton Town

(For the 2004-05 season, Division Two was disbanded and Division One North and South were reorganised into new Divisions One and Two.)

	Division One	Division Two
2004-05	AFC Wimbledon	Ilford
2005-06	Ramsgate	Ware

(For the 2006-07 season, Divisions One and Two were reorganised into Division One North and South regions. See page 176.)

Former Conference clubs now in the Football League

Club	Years in the Conference	Now in (2010)
Accrington Stanley	2003-2006	League Two
Aldershot Town	2003-2008	League Two
Barnet	1979-1991; 2001-2005	League Two
Burton Albion	2002-2009	League Two
Carlisle United	2004-2005	League One
Cheltenham Town	1985-1992; 1997-1999	League Two
Colchester United	1990-1992	League One
Dagenham & Redbridge	1992-1996; 2000-2007	League One
Doncaster Rovers	1998-2003	Championship
Exeter City	2003-2008	League One
Hereford United	1997-2006	League Two
Lincoln City	1987-1988	League Two
Macclesfield Town	1987-1997	League Two
Morecambe	1995-2007	League Two
Oxford United	2006-2010	League Two
Shrewsbury Town	2003-2004	League Two
Stevenage Borough	1994-2010	League Two
Torquay United	2007-2009	League Two
Wycombe Wanderers	1985-1986; 1987-1993	League Two
Yeovil Town	1979-1985; 1988-1995; 1997-2003	League One

Of the former Conference clubs now in the Football League, Colchester United and Doncaster Rovers are the most successful, the former having reached the Championship in 2006, 14 years after being Conference champions. Colchester were relegated to League One in 2008. Doncaster Rovers played for five years in the Conference and were promoted to League Two as promotion play-off winners in 2003. They were promoted to League One as champions in 2004 and to the Championship as promotion play-off winners in 2008. They played in the Championship in the 2008-2009 season, 50 years after they last played in the second tier.

Yeovil Town are now in League One after they were promoted from the Conference in 2003, and gained promotion again in 2005. Newly promoted Wycombe Wanderers briefly graced League One in 2009-10, making a return to the third tier where they last played between 1994 and 2004.

Cheltenham Town finished their second stint in League One when they were relegated at the end of 2008-09 after three largely miserable seasons at the higher level. Hereford United also dropped back to League Two, having struggled throughout the season, their first in the third tier since passing briefly through in 1977-78 on their rapid descent from the old Division Two to Division Four.

Accrington Stanley have yet to progress beyond the Football League's basement division, while Barnet have yet to do so since regaining League status in 2005, although they did progress to the third tier in their first spell of Football League membership.

Both Dagenham & Redbridge and Morecambe reached the Football League for the first time in their history for the 2007-08 season, a feat emulated by Burton Albion for the 2009-10 season.

Amateur Cup Winners and Runners-up, 1893 to 1974

Season	Winner	Runner-up	Result
1893-94	Old Carthusians	Casuals	2-1
1894-95	Middlesbrough	Old Carthusians	2-1
1895-96	Bishop Auckland	RA (Portsmouth)	1-0
1896-97	Old Carthusians	Stockton	1-1, 4-1
1897-98	Middlesbrough	Uxbridge	2-1
1898-99	Stockton	Harwich & Parkeston	1-0
1899-1900	Bishop Auckland	Lowestoft Town	5-1
1900-01	Crook Town	King's Lynn	1-1, 3-0
1901-02	Old Malvernians	Bishop Auckland	5-1
1902-03	Stockton	Oxford City	0-0, 1-0
1903-04	Sheffield	Ealing	3-1
1904-05	West Hartlepool	Clapton	3-2
1905-06	Oxford City	Bishop Auckland	3-0
1906-07	Clapton	Stockton	2-1
1907-08	Depot Battalion RE	Stockton	2-1
1908-09	Clapton	Eston United	6-0
1909-10	RMLI Gosport	South Bank	2-1
1910-11	Bromley	Bishop Auckland	1-0
1911-12	Stockton	Eston United	0-0, 1-0
1912-13	South Bank	Oxford City	1-1, 1-0
1913-14	Bishop Auckland	Northern Nomads	1-0
1914-15	Clapton	Bishop Auckland	1-0
1915-19	Competition not held due to the First World War		
1919-20	Dulwich Hamlet	Tufnell Park	1-0
1920-21	Bishop Auckland	Swindon Victoria	4-2
1921-22	Bishop Auckland	South Bank	5-2
1922-23	London Caledonians	Evesham Town	2-1
1923-24	Clapton	Erith & Belvedere	3-0
1924-25	Clapton	Southall	2-1
1925-26	Northern Nomads	Stockton	7-1
1926-27	Leyton	Barking Town	3-1
1927-28	Leyton	Cockfield	3-2
1928-29	Ilford	Leyton	3-1
1929-30	Ilford	Bournemouth Gasworks Ath.	5-1

1930-31	Wycombe Wanderers	Hayes	1-0
1931-32	Dulwich Hamlet	Marine	7-1
1932-33	Kingstonian	Stockton	1-1, 4-1
1933-34	Dulwich Hamlet	Leyton	2-1
1934-35	Bishop Auckland	Wimbledon	0-0, 2-1
1935-36	Casuals	Ilford	1-1, 2-0
1936-37	Dulwich Hamlet	Leyton	2-0
1937-38	Bromley	Erith & Belvedere	1-0
1938-39	Bishop Auckland	Willington	3-0
1939-45	Competition not held due to the Second World War		
1945-46	Barnet	Bishop Auckland	3-2
1946-47	Leytonstone	Wimbledon	2-1
1947-48	Leytonstone	Barnet	1-0
1948-49	Bromley	Romford	1-0
1949-50	Willington	Bishop Auckland	4-0
1950-51	Pegasus	Bishop Auckland	2-1
1951-52	Walthamstow Avenue	Leyton	2-1
1952-53	Pegasus	Harwich & Parkeston	6-0
1953-54	Crook Town	Bishop Auckland	2-2, 2-2, 1-0
1954-55	Bishop Auckland	Hendon	2-0
1955-56	Bishop Auckland	Corinthian Casuals	1-1, 4-1
1956-57	Bishop Auckland	Wycombe Wanderers	3-1
1957-58	Woking	Ilford	3-0
1958-59	Crook Town	Barnet	3-2
1959-60	Hendon	Kingstonian	2-1
1960-61	Walthamstow Avenue	West Auckland Town	2-1
1961-62	Crook Town	Hounslow Town	1-1, 4-0
1962-63	Wimbledon	Sutton United	4-2
1963-64	Crook Town	Enfield	2-1
1964-65	Hendon	Whitby Town	3-1
1965-66	Wealdstone	Hendon	3-1
1966-67	Enfield	Skelmersdale United	0-0, 3-0
1967-68	Leytonstone	Chesham United	1-0
1968-69	North Shields	Sutton United	2-1
1969-70	Enfield	Dagenham	5-1
1970-71	Skelmersdale United	Dagenham	4-1
1971-72	Hendon	Enfield	2-0
1972-73	Walton & Hersham	Slough Town	1-0
1973-74	Bishop's Stortford	Ilford	4-1

Summary of winners:
10 – Bishop Auckland
5 – Clapton, Crook Town
4 – Dulwich Hamlet
3 – Bromley, Hendon, Leytonstone, Stockton
2 – Enfield, Leyton, Middlesbrough, Old Carthusians, Pegasus, Walthamstow Avenue
1 – Barnet, Bishop's Stortford, Cardiff City, Casuals, Depot Battalion RE, Ilford, Kingstonian, London Caledonians, North Shields, Northern Nomads, Old Malvernians, Oxford City, RMLI Gosport, Sheffield, Skelmersdale United, South Bank, Walton & Hersham, Wealdstone, West Hartlepool, Willington, Wimbledon, Woking, Wycombe Wanderers

FA Vase Winners and Runners-up, 1974 to date

Season	Winner	Runner-up	Result
1974-75	Hoddesdon Town	Epsom & Ewell	2-1
1975-76	Billericay Town	Stamford	1-0 (aet)
1976-77	Billericay Town	Sheffield	1-1, 2-1 (aet)
1977-78	Newcastle Blue Star	Barton Rovers	2-1
1978-79	Billericay Town	Almondsbury Greenway	4-1
1979-80	Stamford	Guisborough Town	2-0 (aet)
1980-81	Whickham	Willenhall Town	3-2
1981-82	Forest Green Rovers	Rainworth Miners Welfare	3-0
1982-83	VS Rugby	Halesowen Town	1-0
1983-84	Stansted	Stamford	2-0
1984-85	Halesowen Town	Fleetwood Town	3-1 (aet)
1985-86	Yeading	Southall	3-0
1986-87	St Helens Town	Warrington Town	3-2
1987-88	Colne Dynamoes	Emley	1-0
1988-89	Tamworth	Sudbury Town	1-1, 3-0
1989-90	Yeading	Bridlington Town	0-0, 1-0
1990-91	Guiseley	Gresley Rovers	4-4, 3-1
1991-92	Wimborne Town	Guiseley	5-3
1992-93	Bridlington Town	Tiverton Town	1-0
1993-94	Diss Town	Taunton Town	2-1 (aet)
1994-95	Arlesey Town	Oxford City	2-1
1995-96	Brigg Town	Clitheroe	3-0
1996-97	Whitby Town	North Ferriby United	3-0
1997-98	Tiverton Town	Tow Law Town	1-0
1998-99	Tiverton Town	Bedlington Terriers	1-0
1999-2000	Deal Town	Chippenham Town	1-0
2000-01	Taunton Town	Berkhamsted Town	2-1
2001-02	Whitley Bay	Tiptree United	1-0 (aet)
2002-03	Brigg Town	AFC Sudbury	2-1
2003-04	Winchester City	AFC Sudbury	2-0

2004-05	Didcot Town	AFC Sudbury	3-2
2005-06	Nantwich Town	Hillingdon Borough	3-1
2006-07	Truro City	AFC Totton	3-1
2007-08	Kirkham & Wesham	Lowestoft Town	2-1
2008-09	Whitley Bay	Glossop North End	2-0
2009-10	Whitley Bay	Wroxham	6-1

Summary of winners:
3 – Billericay Town, Whitley Bay
2 – Brigg Town, Halesowen Town, Tiverton Town
1 – Arlesey Town, Bridlington Town, Colne Dynamoes, Deal Town, Didcot Town, Diss Town, Forest Green Rovers, Guiseley, Hoddesdon Town, Kirkham & Wesham, Nantwich Town, Newcastle Blue Star, St Helens Town, Stamford, Stansted, Tamworth, Taunton Town, Truro City, VS Rugby, Whickham, Whitby Town, Wimborne Town, Winchester City, Yeading

Clubs who have played in all Vase competitions:
Bourne Town, Brockenhurst, Calne Town, Chadderton, Eastbourne Town, Herne Bay, Hoddesdon Town, Holbeach United, Horsham YMCA, Merstham, Ringmer, Saffron Walden Town, Sheffield, Stansted, Stotfold, Tiptree United, Tunbridge Wells, Westbury United, Witham Town, Wootton Blue Cross

FA Trophy Winners and Runners-up, 1969 to date

Season	Winner	Runner-up	Result
1969-70	Macclesfield Town	Telford United	2-0
1970-71	Telford United	Hillingdon Borough	3-2
1971-72	Stafford Rangers	Barnet	3-0
1972-73	Scarborough	Wigan Athletic	2-1
1973-74	Morecambe	Dartford	2-1
1974-75	Matlock Town	Scarborough	4-0
1975-76	Scarborough	Stafford Rangers	3-2
1976-77	Scarborough	Dagenham	2-1
1977-78	Altrincham	Leatherhead	3-1
1978-79	Stafford Rangers	Kettering Town	2-0
1979-80	Dagenham	Mossley	2-1
1980-81	Bishop's Stortford	Sutton United	1-0
1981-82	Enfield	Altrincham	1-0
1982-83	Telford United	Northwich Victoria	2-1
1983-84	Northwich Victoria	Bangor City	1-1, 2-1
1984-85	Wealdstone	Boston United	2-1
1985-86	Altrincham	Runcorn	1-0
1986-87	Kidderminster Harriers	Burton Albion	0-0, 2-1
1987-88	Enfield	Telford United	0-0, 3-2
1988-89	Telford United	Macclesfield Town	1-0

1989-90	Barrow	Leek Town	3-0
1990-91	Wycombe Wanderers	Kidderminster Harriers	2-1
1991-92	Colchester United	Witton Albion	3-1
1992-93	Wycombe Wanderers	Runcorn	4-1
1993-94	Woking	Runcorn	2-1
1994-95	Woking	Kidderminster Harriers	2-1
1995-96	Macclesfield Town	Northwich Victoria	3-1
1996-97	Woking	Dagenham & Redbridge	1-0
1997-98	Cheltenham Town	Southport	1-0
1998-99	Kingstonian	Forest Green Rovers	1-0
1999-2000	Kingstonian	Kettering Town	3-2
2000-01	Canvey Island	Forest Green Rovers	1-0
2001-02	Yeovil Town	Stevenage Borough	2-0
2002-03	Burscough	Tamworth	2-1
2003-04	Hednesford Town	Canvey Island	3-2
2004-05	Grays Athletic	Hucknall Town	1-1 (6-5 on pens)
2005-06	Grays Athletic	Woking	2-0
2006-07	Stevenage Borough	Kidderminster Harriers	3-2
2007-08	Ebbsfleet United	Torquay United	1-0
2008-09	Stevenage Borough	York City	2-0
2009-10	Barrow	Stevenage Borough	2-1

Summary of winners:
3 – Scarborough, Telford United, Woking
2 – Altrincham, Barrow, Enfield, Grays Athletic, Kingstonian, Macclesfield Town, Stafford Rangers, Stevenage Borough, Wycombe Wanderers
1 – Bishop's Stortford, Burscough, Canvey Island, Cheltenham Town, Colchester United, Dagenham, Ebbsfleet United, Hednesford Town, Kidderminster Harriers, Matlock Town, Morecambe, Northwich Victoria, Wealdstone, Yeovil Town

The Barassi Trophy

The Anglo-Italian Cup, founded in the late sixties, is still remembered. Yet it was pre-dated by the non-League Coppa Ottorino Barassi, named after the Italian Vice-President of FIFA who, when the World Cup was held by Italy during the Second World War, hid the Jules Rimet Trophy in a shoebox under his bed for safe keeping.

The slightly less prestigious Barassi Trophy was contested by the winners of the English and Italian Amateur Cups. Leytonstone were the first winners of the competition in 1968 on away goals, while the following year saw it won by North Shields on the toss of a coin after home and away legs against Almas of Italy led to a 2-2 stalemate.

After the English Amateur Cup was abolished in 1974, the champions of the Isthmian League Division 2 represented England, the Isthmian having produced all previous English representatives with the exception of 1969 and 1971. Simultaneous with this change in 1975, another competition was created, the Anglo-Italian Semi-professional Cup, which had the Italian Semi-professional Cup winners play the champions of the Isthmian League Division One (in 1975) and the FA Trophy winners (in 1976).

Both these tournaments disappeared when the Gigi Peronace Memorial continued as a competition between semi-professional teams from both countries in 1976. It was held as such for about a decade until another interruption followed. It was revived again in 1992-93 and played between minor fully-professional sides, with finals always played at Wembley Stadium, London. It seems to have been abandoned again after four more competitions.

Coppa Ottorino Barassi
Competition for semi-professional teams

	Venue	Winners	Score	Runners-up
1968	home/away	Leytonstone	1-1/2-2	Stefer Roma
		[Leytonstone won on away goals]		
1969	home/away	North Shields	2-0/0-2	Almas Roma
		[cup shared]		
1970	home/away	Enfield	3-0/1-2	Ponte San Pietro
1971	home/away	Skelmersdale Utd	2-0/0-1	Montebelluna
1972	home/away	Hendon	2-0/1-1	Monsummano
1973	home/away	Walton & Hersham	4-0/2-0	Jesolo
1974	home/away	Miranese	---- ----	Bishop's Stortford
		[not played due to organisational problems]		
1975	away/home	Staines Town	1-0/2-0	Banco di Roma

1976	away/home	Sorinese [Sorinese won 5-3 on penalties]	1-1/1-1	Tilbury

Anglo-Italian Semi-Professional Cup

	Venue	Winners	Score	Runners-up
1975	away/home	Wycombe Wanderers	0-1/2-0	Monza
1976	away/home	Lecce	0-1/4-0	Scarborough

Anglo-Italian League Cup

	Venue	Winners	Score	Runners-up
1969	away/home	Swindon Town	1-2/4-0	Roma
1970	home/away	Bologna	1-0/2-2	Manchester City
1971	away/home	Tottenham Hotspur	1-0/2-0	Torino
1972	not held			
1973	not held			
1974	not held			
1975	home/away	Fiorentina	1-0/1-0	West Ham United
1976	away/home	Napoli	0-1/4-0	Southampton

Anglo-Italian Cup

	Venue	Winners		Runners-up
1970	Napoli [Match abandoned in the 79th minute]	Swindon Town	3-0	Napoli
1971	Bologna [After extra time]	Blackpool	2-1	Bologna
1972	Roma	Roma	3-1	Blackpool
1973	Firenze	Newcastle United	2-1	Fiorentina

The Anglo-Italian Cup continued as a competition for semi-professional teams (under various sponsor names).

1976	Monza	Monza	1-0	Wimbledon
1977	Lecco	Lecco	3-0	Bath City

Alitalia Challenge Cup

1978	Udine	Udinese	5-0	Bath City
1979	Chieti	Sutton United	2-1	Chieti
1980	Trieste [After extra time; Triestina won 5-4 on penalties]	Triestina	0-0	Sutton United

Talbot Challenge Cup

1981	Modena	Modena	4-1	Poole Town

Gigi Peronace Memorial

1982	Modena	Modena	1-0	Sutton United

1983	Cosenza	Cosenza	2-0	Padova
1984	Francavilla	Francavilla	2-0	Teramo
1985	Livorno	Pontedera	2-1	Livorno
1986	Piacenza	Piacenza	5-1	Pontedera
1987	not held			
1988	not held			
1989	not held			
1990	not held			
1991	not held			
1992	not held			
1993	Wembley	Cremonese	3-1	Derby County
1994	Wembley	Brescia	1-0	Notts County
1995	Wembley	Notts County	2-1	Ascoli
1996	Wembley	Genoa	5-2	Port Vale

Attendance record for a match between non-League sides
36,232: Truro City v AFC Totton (FA Vase Final, 2007)

Attendance record for an FA Cup match between non-League sides
24,526: Wigan Athletic v Hereford United (second round, 1953-54)

Conference highest attendance record
11,065: Oxford United v Woking (26 December 2006)

Conference lowest attendance record
121: Gateshead v Trowbridge Town (10 December 1983)

Midweek Conference attendance record
10,613: Oxford United v Luton Town (8 September 2009)

Unsuccessful applications for election to the Football League by English and Welsh non-League clubs to 1987

18 applications – Bedford Town, Chelmsford City
16 applications – Kettering Town
15 applications – Worcester City
14 applications – Telford United (Wellington Town)
13 applications – Bath City
12 applications – Romford
11 applications – Cambridge City, North Shields, South Liverpool
9 applications – Guildford City, Llanelly (Llanelli), Nuneaton Borough
7 applications – King's Lynn